GIAMBATTISTA
BODONI

GIAMBATTISTA
BODONI

HIS LIFE AND HIS WORLD

BY

Valerie Lester

DAVID R. GODINE, PUBLISHER
BOSTON

First published in 2015 by
DAVID R. GODINE, PUBLISHER
Post Office Box 450
Jaffrey, New Hampshire 03452
www.godine.com

FRONTISPIECE
Bust of Bodoni by Gabriele Ambrosio.
Liceo Ginnasio Statale G. Bodoni, Saluzzo. Photo: VL.

FRONT ENDPAPER:
Antonio Pasini. Conversazione in Casa Bodoni. Parma, Museo Bodoniano.
Alessandro Bianchi/Archive Franco Maria Ricci.
Seated, left to right: Bodoni, Giuseppe De Lama, Vincenzo Jacobacci, Gaetano Ziliani,
Count Giovanni Bonaventura Porta, Margherita Dall'Aglio Bodoni,
and the composer Ferdinando Paër.
Standing: Dalmastro (Bodoni's manservant) and Giambattista Zambiagi.

BACK ENDPAPER:
Anonymous, beginning of eighteenth century.
View of the Pilotta and the Ducal Palace. Parma, Museo Bodoniano.
Alessandro Bianchi/Archive Franco Maria Ricci.

LIBRARY OF CONGRESS CATALOGING-IN-PUBLICATION DATA
Lester, Valerie Browne, 1939-
Giambattista Bodoni : his life & his world / Valerie Lester.
  pages cm
Includes bibliographical references and index.
ISBN 978-1-56792-528-9 (alk. paper)
1. Bodoni, Giambattista, 1740-1813. 2. Printers--Italy--Parma--Biography.
3. Printing--Italy--Parma--History--18th century. 4. Printing--Italy--Parma-
-History--19th century. 5. Type and type-founding--Italy--Parma--History-
-18th century. 6. Type and type-founding--Italy--Parma--History--19th
century. I. Title.
                                        Z232.B66L47 2014
                                        686.2092--dc23

First edition
Printed in the China

For Jim

CONTENTS

PRINCIPAL CHARACTERS

In Saluzzo

GIAMBATTISTA BODONI, leading man, printer and director of the royal press at the court of Parma

GIANDOMENICO BODONI, Bodoni's grandfather, a printer

FRANCESCO BODONI, Bodoni's father, a printer

PAOLA MARGARITA GIOLITTI, Bodoni's mother

CARLO BODONI, Bodoni's uncle, a priest

DOMENICO BODONI, Bodoni's older brother, a printer

ANGELA BODONI, Bodoni's older sister

BENEDETA BODONI, Bodoni's next sister

GIUSEPPE BODONI, Bodoni's younger brother, his assistant in Parma

IGNAZIO CAPPA, school friend

DOMENICO COSTA, school friend who accompanied Bodoni to Rome

In Rome

CARDINAL SPINELLI, prefect of the Propaganda Fide

COSTANTINO RUGGIERI, superintendent of the press at the Propaganda Fide

PAOLO MARIA PACIAUDI, priest, archaeologist, librarian, responsible for bringing Bodoni to Parma

JOSÉ NICOLÁS DE AZARA, Spanish diplomat, Bodoni's patron in later life

In Parma

FERDINANDO I, duke of Parma, Piacenza, and Guastalla

MARIA AMALIA, archduchess of Austria, duchess of Parma

GUILLAUME DU TILLOT, prime minister of Parma

ENNEMOND PETITOT, architect at the court of Parma

JEAN BAPTISTE BOUDARD, sculptor at the court of Parma

JEAN GEORGE HANDWERCK, bursar at the royal press in Parma

Margherita Dall'Aglio (Ghitta), Bodoni's wife

Giuseppe De Lama, Bodoni's biographer and close friend

Dalmastro, Bodoni's manservant

Luigi Orsi, Bodoni's foreman

Francesco Rosaspina, engraver and close friend

Médéric Louis Élie Moreau de St Méry, administrator general of Parma and close friend

Napoleon Bonaparte, emperor of France

Josephine de Beauharnais, empress of France

Joseph Bonaparte, French ambassador to Parma

Marie Louise, Napoleon's second wife, empress of France, became Maria Luigia, duchess of Parma

Count Adam Albert von Neipperg, second husband of Maria Luigia

Elsewhere

Eugène de Beauharnais, Napoleon's stepson, viceroy of Italy

Caroline Murat (née Bonaparte), Napoleon's sister, queen of Naples

Joachim Murat, Bodoni's patron and friend, Napoleon's brother-in-law, king of Naples

Bodoni's Italy

Milan

Turin

Saluzzo Genoa

Parma

Bologna

● **Rome**

Naples

PROLOGUE

I HEARD *the word Bodoni for the first time at a dinner party in California, over a meal of pork loin, roast potatoes, and asparagus. As we lingered over dessert, strawberries and* crème fraîche, *our host suddenly announced: "I recently had a call from a bookseller who told me I am the owner of a 'hot' book." He shuddered painfully. "It's the jewel of my collection, and I must return it to its rightful owner."*

I felt the sudden prickle of interest. I had been casting about for a new project, fooling around with this and that — articles, a translation, newsletters — but nothing major had grabbed my attention. Here's an approximation of the conversation that ensued.

"What's the book?" I asked.

"Bodoni's Manuale tipografico, *the sum, the summit, the* chef d'oeuvre, *the masterpiece, the work of all his works."*

"Who is Bodoni?"

"The illustrious Italian printer and type designer, born 1740, died 1813."

"Why is the book 'hot'?"

"I bought it from a dealer, who bought it from a dealer, who bought it from a dealer, who bought it at auction, where it had been put up by a 'collector' who had stolen it from a university's rare book collection. It's 'hot' not because it's naughty; it's hot because it's swag."

A ripple of excitement shivered up my spine.

Bodoni, Italy, swag. I knew I had found my topic.

At first I was distracted by the theft of the book rather than by Bodoni himself, and I spent time wandering down that particular street of thieves. I importuned my husband Jim, a psychologist, to go to the Library of Congress to research book theft in general. The most salient fact he gathered was that book thieves were almost invariably men, with the occasional moll sitting quietly in the getaway car. But the convicted thief of the Manuale tipografico *was a woman.*[1]

Mimi Meyer worked as a volunteer in the book conservation department of the Harry Ransom Research Center at the University of Texas at Austin. A short, smiling, self-effacing woman with brown hair, she blended in with her background like a nondescript little bird. She had free rein in the library, and she was often seen in the company of the Professional Librarian (who happened to be her romantic partner). Over a period of years during the 1980s and until 1992, Meyer stole literally hundreds of rare books. The choice of subject matter was eclectic; it included topics such as printing, horses, Oxford, and rowing. (Meyer and her partner were rowing enthusiasts.) Some volumes were clearly chosen for their value: a quarto edition of Audubon's Birds of America; *Japanese art books; works by Lewis Carroll; and, of course, Bodoni's* Manuale tipografico. *Others were chosen because of the beauty of their bindings.*

How did she manage these thefts, and on such a grand scale? She admitted that she stowed books under her clothes, but it is hard to imagine a small woman tucking Birds of America *or the large, two-volume* Manuale tipografico *under her dress and getting away with it; it is easy to imagine, but impossible to prove, alternative scenarios.*

Day by day, the collection grew, but one day she slipped up; she was found with a rare book outside *the secure area. This was a flagrant transgression, and she was summarily dismissed. Although the librarians had already begun to notice the absence of certain books, the university was unable to prove her guilty of theft at that time.*

Meyer guarded the books carefully, but eventually found herself in financial straits, so she put her conservation skills to use and started removing evidence of provenance, sometimes covering existing bookplates with other bookplates, sometimes even removing incriminating pages. She then sought out high-end dealers and auction houses, and over time became known as a serious collector who had inherited rare books from a relative. But eagle-eyed and educated dealers have long memories and are often well-acquainted with individual books, and the appearance in a Swann Galleries' auction catalog of a rare Il Petrarcha *caught the eye of such a dealer. He knew the book well — it was the beautiful vellum edition bound in red goatskin, containing Petrarch's sonnets to Laura, published by Aldus Manutius in 1514 — and he knew where it belonged. He immediately reached out to the librarians at the University of Texas, who double-checked and found it missing. They in turn made contact with the FBI, who followed the trail to Meyer, and swooped.*

Mimi Meyer confessed to her crime, and agreed to cooperate with the FBI. By this time, not only had she provided Swann Galleries with 46 volumes, but she had sold another 57 volumes through Sotheby's in New York, Heritage Book Auctions in Los Angeles, and Pacific Book Auction Galleries in San Francisco, thus earning herself a tidy sum of money. The FBI catalogued another 781 stolen books still at her home.

On 30 January 2004, U.S. District Judge Sam Sparks issued Mimi Meyer a three-year probation and ordered her to pay $381,595 in restitution fees. She escaped a prison sentence because of her co-

operation with the investigation and because she was then being treated for alcoholism and mental problems. Witnesses at her trial remarked that Meyer, then 57, was a small woman with surprisingly large red hands.

The good news is that, even though my host had to return his copy of Bodoni's Manuale tipografico *to the University of Texas, he was reimbursed the cost of the book through the State of Texas restitution fund. He was then able to locate another copy of the* Manuale *that he likes just as well as the first. So the jewel was in fact restored as the crown of his collection.*

As for me, after that flurry of interest in book theft, I found myself more and more drawn to the robust Bodoni himself, to his career, his geography, and his cuisine. To my dismay, however, when I started trying to discover something, anything at all, about him, I learned that, while plenty had been written about him in Italian two hundred years ago and then again at the centennial of his death one hundred years ago, precious little apart from T.M. Cleland's 1913 biographical essay had ever been written in English.[2] What could I do? How could I learn more?

I did what any person totally out of her mind would do. I shook off my fascination with book thievery, brushed up my vestigial Italian, and set course for Italy, the eighteenth century, and the life and times of Giambattista Bodoni.

V.L.

SEPTEMBER 2014

BODONI

His Life and His World

Bodoni's birthplace. The plaque reads "Giovanni Batt' Bodoni born in this house on 26 February 1740 died in Parma 30 November 1813."

Saluzzo with Monviso in the background.

I

Saluzzo

PICTURE HIM! He is a vivacious child with wavy, light brown hair, and hazel eyes. Like other boys of his generation, he wears a long frock coat with large cuffs, breeches to the knee, stockings, and square-toed, buckled shoes. Diligent of hand and quick of wit, he soon reveals what the future holds for him. His toys are his grandfather's punches and matrices, and under his father's tutelage, he learns the rudiments of printing and takes to it with astonishing facility, often working with type when his schoolmates are at play. At school he rises to the top of the class and displays his passion for words, soon producing reams of prose and verse. He is well liked by his teachers and fellow students, many of whom grow up to be famous in their own right, in politics, the church, science, and academia. These fellow students have one particularly vivid memory of their childhood friend. During a religious festival with illuminations in Saluzzo, Giambattista created moving figures, representing scenes from the New Testament, on one of the exterior walls of his home.[3]

This early precursor to Italian moviemaking took place some time before his twelfth birthday, and is one of the few actual incidents on record from Bodoni's childhood. However, a glance at his hometown, his family, the institutions and patterns of the age, (and the food he ate) go far to reveal the boy's background and his destiny.

Saluzzo! Even the word sounds salutary, like a blessing for a sneeze. Bodoni's birthplace is notched into a foothill of the Cottian Alps, close to Italy's western border with France; its air is bracing and its view is wide. The cobbled streets rise sharply to the fourteenth-century castle that dominates the historic center, while lofty, snow-covered Monviso, which the Romans called Vesulus, lords it over the entire region. The house where Bodoni was born still stands at the start of a road now aptly named Via Bodoni, but the plaque on the front wall celebrating his life is today outshone by strident signs declaring *"Lavasecco"* and *"Tintoria."* The ground floor is now a dry cleaning and dyeing establishment.

According to the register in Saluzzo's Cathedral of Santa Maria Assunta and San Chiaffredo (Saluzzo's patron saint), Bodoni was born on 26 February 1740 and baptized Giovanni Battista by his uncle Carlo, a young priest. Dates of birth, so dear to the heart of biographers, are notoriously slippery. Even though Bodoni's biographer, Giuseppe De Lama, presumably getting it straight from the horse's widow's mouth, holds firm for 16 February, the *Dizionario Biografico degli Italiani* states firmly "Naque a Saluzzo il 26 (non il 16) febbr. 1740."

The Bodoni family had moved to Saluzzo from Asti (of Asti Spumante fame) in the seventeenth century, and Bodoni himself tells this story about his grandfather, Gian Domenico:

> . . . *types were cut and cast in Saluzzo, in the workshop of my grandfather Gian Domenico Bodoni. When he was young, during the pontificate of Innocent XI [1676-89], he went to Rome and stayed there some years as a compositor in the Stamperia Camerale. He made friends with an engraver whose name I do not know, and learned punchcutting. When he returned home he spent his fortune and even sold a vineyard to support his passion for cutting punches and casting type. My father told me more than once that he had seen types being cast for a Garamone [sic] body, and I myself found a furnace set up on the gallery of our house, and moulds, counterpunches, a few punches and several matrices of little value.*[4] (See Appendices I, II and III for printing terms and an explanation of the printing process.)

Gian Domenico Bodoni married into a printing family when he wed Francesca Benedetta, the daughter of the printer Nicolà Valauri, an only child who inherited her father's printing business. Unfortunately, Gian Domenico died in 1723 and the boy never had a chance to meet his grandfather in person; it would be a mistake, however, to underestimate the influence of being able to play with his grandfather's printing equipment. The printing business was in turn inherited by Bodoni's father, Francesco Agostino Bodoni, who improved and enlarged it. According to Stephan Füssel, Francesco Bodoni specialized in popular writings on cheap paper at affordable prices and "... all production stages were vertically integrated; not even the formes were bought from suppliers but were developed and cast in-house."[5] Bodoni's mother, Paola Margarita Giolitti, came from a well-known family in Cavallermaggiore, about 80 miles from Saluzzo. She was said (perhaps wishfully) to have been descended from the famous Giolito family, illustrious Piedmontese printers of the sixteenth century who made their fortune in Venice and Monferrato.

Examples of printing by Bodoni's grandfather (left) and father (right).

Giovanni Battista (whose name later became Giambattista) was the seventh child and fourth son of eleven children. Three died in infancy before his birth and one died shortly after, but he was robust and navigated the dangerous shoals of childhood with vigor, even though he was probably premature. His closest sibling in age, Angela Maria Rosalia, was born and died in May 1739; Bodoni arrived in the following February, a mere nine months later.[6]

Millennia before the Bodonis lived and died there, Saluzzo was a tribal city-state, inhabited by the mountain tribes of the Vagienni and the Salluvii. The Vagienni proved to be an irritant to Rome and were summarily annihilated in the third century B.C. As for the Salluvii, when they descended from the Alps and floated down the Durance to prey on Marseilles around 125 B.C., the Roman consul, Marcus Fulvius Flaccus, retaliated by marching into Saluzzo and taking control. At that point the Salluvii vanished into the mists of history, leaving nothing behind but a wisp of memory that survives in the word Saluzzo.

After the fall of Rome and the Dark Ages, Saluzzo became the site of territorial tugs-of-war, but during the relatively settled era of the marquisates from 1142 to 1548, the town burst into flower. Its altitude, good air, and abundance of food from nearby fertile plains provided a bulwark against decline. The marquises of Saluzzo left a legacy of impressive buildings, art, and chivalric romance. One of their most astonishing engineering feats, the first transalpine tunnel, was completed in 1481 during the marquisate of Ludovico II. This tunnel, affectionately known as *Buco di Viso* [Viso's Hole], is 75 meters long, 2.5 meters wide, and 2 meters high; it burrows under Monviso at 2,882 meters above sea level and links Italy with France. The tunnel provided a necessary and effective trade route for the transportation of salt from Provence, as well as fabric, furniture, horses, and other livestock. In return, Italy exported rice, wool, and leather to France.[7] By the middle of the eighteenth century, the tunnel had suffered many internal rock falls, so it is unlikely that the young Bodoni or his friends ever made the journey through it. Since then the tunnel has been repeatedly cleared and reopened.

Monviso, at 3,841 meters, is the highest mountain in the Cottian Alps. It is the site of the three sources of the Po, a river that persistently seeks out the East, rising near Italy's border with France, flowing past Saluzzo and then across the entire north of Italy, finally mouthing its way into the Adriatic south of Venice.

In the late fourteenth century, the Marquis Tommaso III propelled Saluzzo onto the world scene with *Le Chevalier Errant,* his rambling, allegorical, chivalric "novel," written in French, in both prose and poetry, and full of fables, legends, and peculiar science. It traces the travels and adventures of a dissolute but, of course, ultimately redeemed knight, and the concomitant dangers of earthly love. As contemporary portraits attest, the tale spawned generations of boys who rushed around on hobbyhorses, waving wooden swords.

Saluzzo and its lovely surroundings had already provided the scene for other literary adventures. Virgil mentions Vesulus (Monviso) in the *Aeneid* (X, 708). In the *Decameron*, Boccaccio tells the tale of cruel Gualtieri, marquis of Saluzzo, and his lovely wife, the infinitely patient Griselda. Petrarch tells the same tale in his *De obedientia ac fide uxoria mythologia* and his *prohemium* begins *"Est ad Italiae latus occidum Vesulus, ex Apennini iugis mons unus altissimus."*[Vesulus/Monviso on the western side of Italy is the single highest mountain in the range of the Apennines.] Petrarch attracts Chaucer, who repeats the tale of the marquis of Saluzzo, now Walter, and patient Griselda almost word for translated word in "The Clerk's Tale." Here is Chaucer's lovely description of Saluzzo (Saluces):

> *Ther is, right at the west syde of Ytaille,*
> *Doun at the roote of Vesulus the colde*
> *A lusty playn, habundant of vitaille,*
> *Where many a tour and toun thou mayst biholde,*
> *That founded were in tyme of fadres olde,*
> *And many another delitable sighte,*
> *And Saluces this noble contree highte.*
>
> The Clerk's Tale, 57-63

These lines breed speculation: might Chaucer have visited Saluzzo when he traveled to Genoa and Florence in 1373?

Bodoni called Saluzzo his sweetest, most venerated birthplace, and retained a constant affection for it throughout his life. The beauty of the landscape, the literary and artistic tradition, and the opportunity to start printing at a very early age indelibly influenced the child who would become the greatest Italian printer of his era, and arguably of all time. This then was Bodoni's patrimony: a small but important town set strategically on the top of a hill, on a trade route between France and Italy; an extravagantly fertile plain below; towering, gorgeous Monviso, one of the most perfectly shaped mountains in the world, a castle, beautiful civic and private buildings, some with terraces and exterior frescoes, including one of a particularly elegant Lady Geometry wielding an enormous pair of compasses; the hangover from chivalric romance; literary respect for patient women; and, most importantly, an already thriving printing tradition in which his own family played a major part.

In 1729, the much-titled Vittorio Amedeo II (duke of Savoy, marquis of Saluzzo, marquis of Monferrato, prince of Piedmont, count of Aosta, Moriana and Nizza, king of Sicily, king of Sardinia) issued new legislative orders to his realm concerning education. The Comune of Saluzzo was directed to locate a bright and well-illuminated house with at least five rooms to act as classrooms. The Comune chose to rent the house of Signor Cavassa, heir of a powerful Renaissance family. The Casa Cavassa was built in the fifteenth century, carved and frescoed, and accommodated the steep nature of its site by flowing down six floors. The school, operated by the Jesuits and known as the Collegio Regio, was attended by Giambattista Bodoni and his brothers. In no way a backwater establishment, it attracted famous teachers from other parts of the country.

The Casa Cavassa, where Bodoni went to school.

The school year ran from November to August or September, at which point students were required to help with the harvest. No lessons were held on Thursdays and Sundays. The bell of the civic tower rang out each school morning to announce the start of lessons, a bell that served the useful purpose of informing parents of the time and thus preventing the boys (no girls, of course) from leaving home too early and making a nuisance of themselves in the town before classes. They attended Mass at school, and each morning recited a Latin prayer in unison, giving thanks to God, requesting help from the Blessed Virgin, and invoking protection for the sovereign. During holidays, they were obliged to attend Mass in their own parish.

The legislation of 1729 had ironclad rules: students were prohibited from playing ball; from frequenting cafés, inns, and theaters; from bearing firearms and knives; and from going to balls and wearing masks. Boys who failed to respect teachers and parents were harshly punished, and those who were incompetent or irreligious faced expulsion. These regulations were instituted deliberately to help to ensure the power of Savoy, and the sovereign, expecting complete obedience, left nothing to chance. Teachers were advised what classes to include; what textbooks to adopt; how to organize the school's timetable; the way in which to correct and comment; the criteria for promoting boys from one class to the next; and the number of students per class. The regulations even went so far as to decree what homework the boys were assigned.[8]

A student was given seven years of education, but did not attend the actual school during his first year, working instead with tutors to learn how to read and write. Once installed at school, he began the study of Latin, Greek, Italian and French. Because of Saluzzo's proximity to the French border, Bodoni grew up speaking Italian and French as well as the local dialect, which was seeded with both languages. Later, mathematics, history, geography, and mythology were introduced, and finally rhetoric, science, and humanities.

Bodoni's sisters were taught to cook, mend, knit, and spin, and as members of the bourgeoisie, they could count on private tutors to teach them to "calculate" for the purpose of doing household accounts, and to read and write, as attested to by the letter of 22 September 1801 with its firm handwriting that Bodoni received from his sister Benedeta, saying "I have already written to you regarding the marriage that my son Francesco wants to make, without our consent . . . and your sister Angela has written to you . . ."[9]

Daughters of the nobility received a higher level of education. After learning to read and write, they studied French, the language of the court, reading mostly books of devotion and moral tales. They were taught to play a musical instrument, to draw, to paint, and to embroider. Poor girls were out of luck. Their job was working in the home; their challenge was to learn by example.

When the Comune first acquired the Casa Cavassa, the students and teachers endured long school hours in an unheated building with high ceilings and soaring windows, a building that threatened to collapse. The archives of the Comune contain a note of expenses for the acquisition of paper, flour, and oil for "breading" in the winter months. Breading refers to an early attempt at insulation in which paper imbued with oil and flour was placed over windows. Fortunately, in 1742, about five years before Bodoni entered the school, inspectors perceived the sorry state of the building and instituted desperately needed but minimal repairs.

The Casa Cavassa still stands, and functions as Saluzzo's delightful municipal museum. It underwent serious restoration in the nineteenth century, and visitors today can enjoy its fifteen rooms, its frescoed chamber, Hans Klemer's[10] grisaille frescoes in the inner courtyard, painted wooden ceilings, period furniture, and the thought of young Giambattista Bodoni honing his already sharp intelligence within its walls.

As well as the influence of his family and his teachers, Bodoni was subject to the influence of the ruler of Savoy, in this case the long-lived Vittorio Amedeo III, a ruler known for his military courage, honesty, hard work, and wisdom. Giambattista grew up conservatively, respecting his ruler, his teachers, the church, and his family. He profited from a fine education in a small town where printing was already well established, and he lived in beautiful surroundings. With such a childhood behind him, he became a confident, ambitious young man, unafraid to seek fame and to boldly look it in the face.

Although no portraits exist of Bodoni as a boy, those that appear after his arrival in Parma reveal a handsome man who steadily gains girth as he grows older. He clearly relished his food; perhaps he enjoyed it too much, as gout would later suggest. One thing is certain: the food on offer in Saluzzo in his early years was of the highest quality, reflecting the cosmopolitan nature of the place.

Il cuoco piemontese perfezionato a Parigi[11] is a marvelous book, published in Turin in 1766, and giving an idea of the kind of food available to the growing Bodoni family. Its anonymous author (most likely a man) follows the order of the seasons, starting with spring, which he calls the most pleasant season of all, but sadly lacking in chicks and ducklings, small birds, vegetables, and fruit. However, young hares and rabbits, piglets, lambs, calves, and kids abound, and fortunately beef has no season. Nor do eels or frogs. (Frog fricassée is a featured recipe.) Freshwater and saltwater fish are available. Artichokes, asparagus, certain kinds of mushrooms, peas, cardoons, spinach, lettuce, turnip tops, sorrel, and chervil come into season, as do strawberries, gooseberries, and cherries.

Summer sees an increase in poultry, game, and other birds, including songbirds. Beans, cauliflower, cabbage, and onions appear, along with peaches, plums, apricots, figs, currants, mulberries, melons, and pears. Autumn brings a bounty of fish, meat, cool weather vegetables and fruit, with the welcome addition of nuts, olives, and a huge variety of grapes. The lean winter months of December, January, and February, see an increase in the consumption of dairy products and dried and preserved food.

Even in 1766 Italians were already preoccupied with the preparation of coffee. The author insists that the beans be fresh and not vitiated by seawater (presumably on their perilous voyage from the Levant), should not smell moldy, and should be freshly ground. An ounce and a half of coffee per pint of water was the correct proportion, and if served with milk, that liquid had to be steaming before being poured on top of the coffee. How tempting, but forbidden, the local cafés must have been for the young Bodoni, and how delightful to celebrate the last of his schooldays by heading out to a previously forbidden café to celebrate with friends.

Yes, good food was certainly available for the growing boy. Wine, too. The area around Saluzzo was, and still is, rich in a variety of autochthonous vines, and is nowadays a center for the preservation of these ancient varietals. One light, sweet wine, *pellaverga*, was very popular in Bodoni's day and has an interesting history. Every year, one of the marchionesses of Saluzzo, Margherita di Foix, would send thirty bottles to Pope Julius II, who appreciated the wine so much that in 1511 he made Saluzzo an episcopal seat.

Religion also played its customary part in the life of the Bodoni family, and Saluzzo's dashing patron saint, the aforementioned San Chiaffredo, loomed large in the children's lives. He was easy enough for them to recognize because of his attributes of sword, standard, elm, and military attire. His handsome portrait by Hans Klemer hung in the cathedral, and his shrine in nearby Crissolo attracted pilgrims in search of miracles. Legend has him born in Egypt and a soldier in the famous Theban legion, most of whose members were Christian. In 285 A.D., the co-emperors Maximian and Diocletian, wanting to quell a revolt in Gaul, shipped the entire Theban legion, 6,600 strong, from Egypt to Rome, and then marched it north through Italy and over the Saint Bernard pass into Switzerland. After successfully crushing the revolt, the soldiers camped in nearby Agaunum (now the Swiss town of St. Maurice-en-Valais) and were ordered to celebrate their victory with sacrifices to the Roman gods. To a man, the Theban legion refused, whereupon they were decimated (that is, a tenth of them was slaughtered). When the remaining troops still refused to comply, another tenth was slaughtered, and so on. Chiaffredo escaped. He made his way back over the Alps, finally reaching Crissolo, about 30 kilometers due west of Saluzzo, where he met eventual martyrdom.

In about 522, a man fell over a precipice near Crissolo and landed miraculously unhurt. The local populace attributed the miracle to his having fallen on the very spot where a skeleton had been plowed up by a peasant, its bones attributed to San Chiaffredo. The cult of San Chiaffredo is still very much alive today, and the sanctuary in Crissolo contains his relics and a vast number of votive offerings.

AT SOME TIME during Bodoni's teenage years, just when he was finishing his course in "philosophic studies,"[12] his brother Nicolino died. Nicolino, nine years older than Giambattista, had shown enormous promise. Not only had he taken holy orders, but he had become a doctor of law, on top of which he received high honors in the public examination at the University of Turin. These achievements opened the door to his becoming tutor to the children of the marquis of San Germano. His death occurred just a year after he entered the marquis's household.

Giambattista, until then committed to the study of philosophy, immediately changed his mind in favor of following his brother into the Church. This plan was summarily scotched by the bishop of Saluzzo, who was well aware of Bodoni's overwhelming liveliness [*la soverchia sua vivacità*[13]]. After talking things over with the bishop, the youth decided to enter his father's business and train as a printer, a natural decision considering his early prowess. He also showed exceptional skill making wood engravings, often using San Chiaffredo as his subject. Everyone, but in particular the bishop, was astonished by the ease with which he accomplished his designs and how quickly he achieved results. Giambattista, too, was well satisfied with his work and, always ambitious, decided he needed a wider market than Saluzzo. Off he went to Turin, where his prints found ready buyers. He stayed for a while in that city, pleasing his father by furthering his education under the guidance of the printer Francesco Antonio Maiaresse.

Ambition had taken hold of him. Turin was all very well, but Rome would offer him greater opportunities for glory — glory for himself, for his family, for Saluzzo, for Italy. Hadn't grandfather Gian Domenico already paved the way? Bodoni returned to Saluzzo to make preparations for travel to Rome, determined to follow in his grandfather's footsteps. The bishop endorsed his plan and encouraged him to acquire training in engraving while he was there, recommending that he seek instruction from the engraver Lucchesini.

As a traveling companion, Giambattista chose his friend Ignazio Cappa, a discerning and capable young man who had also worked with his own father, a specialist in wrought iron. Bodoni beguiled him into joining the adventure, but just before they were ready to leave, Cappa lost his nerve. This did not deter Bodoni. He quickly assessed the rest of his comrades, and his eye lit on Domenico Costa, a young man destined for the Church, for whom the idea of Rome had a strong attraction. Costa turned out to be a better choice than the anxious Cappa, being filled with a soaring ambition that more than matched Bodoni's. While Bodoni intended to become the pride and joy of all Italy, Costa saw himself as an exemplary shepherd of souls and the pride and joy of God. Both came from that breed of Piemontese whom their fellow Italians described as tough and self-reliant, and both certainly lived up to this reputation.

The young men raised money for their journey however they could. Bodoni went into a frenzy of wood engraving and printing, producing a series of vignettes and decorations to sell when they arrived in Rome. He and Cappa were breezily confident about finding accommodation with family members. Costa had an uncle who was secretary to Abbot Lagnasco, the Polish ambassador to the Pontificate, and Bodoni counted on his uncle Carlo, then living in Rome, and the same priest who had baptized him.

Giambattista and Domenico chose to leave Saluzzo on Ash Wednesday, which in 1758 fell on 8 February.[14] The day before, *martedi grasso*, the Bodoni family would have prepared an enormous farewell meal that would hold Bodoni over for a lean Lent, and they would also have made sure that his knapsack was stuffed with cheese, salted anchovies, and bread for the journey.

"*Dopo aver asciugato coi loro baci le lacrime delle rispettive mamme . . .*"[15] [After having dried with their kisses the tears of their respective mammas], they said goodbye to the rest of their families. Giambattista embraced his brother Domenico, who would work for most of his life in the family printing business in Saluzzo; his sister Benedeta, just married to Angelo Lobetti (she was the only member of that generation of the Bodoni family to produce heirs); his brother, the mysterious Felice Vincenzo, about whom nothing is known; his sister, Angela; and Giuseppe, the brother who would work shoulder to shoulder with him in later years.

Then Bodoni and Costa turned their backs on Saluzzo. Giambattista was not yet eighteen years old.

IT IS ANNOYING not to know precisely by what means the boys traveled. The possibilities were: foot, horseback, diligence (a public stagecoach), and private coach, this last being extremely unlikely due to its cost. The most likely choice would be a local diligence to Turin before a long-distance diligence from Turin to Genoa, then a sailing vessel from Genoa to Civitavecchia, and another diligence from there to Rome. "*Viaggio lungo, faticoso, interminabile*"[16] says Carlo Martini. Yes—long, exhausting, and seemingly interminable for two eager young men.

The entire journey lasted from at least eight days to as much as two or three weeks, depending on the length of their stay in Genoa and their means of transportation. The diligence from Turin to Genoa stopped overnight along the way, and passengers descended to eat their meal of the day and to stay in local establishments of varying degrees of sleaziness. On offer were inns, guesthouses, and rooms in private homes. Sometimes travelers were given dirty hay to sleep on, but this might have been preferable to the *letto abitato*, a bed shared with other people and bed bugs. Tobias Smollett, the dyspeptic Scottish author, traveling in Italy at almost the same time as Bodoni, grumbles: "The hostlers, postilions, and other fellows hanging about the post-houses in Italy, are the most greedy, impertinent, and provoking. Happy are those travelers who have phlegm enough to disregard their insolence and importunity: for this is not so disagreeable as their revenge is dangerous."[17] Invariably, travelers came away feeling exploited, and quickly learned to negotiate a price before agreeing to spend the night.

Lenten fare along the way would have consisted mainly of vegetable soup, which relied heavily on field greens and a variety of legumes such as kidney beans, chickpeas, lentils, and above all fava beans. Bread, omelets, anchovies, frogs, snails, crabs, plus fresh water fish caught in local ditches and streams, would also be available[18] – for prices the boys may not have been able to afford.

At Genoa, Bodoni had his first sight of the sea; until then, his experience with important bodies of water had been exposure to a rather petite Po flowing through the lower reaches of Saluzzo and a plumper Po flowing through Turin. At Genoa, *la Superba*, with the Appenines at her back and the Mediterranean at her feet, Bodoni came into contact with a city filled with gorgeous palaces and parks plus all the seaminess of a port that was home to sailing vessels plying their trade from port to port in the Mediterranean.

Bodoni and Costa remained in Genoa waiting for transportation to take them south. Bodoni spent his time wisely: he quickly found work with a printer. (Genoa has a history of printing dating back as far as 1471.) There he earned more funds for the continuation of the journey. Finally, in the most likely scenario, he and Costa set sail for Civitavecchia, the port for Rome, rather than traveling overland.

On arrival at Civitavecchia, after a fast, stomach-churning winter sail, with the north wind racing down the coast of Italy, they would pick up a diligence for the last stage of their journey of 85 kilometers along the Via Aurelia to Rome. The closer they approached Rome, the more desolate the landscape became, a landscape exhausted by its own glorious past, now nothing more than an unproductive wasteland. After the sweet orderliness of Saluzzo, the long approach to Rome through this miserable malarial wilderness would have been disconcerting and disappointing. At last the diligence passed through the Porta San Pancrazio and into Rome, near the top of the Janiculum hill.

Now we must imagine the moment: a few paces more and the boys can quench their thirst in the huge, gushing Acqua Paola fountain, and then, looking east, they see the city unfolding in the valley below. Look! There's the Tiber! I see the Pantheon! Is that the Forum? Over there on that hill, that's Trinità dei Monti! Look at the snowcapped mountains beyond!

They had arrived at last, and all Rome lay at their feet as they gazed out across the Tiber.

The Palazzo Valentini, Bodoni's home in Rome, directly behind Trajan's column.

PLATE 1 Don Ferdinando di Borbone, Duke of Parma. Circa 1770. By Pietro Melchiorre Ferrari.

PLATE 2 Father Paolo Maria Paciaudi. By Giuseppe Lucatelli.

PLATE 3 Ennemond Petitot. By Domenico Muzzi.

PLATE 4 Guillaume Du Tillot, Prime Minister of Parma. By Pietro Melchiorre Ferrari.

PLATE 5 Don Ferdinando di Borbone, Duke of Parma. By Johann Zoffany.

PLATE 6 Maria Amalia of Austria, Duchess of Parma. By Johann Zoffany.

PLATE 7 José Nicolás de Azara. By Anton Raphael Mengs.

PLATE 8 Joachin Murat, King of Naples.

PLATE 9 Is it or isn't it Bodoni? This unnamed portrait of a young man, attributed variously
to the artists Giuseppe Baldrighi and Andrea Appiani, was long assumed to be of Bodoni.
Recently, experts in the history of clothing have dated it to the 1790s rather than the 1770s, so
unless either artist were drawing from memory, it is probably not Bodoni. However, the young
man's features so closely resemble those in Appiani's later portrait that a face-match on iPhoto
paired the two images.

PLATE 10 Giambattista Bodoni. By Andrea Appiani.

PLATE 11 Napoleon in the Robes of the King of Italy. By Andrea Appiani.

PLATE 12 Empress Marie Louise of France. Later Duchess of Parma. By Robert Lefèvre.

PLATE 13 Don Ferdinando in Maturity. Artist
unknown.

PLATE 14 Maria Amalia in Maturity. Artist
unknown.

PLATE 15 Giambattista Bodoni in 1792. By Giuseppe Turchi.

PLATE 16 Giambattista Bodoni. By Giuseppe Lucatelli.

PLATE 17 Margherita Dall'Aglio Bodoni. By Giuseppe Bossi.

PLATE 18 Camera di San Paolo by Correggio.

College of the Propaganda Fide.

2

Rome 1758–1766

The man fit to make a fortune in this ancient capital of Italy must be a chameleon sensitive to all the colors which the light casts on his surroundings. He must be flexible, insinuating, a great dissimulator, impenetrable, obliging, often base, ostensibly sincere, always pretending to know less than he does, keeping to one tone of voice, patient, in complete control of his countenance, cold as ice when another in his place would be on fire; and if he is so unfortunate as not to have religion in his heart, he must have it in his mind, and, if he is an honest man, accept the painful necessity of admitting to himself that he is a hypocrite. If he loathes the pretense, he should leave Rome and seek his fortune in England.

GIACOMO CASANOVA

I T RAINS once or twice a week in Rome in February, torrential, lashing rain. Water gushes and spews, and not just from fountains. A person can be walking along, completely unprepared for rain and, all of a sudden, sodden. Rain streams through the eye of the Pantheon, the Tiber swells, and trees along its banks drown in the swift, swirling, muddy water. The usually easy-going river becomes a raging torrent, and floods the city. Plaques on churches record the heights reached by the water over the centuries, and you crane your neck to see some of them.

Rain may have streamed down on Giambattista and Domenico as they made their way down the Janiculum hill, across the Tiber, and into the thick of things, but if they were lucky it was a sparkling winter day in which the air was mild and bright, the ochre and red buildings glowed in the sunshine, the white of ancient columns drew the eye skyward, almond and cherry trees were in blossom, and oranges were ripening on trees all over the city.

Gorgeous though it appeared, the city stank.

The population, which during the heady years of the Roman empire had reached more than two million, had declined precipitously to approximately 160,000 by 1758. Rome was experiencing rural sprawl as the countryside crept back into the city and weeds sprouted among the ruins. Previously inhabited land returned to pasture, vineyards, and wasteland. The Forum became the site of rock-throwing battles. Farm animals mooed, baa-ed, and honked their way through the streets, leaving a trail of excrement behind them. Despite the considerable available space, the Roman people crowded together near the bend in the Tiber and on the Quirinal hill, their homes surrounded by elegant churches and palazzi, even as they lived cheek by jowl with their livestock. "The corridores [sic], arcades, and even staircases of their most elegant palaces, are depositories of nastiness, and indeed in summer smell as strong as spirit of hartshorn,"[19] grumbled Smollett, and with justification.

Certainly, Rome was warmer, smellier, louder, more crowded, and more be-witching than Saluzzo. The new arrivals found it crammed with clerics, venders, artists, dealers, writers, aristocrats, foreigners, shepherds and shepherdesses (often elegantly dressed and without sheep), servants, and the omnipresent poor. They had landed in the religious *omphalos*, the cultural magnet, the academy of Europe, at a moment when Rome was the apogee of the Grand Tour. Participants in the Tour were drawn to Rome by Piranesi's engravings, which circulated all over Europe and lured pale, northern moths to a city that reeked of the decay that accompanies monumental splendor and the sweat of romantically inspired artistic endeavor. But the Grand Tourists were mainly drawn to Rome by the itch for possession. They wanted to see Rome and buy, and agents like the Scottish artist/archaeologist Gavin Hamilton were only too pleased to assist them.

That the city was crammed with clerics is no overstatement; forty percent of the population consisted of clergy, including at least thirty orders of monks. The

Capuchins, with their recognizable hoods, brown habits, beards, and bare feet, were the most beloved. They took on tasks that others avoided: pulling teeth, attending the funerals of the poor, and acting as models for artists who could ill afford the going rate. Even men who were not members of the clergy often dressed as if they were. Ministering to the poor by both clergy and lay people was a Christian duty and taken seriously for the indulgences it bestowed, but the beggars' omnipresence struck visitors forcibly. "It is execrable to see the amount of beggars by whom one is assailed in the streets of Rome," laments Charles de Brosses, on his visit to Rome in 1739.[20]

When Bodoni arrived in 1768, Pope Benedict XIV (Prospero Lambertini) was nearing the end of his reign. Regarded as the most erudite of all the popes, he made his particular mark with his ecclesiastical writings. Learned in a wide range of topics including science and mathematics, he was also a diplomat and skilled negotiator, even on occasion capable of reconciling Catholics and Protestants. A witty and sometimes racy conversationalist, he sought the company of clever people in all levels of society. He was well acquainted with the poor with whom he conversed during his walks into the more unsavory parts of Rome.

Horace Walpole, one of Pope Benedict's most dedicated admirers, composed the following words about him for an inscription: "A priest without insolence, a prince without favorites, a pope without nepotism, an author without vanity. In short, a man whom neither wit nor power could spoil."[21] When the pope saw a copy of this inscription, he is said to have smiled and shaken his head, declaring, "Alas! I am like the statues of the Piazza S. Pietro — admirable at a distance but monstrous when seen at close quarters!"[22]

Benedict XIV was determined that Rome should be the city where art and religion flourished in seamless magnificence. He supervised urban beautification projects, including most of the construction of the Trevi fountain, and initiated the restoration of many of Rome's major churches. He spent time and money supporting archaeological excavations, procuring antiquities, and buying hundreds of paintings for his new public museums. Giambattista Bodoni had arrived in a city that was humming with activity.

Even as foreigners chafed against a government ruled entirely by a clerical gerontocracy, they thrived

Pope Benedict XIV.

on Rome's artistic opportunities. Collectors and dealers found treasures to buy and sell. Artists profited from ecclesiastical commissions; there was no apparent prejudice against foreign artists, although they were required to bow to a timetable that ordained countless feast days and elaborate religious festivals that included processions, ephemeral buildings, street theatre, fireworks, and free wine and food, all of which, though enjoyable, resulted in time wasted and lost productivity.

Other pastimes included *conversazioni*, nocturnal parties where sparkling conversation was enhanced by gaming, music, and refreshments. Pleasure could be had, too, in cafés and the city squares, but sometimes the entertainment could be gruesome when the squares became sites for public punishments such as flagellation and execution.

In opposition to any lack of taste (say over-enthusiasm for flagellation and execution), the Accademia dell'Arcadia was formed in Rome in 1690 and waved its banner on behalf of good taste. Arcadia refers to an actual, secluded, pastoral region of the Peloponnesus in Greece that became a proverbial utopia, immortalized by Virgil in his *Eclogues*. Members of the Accademia considered Arcadia their spiritual homeland, chose a district in Arcadia to hail from, took names from bucolic classical literature, and dressed up as those *pastori* and *pastorelle* (shepherds and shepherdesses) who could be seen herding their imaginary sheep all over town.

At the time of Bodoni's arrival, Arcadianism was in full flower, and it permeated fashion and the arts. The Accademia's aims were a return to a simpler way of life and the promotion of good taste according to classical precepts; its members were required to find a sensible balance between nature and reason, passion and intellect, truth and imagination. It is hard to overestimate its influence during the eighteenth century and the prestige it conferred upon its members. An Arcadian possessed an automatic entry into society. Naturally enough, the ever-ambitious Bodoni eventually became a member.

Giambattista Bodoni and Domenico Costa stumbled into this roiling, seamy stew of ecclesiastical fervor, Arcadianism, and assertive commerce. They shouldered their way past beggars, jumped out of the paths of rich men's carriages, and inhaled the heady aromas of grilled fish and meat, and boiled cabbage. Even as they admired the column of Marcus Aurelius, they were overwhelmed by the smell of coffee. The foot of the column was the preferred site for roasting beans for the entire city.

Rome was indeed a city of smells, in part because eighteenth-century Romans did not appreciate the smell of food being prepared inside their houses (or, indeed, smells of any kind indoors, particularly perfume, which they regarded as a disgusting French phenomenon). Grilling was performed out of doors at fish or meat stalls, with separate stalls for sauces. Huge vats of tripe, enough to satisfy the entire city, were stewed in front of the church of San Marcello,[23] and special cabbage cooks set up cauldrons in the Piazza Colonna, sometimes enhancing the flavor of the vegetable with bacon fat and garlic. Young boys would then hurry the aromatic, steaming cabbage to its destination, in the manner of pizza delivery today.

In the Piazza Navona, the din of venders even overpowered the sound of Bernini's gigantic Fountain of the Four Rivers. Because it was still Lent when Bodoni arrived, bakers loudly hawked their *maritozzi*, specially baked but extremely dry buns. Farmers from the countryside and fishermen from the shore jostled with each other, yelling out their wares: eggs, fish, eels, snails, cheese, corn meal, bread, and vegetables, especially those of the early spring season, such as artichokes and a variety of salad greens. The true star of the spring was *puntarelle*, a form of chicory even now deeply loved in Rome and eaten with a pesto of anchovies, garlic, and olive oil.

Everywhere they looked, the boys saw new sights: a barber holding high his blade as he shaved a customer; a scrivener dutifully writing letters at the bidding of the illiterate; Jesuits praying; acrobats; fortune tellers; drummers (useful for their ability to mask the screams of those having their teeth pulled); quacks touting their miracle cures; performing goats; lottery ticket sellers; lemonade venders; astrologers; strolling musicians; and the *cavalletto,* a torture rack with a mechanical thrashing component that acted as a threat to and a punishment for wrongdoers.[24] The sheer number of clerics on the streets was stunning, but most important for Bodoni was the stone lettering everywhere, beautiful letters, square and clear, huge capital Roman letters, marching across facades, advertising the city itself.

Tired, stunned, hungry, and almost penniless, Bodoni and Costa sought out their uncles. First they hunted down Costa's, *"ma l'effeto non corrispose"* (to no effect).[25] But surely Bodoni's uncle, the very man who had baptized him, his father's own dear brother, would prove more welcoming? No. Carlo Bodoni was nowhere to be found in Rome. He was away in the Sabine hills outside the city, working as a Lenten preacher.[26] (It turns out that his greatest claim to fame was his indefatigable effort in trying to convert Jews to Christianity.)[27]

No record remains of where the boys found lodging, but during the days that followed, an increasingly destitute Bodoni went from print shop to print shop, selling the last of his wood engravings. In a squishily hagiographic piece celebrating the two-hundredth anniversary of Bodoni's birth, Alfonso M. Begheldo says that Bodoni gave Rome his little works in wood and that Rome gave him its spirit and a sense of catholicity that knew no bounds.[28] At this point Bodoni would more likely have appreciated a loaf of bread; but perhaps the situation was not too dire. Modesto Paroletti, a lawyer and author from Turin, claims that a man named Bima decided to become a Capuchin monk and, upon taking his vow of poverty, handed over a healthy sum to Bodoni.[29] Bodoni had an uncanny knack for bettering himself through the benefit of clergy.

Pope Clement XIII.

With the rest of Rome, he and Costa celebrated Easter on 26 March 1758. Weeks passed. With the rest of Rome, they became obsessed with the death on 3 May of Pope Benedict XIV and the subsequent rituals to ensure his safe passage to heaven. With the rest of Rome they waited through June and July for the election of a new pope. Finally, on July 16, puffs of white smoke emerged from the roof of the Sistine chapel. The cardinals had chosen Carlo della Torre di Rezzonico, the super-modest Pope Clement XIII, who today is best remembered for his moral strength, for championing the Jesuits in the face of increasing opposition, and for fig-leafing Vatican statuary, all the while resembling, in James Boswell's words, "a jolly landlord."

None of the boys' ambitious plans for advancement and fame bore fruit. Finally, rejecting the idea of an ignominious retreat to their maternal bosoms, they decided to seek their fortunes elsewhere and move to another city.[30] Bodoni was well aware that Rome and its surroundings were no longer the hotbed of Italian printing, even though Subiaco, just 40 kilometers away had been the first city in Italy to attract printers from Germany, shortly after Gutenberg's invention of moveable type in 1450. Perhaps they would have better luck in Florence, Milan, or Venice.

Bodoni made one last ditch visit to the distinguished press of Generoso Salomini.[31] Although Salomini had no work to offer Bodoni, he was impressed by the boy's lively personality and way with words, and immediately saw a future for him. He decided to introduce him to Abbé Costantino Ruggieri, the superintendent of the press at the Sacra Congregatio de Propaganda Fide (the Sacred Congregation for the Propagation of the Faith), which was the missionary arm of the Vatican.

Ruggieri was also the secretary to Cardinal Spinelli, the prefect of the Propaganda Fide. Salomini marched Bodoni over to the cardinal's palace, where they had the good fortune to run into Abbé Ruggieri on the main staircase. Salomini asked Ruggieri if he would intervene with the cardinal and seek help and protection for the young man. Ruggieri questioned Bodoni closely on various aspects of printing, and particularly about his woodcuts. As it was midday, he gave Bodoni some money for lunch, and told him to come back afterwards to meet the cardinal.

Cardinal Giuseppe Spinelli.

When Cardinal Spinelli saw Bodoni's woodcuts, he felt they were too good to have been created by such a young man. He decided to put him to the test. He set him up in a room alone, and asked him to prove his worth by cutting a coat of arms. Bodoni first drew the design, and then with just a few tools managed to incise a perfect woodcut in the space of three hours. The cardinal and the abbé were astonished and delighted with the result.[32] They were so pleased that they hired Bodoni on the spot as an assistant compositor (typesetter), and Cardinal Spinelli even invited Bodoni to live with him at the Palazzo Valentini.

The Palazzo Valentini is monumental. Now the seat of the Province of Rome, it is situated on the Via IV Novembre near the Piazza Venezia,[33] just a stone's throw from where Ruggieri lived in the Piazza SS. XII Apostoli. The palace is built around a rectangular courtyard, with its back flanking Trajan's forum. Cardinal Spinelli established a library of 28,000 volumes on the ground floor, a library not just for the use of scholars such as J. J. Winckelmann, who had already been working with Spinelli for years, but also for the general public.

With Trajan's column just a few meters away, Bodoni could simply roll out of bed in the morning, let himself out the back door of the palace, and come face to face with bas reliefs of the Dacians and the Romans fighting their way up the column. A few steps more, around to its front, he could read the inscription, cut in large Roman capitals, strong and pure, those famous letters that have imprinted themselves on the minds of generations of type designers.

Bodoni had landed on his feet. Living in a cardinal's palace suited him very well and, as Carlo Martini so charmingly concludes, the Propaganda Fide press was the springboard for his immortal flight.[34]

Meanwhile, Costa gave up on finding his way in Rome, but he did not give up

The inscription at the base of Trajan's column.

on the church. He returned to Piedmont, became a parish priest, and remained in close contact with his friend.

The press buzzed with activity. It was housed in the building owned by the Propaganda Fide, itself an organization established by Pope Gregory XV in 1622 as a means of strengthening and uniting the various missions that were spreading the Catholic faith throughout the world. This missionary work was particularly important in the battle for souls in Africa and Asia, where Protestantism was beginning to take hold as a result of Dutch and British commerce and colonialism. Naturally, Catholic missionaries going to those fronts needed weapons — bibles and missals printed in the vernacular — and this requirement meant the Propaganda Fide had a steady need for types cut in non-Latin alphabets in various sizes. Fortunately, it already owned punches and matrices for 23 languages, including an Illyrian face, a gift from Holy Roman Emperor Ferdinand II (1578-1637).[35] For its printer's mark, the press used the armorial bearings of the Propaganda Fide: a globe, a cross, and the words from Saint Matthew 28:19, "*Euntes docete omnes gentes.*" [Go and make disciples of all people.]

The building is even now located at the north end of the Piazza di Spagna.[36] In shape, it is a raffish rhomboid, thanks to its challenging site, to the work of various architects, to additions over time, and to Borromini's high baroque, curvy brilliance. With its shortest side on the Piazza di Spagna, it widens between the Via della Propaganda Fide and the Via Due Macelli. The site was originally occupied by the Palazzo Ferratini, which in 1633 was donated by its owner, a Monsignor Vives, to the Congregation. In the subsequent 30 years, it underwent considerable alteration and construction, overseen at first by the great architect and sculptor Bernini, who added a small, oval chapel to the existing building and redesigned the short façade on the Piazza di Spagna, while the architect Gaspare de Vecchi re-designed the whole east wing. Out went Bernini and in came his rival, Borromini, who designed a flamboyantly original façade on the Via della Propaganda Fide, which is difficult to appreciate because of the narrowness of the street. Then, in an act that was true to his art but grossly unkind, Borromini knocked down Bernini's chapel and replaced it with a larger, rectilinear building of his own design, the Rei Magi chapel (said to have been given that name in honor of the three kings who were Christianity's first converts). Poor Bernini. Each day he had to suffer the ignominy of the destruction of his chapel and the erection of Borromini's, all of which he witnessed from the palazzo he had built for himself one street away.

Bodoni started work at the Propaganda Fide press one day near the end of 1758.[37] By chance, it was a perfect moment to arrive. Cardinal Spinelli, the prefect, was deeply committed to spreading the Catholic faith and enlarging the press. On 1 September 1758, he had appointed the indefatigable Costantino Ruggieri as superintendent. Ruggieri hailed from Santarcangelo, a small town on the Via Emilia in Romagna, not far from Rimini. He was a philologist, a man of intelligence and erudition, who had the respect of a range of scholars, among them the pope himself.[38] He was also referred to as a *tipo cupo*, a gloomy chap. He came to Rome from Padre Martini's enormous music library in Bologna to work in the library of Cardinal Pietro Ottoboni (1667-1740). Here was a cardinal devoted to music, art, architecture, and sexual congress. (It is said that his bedroom sported portraits of his mistresses dressed up as saints, and that he fathered between 60 and 70 children.)

Ottoboni had a particular task in mind for Ruggieri. As cardinal-bishop of

Piazza di Spagna. The Propaganda Fide is the building in the central background and the Spanish Steps are on the left.

Portus, he had become interested in Saint Hippolytus, an earlier bishop of that town, and he needed someone to write a dissertation on the saint, proving for all time Hippolytus's connection with Portus and not Aden (on the southwest tip of the Arabian peninsula) as had been claimed. Ruggieri proved to be the perfect man for the task. Already an antiquarian, an accomplished scholar, and a scrupulous researcher, and with Ottoboni's huge collection of books and historical material at his disposal, he set to work with enthusiasm. By 1740, the dissertation was deemed ready for printing by the Vatican press. Just before this could happen, Ottoboni fell sick of a fever and died, and the dissertation languished for decades before it was published. The sensitive Ruggieri sank into a spell of deep melancholy. However, his reputation for competence and scholarly exactitude preceded him, and his melancholy lifted when Cardinal Spinelli invited him to Rome to run the Propaganda Fide press.

With the return of physical and intellectual vigor, Ruggieri began to breathe new life into the establishment. He quickly recognized that a great deal of hard work was necessary to bring the press back to its former glory and capacity after years of decline. He was the new broom sweeping clean; he had grand ideas for the press, and they required talented helpers.

BODONI, THE YOUNG MAN preparing to step across the threshold of his new life, was tall, virile, well proportioned, and so agile that, during his years in Rome, he was nicknamed "the deer."[39] He had a head of rich, reddish-brown hair; his forehead was wide; his nose was rather long (but dignified); his eyes were moderately large, keenly expressive, and contained the glint of ambition; his mouth was ready to smile.[40] Think, then, of a dashing Bodoni with that glint in his eye striding through Borromini's enormous entrance, with the chapel of the Rei Magi to his left, the grand staircase to his right, and the enormous courtyard facing him. The place was alive: missionaries, functionaries, librarians, servants, and proto-priests from all over the world bustled around. Bodoni sought out the press and found it on the opposite side of the courtyard, established in two dark, cramped rooms on the ground floor.[41] The setting was far too small to contain the superintendent's ambitious plans.

Ruggieri was determined that the compositors and printers should have space and light so they could do their work with exactitude. He ordered new presses, and in January 1759, shortly after Bodoni's arrival, he moved the printing house to five spacious, light-filled rooms on the fifth floor, allotting one room to the two compositors, and the rest to the three casters, four punchcutters, an engraver, and the presses themselves.[42] The book store remained on the first floor where it attracted street trade, while customers could visit a room on the second floor to browse through examples of all the publications published by the Propaganda Fide press. Arriving just as Ruggieri's new broom was sweeping clean, Bodoni's timing was impeccable. He soon became indispensable both as a technician and an artist, fulfilling any task he was given with confidence and skill: assistant, printer, compositor, and woodcutter of letters and decorations. Passerini, writing in 1804, notes that the woodcuts Bodoni made there "are still today jealously guarded and saved because they are of a fineness just less than if they had been made on copper."[43]

The prefect and the superintendent kept a close eye on Bodoni, noticing his skill and his enthusiasm for typesetting in foreign languages. They quickly recognized that he would be the man for a finicky job that was long overdue. Stuffed away in the nether regions of the Propaganda Fide were boxes and boxes of punches (see Appendix 1, "Cutting a Punch") in a wide variety of languages, all jumbled up, rusted, and filthy.

Like the punches themselves, stories about their provenance are jumbled. The received wisdom, handed down from biographer to biographer, is that Pope Sixtus V (1520-1590), that absolute tornado of ruthless reform, commissioned the Frenchmen Claude Garamond and Guillaume Le Bé to come to Rome and cut punches in the exotic languages (that is, languages other than those in Roman type) necessary to propagate the Catholic faith in countries where Protestantism was gaining an increasing foothold. However, James Mosley, the great historian of type, points out that Garamond never left France, and Le Bé, who may have made it to Rome, is not on record as having cut any punches there. Mosley also comments that Sixtus V, who was pope from 1585-1590, would have had trouble in bringing Garamond to Rome because the Frenchman had died in Paris in 1561. Just where the jumbled punches came from, and who cut them, remains a mystery.[44]

After a flurry of useful activity during the pontificates of Gregory and Sixtus, they had fallen into disuse. A hundred and fifty years later, these were the punches ("an immense typographic arsenal"[45]) that Ruggieri handed over to Bodoni. What a rush of nostalgia for Bodoni as he handled the dirty, rusty objects and recalled his childhood self on the gallery of his home in Saluzzo, playing with his grandfather's collection of old punches. He started to play again, to clean, to repair, to sort this printers' tower of Babel, and to place the letters safely in their proper cases. In the course of this work, fondling and ultimately revivifying neglected objects, Bodoni found his true love.

It was time to design a face and to cut punches himself. Lacking experience with steel (until then he had only cut wood letters and decorations), he enlisted the help of a friend, a German engraver of medals, one Bernardo Bergher. It was a poor choice. Though an expert with medals, Bergher was a dunce with punches. He rushed the job, and the punches ended up shoddily cut and poorly justified. To make things worse, after the proofs were taken, sad affairs that they were, Bodoni examined the pieces of type and found they had completely broken down, either from poor casting or poor metal, or a combination of both. He learned from the experience, and it sharpened his determination to shift for himself. He picked up graver and file, and working entirely on his own, cut a decoration, cast it, and printed it — and it was beautiful. Heady with success, he started to cut and cast more letters, some simple, some elaborate, some exquisitely small. He was critical of his first small typeface, which he cut in the style of Garamond, but it was much admired and praised all over Rome.[46] He became a magician with his tools, and soon acquired a reputation for skill and perfectionism. He joined the ranks of the punchcutters at the press, and was rewarded for his efforts, as the following record of payment attests: "To Gio. Battista Bodoni . . . in payment for various decorations, tailpieces, and miniature alphabets and other services to the said printing office, the sum of 10 scudi."[47]

Cardinal Spinelli decided to broaden Bodoni's skills by sending him to university for the study of exotic languages. The University of Rome, "La Sapienza" [wisdom], was then located in the Palazzo della Sapienza. Set squarely, or rather, rectangularly, between the Pantheon and the Piazza Navona, it was founded in 1303 by Pope Boniface VII, making it almost as old as the Sorbonne.[48] It offered a range of disciplines in addition to its prime subjects, theology and religious history. Law, literature, medicine, and foreign languages flourished, but the hard sciences, although taught, were regarded with suspicion, while natural sciences were largely ignored. Astronomy was anathema.

Bodoni duly reported to the university and plunged into the study of Arabic and Hebrew.[49] Focusing closely on how the scripts were constructed, he quickly gained a visual knowledge of the languages, and this knowledge became the foundation for his lifelong obsession with foreign type.

Bodoni was not only absorbed in the study of languages, he was also influenced by his surroundings at La Sapienza. Each day as he entered the quadrangle, he came face to face with the astonishing university chapel of Saint Ivo. Just as Borromini's Rei Magi chapel at the Propaganda Fide loomed large in Bodoni's personal geography of Rome, so now did Saint Ivo, also designed by Borromini, and completed in 1660. The building is pure geometry: its footprint is a circle and two superimposed equilateral triangles, making up a Star of David. On the other hand, it is a novel masterpiece of the High Baroque, full of striking originality and organic movement, provided in large part by Borromini's signature convex and concave undulations, and the lighthearted riff on Trajan's column that his spire displays.

Saint Ivo's is a bride of a church, white, white, white — a place in which to sit and to dream of paper (if you were Bodoni), as in the pure white of the interior; and of ink, as in the sharp black and white of the floor tiles; and of letters, as in the complex geometry of the structure. But it seems as though something of the coils and countercoils of the High Baroque began to disturb Bodoni. Although his own wood engravings were full of the fashionable twirls and curlicues of the period, he was continually drawn to what he saw in purely classical buildings and monuments, but more importantly, to the inscriptions on them.

In the elegant surroundings of Borromini's High Baroque church and library, Bodoni began to change. The young man from Piedmont was on his way to becoming very classical in his tastes and intentions, very elegant, and very, very grand.

WHEN CARDINAL SPINELLI and Abbé Ruggieri saw how adept Bodoni was at working with exotic alphabets, they decided he should replace the current aged and incompetent compositor of foreign languages. One of the first volumes they assigned to him was Bishop Raffaele Tuki's *Pontificale copto-arabo* (a pontifical contains the rites performed by bishops). For this work, he was greatly assisted by Father Giorgi, his Arabic teacher at La Sapienza. Bodoni was

Saint Ivo. Interior of dome.

required not only to design the book but to provide a title page and various decorations throughout. For the title page, he cut the letters and decorations in wood, but for the text he used metal letters in Coptic and Arabic which were already on hand at the Propaganda Fide.[50] He placed the languages in two columns, and printed the book in two colors, black and red. Ruggieri, on seeing the first printing, insisted that Bodoni place his name and city on the title page of subsequent printings. This was an astonishing accolade for a lowly apprentice and salient evidence of Ruggieri's appreciation of the young man's work (Plates 20 & 21).

Beautiful though Bodoni's bold and colorful title page is, the head- and tail-pieces are disconcerting. They have absolutely nothing to do with pontifical rites in the Arabo/Coptic church and everything to do with High Baroque excess. In one, two lions with human heads flank the torso of a hermaphroditic Flora spewing forth from a sunflower, head laden with a basket of fruit. But look closely, and you'll find a neat Roman B, set in the middle of a triangle below the torso, at what would be knee level if Flora's lower half were not subsumed in a sunflower stalk. With this Roman B, set in a stylistically discordant engraving within a particularly complex and serious religious work, Bodoni revealed his presence. The letter looks superimposed on the engraving, tacked on in a moment of self-congratulation.

Tail-piece with "B" in *Pontificale arabo-copto*.

The only rationale possible for this *jeu d'esprit* (and the excuse is a real stretch) is that the B might reflect the squareness of the Coptic characters, while the Baroque flourishes of the decoration reflect the undulations of Arabic script. Perhaps Bodoni was in a flurry of typesetting when Ruggieri asked him to include some decorations, so he sought out something he had already in hand. Finding a decoration the right size for his purpose, he inserted Flora (a tiny touch of carnality) and his Roman B (Look at me! Look at me!) into the august surroundings of the *Pontificale copto-arabo*.

BODONI WORKED concurrently on another book, the *Alphabetum Tibetanum*, by the aforementioned Father Antonio Agostino Giorgi (1711-1797). A good friend to Ruggieri, Giorgi was director of the Biblioteca Angelica, procurator general of the Augustinians, and a seasoned warrior against any threat that challenged the precepts of his order, especially Protestantism.[51] A professor of exotic languages, a linguistic phenomenon who spoke eleven languages fluently, Giorgi was also an esteemed scholar in Greek and Roman classics, Christian theology, and science. But he was at heart an orientalist, engaged in the preparation of a compendium that eventually became his colossal *Alphabetum Tibetanum*.

The first edition of this work, which came out in 1759 (a year after Bodoni's arrival at the press) is a relatively short 208-page examination of the Tibetan language, but the second edition, to which the first is attached at the end, reaches 820 pages, and is a lengthy discourse on Manichaeism, the evils of divine emanation, the origin of the Buddha, Japanese and Indian divinities, and of course, the power and glory of the Catholic faith.[52] It is based on reports sent back to Rome from Lhasa by the Capuchin missionaries, Francisco Orazio della Penna di Billi and Cassiano di Macerata, and is still in circulation today. Throughout the work, Father Giorgi wastes no time in flaunting the superiority of the Catholic Church over the teachings of the Buddha; nor does he hesitate to make some astonishing, far-reaching cross-cultural linguistic comparisons, thus displaying to advantage his immense erudition, if less than logical judgment.

It comes as no surprise that Bodoni was chosen to work on this book, having studied with Father Giorgi and profited from his help while working on the Arabo-Coptic pontifical. The *Alphabetum Tibetanum* was a brute to typeset, containing as it did many foreign languages interspersed with the Latin narrative, as well as text diagrams and six fascinating engraved plates by Alexius Giardoni of subjects such as prayer wheels, the crucified Indra, and the Bhudda's toenails. Once again, Bodoni provided some ill-suited head- and tail-pieces.[53]

It is hard to assess how many more books Bodoni worked on during his years at the Propaganda press. We know about the *Pontificiale* and the *Alphabetum Tibetanum* because they are mentioned by his biographers and scrupulously scrutinized by Sergio Samek Ludovici,[54] but it is impossible to ascertain what other publications he typeset and decorated. It is, however, easy to speculate that his fellow compositors became resentful about seeing his name on publications while they remained anonymous, and this resentment could have caused Ruggieri to stop singling him out. Whatever the case, Bodoni's subsequent work at the press is unacknowledged. We know he's there, but he's a shadow figure.[55]

YOUNG GIAMBATTISTA was far from dull, and this begs the question: What was he up to in his spare time in a city that was rife with variety and known for its sexual license?

De Lama states that in his hours of leisure Bodoni cut decorations and flowery capitals, and cut tiny characters, which were highly admired in Rome. Is this believable? Certainly, to some extent. But Bodoni was an attractive young man at the height of his sexual powers, living in Rome at a vibrant moment in the city's history, and it is hard to believe that he spent all his time whittling away when all Rome was on offer.[56]

Outside the building lay the Piazza di Spagna, from which the Spanish Steps, like a backdrop for an opera, climbed towards the church of the Trinità dei Monti. The piazza and its immediate surroundings were the favored home of expatriates, including those who had dealings with Cardinal Spinelli and the Propaganda Fide press. Among them was archaeologist, librarian, art historian, and pederast J.J. Winckelmann, who lived in the Palazzo Zuccari, at the top of the Steps, from where he could survey the whole city. His view, however, did nothing to mitigate his complaints about lack of sleep because of the frightful noise of shouting, shooting, and fireworks that often lasted until daybreak.

The Piazza di Spagna was indeed the noisy meeting place of Rome. Working at the Propaganda Fide, Bodoni was aware of its powerful draw during the day, but what about his nighttime activities? After a day's work, all he had to do was to walk out the door of the press to find himself confronted with . . . Life! Gorgeous Roman women! Pretty girls and their mothers! Foreigners! Elegant shepherds and shepherdesses! Homosexuals! Castrati! Transvestites! Harlequins! Actors! (but no actresses—the Church, which turned a blind eye to adultery and courtesans, was firm about outlawing actresses). And pretty young boys dressed as girls, who spoke with flutelike voices and, with some anatomical adjustments, acquired "plump, round hips, buttocks, and necks."[57] It became extremely difficult to tell the boys from the girls as they strutted about the Piazza di Spagna but, as Giacomo Casanova, who was in Rome at the same time as Bodoni, knew only too well, the challenge was *so* enticing.

Roman women, whatever their age or station in life, took care to present "*bella figura.*" That is, they paid close attention to their appearance, but in a far more natural manner than French women, whose opulent, panniered fashions the Roman upper classes admired and emulated to a certain degree, while the lower classes usually wore traditional costumes. Roman women adored unguents but eschewed rouge and perfume, having "an unconquerable revulsion for odors, maintaining that the use of perfume is pernicious in this climate, and makes them faint."[58] The naturalness of Roman women, their air of comfortably inhabiting their bodies, made the rest of Europe suspicious and uncomfortable. Roman matrons frequently had lovers, an arrangement condoned by their husbands, who often married them for money or prestige. However, the chastity of young, unmarried women was zealously guarded by their mothers, and it took the charm, skill, and determination of a Casanova to make a conquest.[59]

While Cardinal Spinelli and Abbé Ruggieri may have averted Bodoni's gaze from Roman women, they certainly made sure that he met cardinals, gentlemen, and scholars, and that he moved in ever higher social, ecclesiastical, and scholarly circles.[60] One of the most influential ecclesiastics he met was a fellow Piemontese, Father Paolo Maria Paciaudi, Cardinal Spinelli's librarian. This meeting with Father Paciaudi was the most important encounter of Bodoni's life.

Born in Turin in 1710, Paciaudi was a fashionable preacher, whose stirring sermons were intended to induce the aristocratic congregations of churches such as Sant' Andrea della Valle into a life of virtue. He was also a highly respected scholar, archaeologist, and librarian. A Theatine monk, he practiced the principles of that order in his efforts to reform Catholic morality, and he waged an ecclesiastical hot war on the teachings of Martin Luther. Paciaudi had a particular interest in the work of the Polyglot Press at the Propaganda Fide because the Theatines were the first order to found papal missions overseas. He kept his eye on Bodoni's progress and was amazed, like everyone else, by the young man's skill. He would remember this skill long after leaving Rome for Parma in 1761.

Another distinguished scholar/archaeologist with whom Bodoni would have come into contact through Father Paciaudi and Cardinal Spinelli was J.J. Winckelmann. Often referred to as the father of art history, Winckelmann worked as Cardinal Albani's librarian and as scriptor and prefect of antiquities at the Vatican. He was known for his particularly beautiful Greek script and his insistence on the use of the clearest possible Greek type for the printing of books. He felt that standards of printing in that language had slipped since the days of Robert Estienne (1503-1559), whose publications in Greek were renowned for their elegance and clarity. Bodoni paid attention to this insistence on clarity and beauty, and took it especially to heart when cutting and printing his own Greek type, said to be his favorite type of all.

The man with whom Bodoni spent most time was, of course, Abbé Costantino Ruggieri. They worked closely together, and Ruggieri witnessed Bodoni's competence quickly outstripping that of his colleagues in the studio. Ruggieri's admiration for Bodoni blossomed into love. Passerini recounts what happened: "So this learned man fell in love with him, and started to feel so much regard for him that he desired his company on his daily walk, all the more so because it seemed to him that the gloom with which he was often assailed was in large part eased by Bodoni's lively and witty company."[61] Early each morning, Bodoni set out from the Palazzo Valentini for Ruggieri's apartment in nearby Piazza SS. XII Apostoli, and together they walked the streets of Rome until Ruggieri was ready to go to work.

Abbé Ruggieri's world was shattered when Cardinal Spinelli died suddenly on 12 April 1763.[62] Bodoni, too, was grief-stricken by the death of that warm and generous man who had done so much for art and archaeology, for the modernization and expansion of the Propaganda Fide press, and for Bodoni himself. Indeed, the cardinal's death saddened the whole city. His body was transported in a cavalcade from the Palazzi Valentini to the church of SS. XII Apostoli. There he lay in state, and after his funeral he was buried below the middle of the nave, resting beneath an elaborately decorated and effusively wordy tombstone, alas now almost illegible.

LIFE IN ROME went swirling on. Visitors kept coming and going, eating and drinking. On the subject of eating and drinking, Smollett notes: ". . . the vitella mongana, which is the most delicate veal I have ever tasted, is very dear . . . Here are the rich wines of Montepulciano, Montefiascone, and Monte di Dragone; but what we commonly drink at meals is that of Orvieto, a small white wine, of an agreeable flavour."[63] Casanova gave a dinner party for the family of Momolo (an ex-gondolier who became a sweeper for the pope) whose daughter he was aiming to seduce, and comments, "The polenta was excellent, the pork superb, the ham perfect. In less than an hour there was no longer any sign that the table had once been covered with things to eat; but the Orvieto wine continued to keep the company cheerful."[64] Charles de Brosses admitted to being bowled over by the exquisite flavor of Tiber sturgeon. Hot chocolate and ices were all the rage.

Tomatoes were a recent phenomenon and were still regarded with suspicion. A few years later, in the poem *"Er pranzo e el minente,"* (translated by Gillian Riley), Giuseppe Gioacchino Belli exulted in the variety and excellence of Roman food.

Just listen to what we had. Rice and peas,
A stew of beef and turkey cock,
Beef topside pot roast with cloves, a right old dish of tripe,
And spit roast sausages and pork liver.
Then a fry-up of artichokes and sheeps' balls,
Some sinful gnocchi to die for,
A puffed-up take-away pizza,
Sweet sour wild boar and game birds.
There were peppers in vinegar,
Salami, mortadella, and a fresh sheep's cheese,
House plonk, [65] *and wine from Orvieto.*
Next some divine rosolio, [66]
Coffee and sweet bread rings,
And radishes to gladden the heart. [67]

Visitors from abroad streamed into the city. On 15 October 1764, Edward Gibbon, author of *The Decline and Fall of the Roman Empire*, wrote: "I was sitting and reflecting among the ruins of the Campidoglio, with the barefoot brothers singing vespers in the temple of Jove, when for the first time the idea of writing about the decline and fall of Rome came to mind." Meanwhile, James Boswell was spending almost all his time with women, but not just prostitutes. On 16 February 1765, he noted that he danced and dined with the young Swiss/Austrian artist, Angelica Kauffmann, and then chatted with her, calling her "paintress singer; modest, amiable," adding "Quite in love." [68]

Bodoni persisted at the press, but he was exhorted by the circle of *virtuosi* in which he moved to think of a life beyond Rome and particularly of a life in England. "In the eighth year of his training, all spent in assiduous study," [69] states De Lama, "in much production, and in extremely costly experimentation, he was seduced by large promises of fortune that certain virtuosi, extolling the generosity of Britain, constantly repeated in his ear." Ambition and curiosity were tempting him north to sharpen his skills in a wider arena than Rome.

At the time, Britain was on its way to becoming a rich and inventive nation. Already a center of world finance, the country was on the brink of the Industrial

John Thomas Baskerville (1706-1775).

Revolution. More important to Bodoni, it was a center of printing ingenuity and home to such luminaries as the Caslons (father and son) and John Baskerville (1706-1775). Their fame had spread to Rome in books carried there by tourists and collectors, and these books were quickly snapped up by bibliophiles like Winckelmann and Cardinal Spinelli. Bodoni, by now 26 years old, was languishing at the Propaganda Fide, no longer challenged at the press, and by 1766 had become infatuated with the idea of going to England and seeing with his own eyes the innovations within the British printing industry. All that held him back was his loyalty to Abbé Ruggieri. Many years later, when he was an old man, Bodoni's brother Giuseppe recalled the tragic incident that happened next (although he was seriously wrong about the year in which it occurred):

Bodoni usually took himself each morning to the home of his Maecenas [Ruggieri]. One day like many others (and if I am not mistaken it was 11 November 1762[70]) finding out that Ruggeri was still in bed, he was detained by the manservant in the antechamber. While he was waiting, he heard a shot from a firearm. He jumped at the explosion, and then found the poor man lifeless from the desperate shot of a pistol. This tragic spectacle affected him like a thunderbolt . . . Thus ended the days of that famous man of letters who, by a thousand titles, deserved a better end.[71]

Passerini continues: "It is impossible to express the fright, the sorrow of the highly sensitive Bodoni. Here lay this man, who had fallen on his side as though struck by lightning or by a huge, deadly rock."[72]

Depression kills, but even so Ruggieri's suicide provokes speculation.[73] First, it seems surprising that he had a pistol in his possession. Second, his timing, at a moment when he knew Bodoni would be arriving for their daily walk, seems thoughtless at best, even willfully cruel. Was he angry with the young man? Had they fallen out? Was his suicide an act of vengeance? We will never know the truth, but poor Ruggieri must have been suffering such exquisite anguish that nothing could prevent him from pulling the trigger that ended his life.

But now Bodoni was free to leave Rome, and no one could change his mind; not Cardinal Castelli, the new prefect of the press; not Marco Ubaldo Bicci, who succeeded Ruggieri as superintendent; not the members of the artistic and literary circles in which he swirled; not his colleagues and friends at the Propaganda Fide. Undeterred by his inability to speak English and in the mistaken belief that (due in part to the popularity of Italian opera and song) all educated Britons would naturally speak Italian, he was confident he would have no difficulty in making himself understood.

Bodoni was primed for his grand adventure, but before leaving Italy for England, he decided to return to Saluzzo to set eyes on—and to embrace—his family and friends for the first time in eight years.

ABCDEFGHIJKLMNOPQR
STUVW&XYZ
abcdefghijklmnopqrstuvwxyz

ABCDEFGHIJKLMNOPQR
STUVW&XYZ
abcdefghijklmnopqrstuvwxyz

ABCDEFGHIJKLMNOPQR
STUVW&XYZ
abcdefghijklmnopqrstuvwxyz

A synopsis of the roman types of William Caslon (top), John Baskerville (center), and Giambattista Bodoni (bottom); all in modern digital renderings.

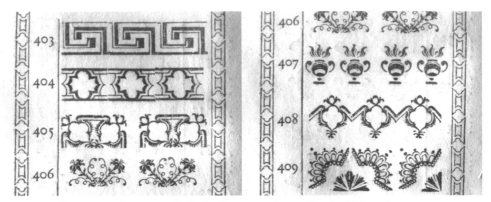

Ornaments from an early Bodoni type specimen, *Fregi e Majuscole*, 1771.

3
The Invitation

He is full of talent, industrious, and honorable.

PAOLO MARIA PACIAUDI

BODONI'S TRIP to England was doomed from the start. Whining in the marshes of the valley of the Tiber lay a formidable enemy, the blood-sucking female *Anopheles* mosquito, vector of malaria, carrier of the deadly parasite *Plasmodium falciparum*. A democratic predator, she was responsible for the deaths of ordinary citizens, cardinals, and popes — and was very nearly responsible for the death of Bodoni himself. Symptoms of malaria include anemia, bloody stools, chills, coma, convulsion, fever, headache, jaundice, muscle pain, nausea, sweating, vomiting. It usually starts with fatigue and weakness, then come the high fever and sweating, which alternate with the chills.

Stung by such a mosquito as he left Rome, Bodoni remained healthy to all appearances during the parasite's incubation period of eight to fourteen days. He made it safely to Turin, where he visited Domenico Costa's mother, and together they set out for Cervignasco, a small town immediately north of Saluzzo, where Costa was serving as parish priest. Not wanting to part from each other too soon, all three then headed to Saluzzo for the grand reunion with Bodoni's family. By the time they reached Saluzzo, Bodoni was suffering from headaches and exhaustion, followed shortly by extremes of body temperature. And then he became very, very ill.

Overjoyed at first to see Bodoni, but all too quickly appalled by the gravity of his illness, the family set about lowering his temperature with cold compresses, the old tried-and-true method for reducing fever. (The new treatment for malaria, quinine, was available in Rome during the 18th century, first sent there from Peru by a Jesuit priest a century beforehand, but it is impossible to know whether it would have been available to the Bodoni family in Piedmont in 1766.) The family could make no headway curing him. One day he was gravely ill, the next day he rallied, and the next he fell gravely ill again. They were learning that malaria was notorious for its repetitive behavior, and the type of malaria Bodoni suffered from was Tertian Fever, so named because it revisits the patient every third day.

Only a catastrophic illness could have deflected Bodoni from his journey and forced him to stay close to home. The weeks and months dragged on, but finally his strong constitution prevailed and the episodes of fever became fewer and further between. Unable to stand the boredom of convalescence, he called for his friend Cappa, the same young man who had wanted to accompany him to Rome a decade earlier but had lost his nerve. In the intervening years, Cappa had joined his father's metalworking business in Saluzzo and was now a smith in his own right. Bodoni showed him that he, too, was a worker in metals but on a far smaller scale, and when he had strength enough to wield file and graver, he demonstrated the art of punchcutting to Cappa. Soon they were working together, and by Easter 1767 Bodoni was able to print with his own type a sonnet in celebration of Christ's resurrection, in this way not only celebrating the risen Christ but his own resurrection from mortal illness.

This printed sonnet became an advertisement for his skill. Orders started flowing in. As he increased in physical vigor, he accepted commissions, working side by side with his father and his brothers, Domenico and Giuseppe. Soon a year had passed. He could easily have settled back into a comfortable existence in Saluzzo, surrounded by family and childhood friends, and marrying a local woman, but that assumes his ambition had died a premature death during his illness. This was definitely not the case. As soon as he was able to travel, he began making forays to Turin to keep abreast of what was happening in the busy and evolving world of European printing.

MEANWHILE, slap in the middle of northern Italy, in the city of Parma, Ferdinando Maria Filippo Lodovico Sebastiano Francesco Giacomo, the young duke of Parma, was being importuned by his prime minister, the Frenchman Guillaume Du Tillot, about the necessity of establishing a royal press as a component in their greater dream of turning Parma into a miniature Paris, with all the accoutrements of the City of Light. Du Tillot pointed out that every self-respecting city in Europe — Paris, Madrid, Vienna, Naples, Turin, and Florence — had a press with which to promote itself. It was time to put Parma on the map, and the way to do this was by founding, and funding, a royal press, a magnificent press that would be the envy of all nations. The malleable 17-year-old duke was persuaded. He charged Du Tillot with finding the right person to establish and run the press, someone who could produce the highest quality work for the glorification of his city.

Du Tillot, being French, naturally sought advice in Paris, then the epicenter of European printing. He specifically addressed Pierre-Jean Mariette, a vastly erudite connoisseur of prints, drawings, and the art of printing, begging him to recommend someone who combined efficiency with artistic brilliance. Mariette responded sagely, advising Du Tillot to choose an Italian rather than a Frenchman, someone who would be able to pay proper attention to works published in Italian. Du Tillot took Mariette's words to heart and sought advice from someone right in his own backyard, none other than the librarian of Parma, Father Paolo Maria Paciaudi, the priest from Piedmont who had earlier recognized Bodoni's talents at the Propaganda Fide. Remembering the extraordinary ability as well as the social acumen of the young man, Paciaudi suggested that Bodoni would be the perfect person for the job — if he could locate him.

Paciaudi wrote first to Father Giorgi in Rome asking for Bodoni's whereabouts. Giorgi informed him that Bodoni had returned to Piedmont and suggested that he try to find him through Francesco Berta, the head librarian in Turin. On 5 January 1758, Paciaudi wrote the letter that changed Bodoni's life. In it, he informed Berta of the duke of Parma's wish to establish a royal press and to find someone sufficiently gifted and competent to run it. He stated that he, Paciaudi, had recommended Giambattista

Pierre-Jean Mariette (1694-1774).

Bodoni of Saluzzo for the post, having met him in Rome with Cardinal Spinelli at the Propaganda Fide. "He is full of talent, industrious, and honorable,"[74] continued Paciaudi, aware that Bodoni would need permission from the duke of Savoy before leaving Piedmont. He implored Berta to find Bodoni and to pave the way with the duke, adding that if the duke's permission were granted, Bodoni must come immediately to Parma, bearing with him punches and matrices for characters of all sizes in Greek and Hebrew as well as an assortment of both Roman and cursive characters. These would then become the property of the press. He would be paid for them; his lodgings would be provided; and all the expenses of the press would be assumed by the duke. Time was of the essence. Bodoni was needed immediately to print a work that was both voluminous and important.[75]

Paciaudi added: "He will be in charge of the press, and will act as compositor on occasion to print items of a secret nature. He will oversee the other compositors, and will always review the first proofs . . . His journey and the cost of transporting his tools and characters will be paid for by the duke." As far as his monthly salary was concerned, it would be neither too little nor too much. "It's better to keep it low at first, so that if he merits more, it can be added to."[76]

Father Berta fulfilled his duties as emissary, and everything went according to plan. He located Bodoni, handed him the invitation from Parma, and gained permission from Vittorio Amedeo III, the duke of Savoy (and later king of Sardinia) for Bodoni to leave Saluzzo; and the contract was signed. Bodoni rushed to Turin to present himself to the duke of Savoy, who received him warmly and showered him with gifts. "I would like to see you again before you take yourself off to the Court of Parma," cried out Carlo Emanuele, the duke's 15-year-old son.[77]

Bodoni returned to Saluzzo to make preparations for his departure and for the shipment of his equipment and tools. Then for the second time in his life, he bade a tearful farewell to his family and friends, and on 8 February 1768, left Saluzzo for Parma, stopping again in Turin for final instructions from the duke and another pledge of royal bounty.

The city of Parma.

La Pilotta from the town.

4
Parma 1768

*City of sweet, enveloping fogs and flat horizons marked by majestic poplars
. . . city of masks and narcissistic poses, sophistication, epicurean appetites,
and earthy realism . . . All in all, the city is gorgeous.*

WALLIS WILDE-MENOZZI

P ARMA in February is damp and cold. On some winter days, fog obscures the distant Apennines; sometimes it obscures the hand in front of your face. On other days, snow and ice turn cobbles into treacherous chutes. The city boasts an air of mystery and chilly grandeur that is swiftly dispelled by shafts of winter sun illuminating red and ochre buildings and the pink Verona marble of the baptistry. Unlike Saluzzo and Rome, Parma is flat, sitting on a bed of gravel 400 meters deep that helps absorb earthquakes. The city bestrides the Parma, a considerable river for most of the year as it snakes its way to join the Po, but which is referred to as a *torrente* rather than a river because of its ability to flood in autumn and dry up completely in summer.

A thriving center of printing as early as 1472, Parma produced a quantity of incunabula, that is, works printed in the 45 years following Gutenberg's first use of a moveable type press in the 1450s. After this flowering, printing in Parma languished, in common with printing in much of the rest of Italy, apart from Turin and Venice. The Farnese family, rulers of Parma from 1545 until 1731, pursued large-scale, wide-ranging projects but had not the slightest interest in publishing books. Meanwhile, printing was flourishing in other European countries, especially in the cities of Paris, Madrid, Lyons, and Basel.

THE COACH bringing Bodoni to Parma arrived at noon on Saint Matthias's day, 25 February 1768.[78] (Usually falling on 24 February, St Matthias's day was celebrated on the 25th in leap years like 1768.) The significance of this date would not have been lost on Bodoni; tradition held that it was the luckiest day of the year because Saint Matthias won the lottery to replace Judas Iscariot as Jesus's twelfth apostle.

Bodoni's first task was to find the site of the new printing office that, with his lodgings one floor above, was located in the palace of the Pilotta on the banks of the river. Prime Minister Du Tillot had informed him that this site would be temporary; he had grandiose plans for a state-of-the-art printing establishment on its own site, but the offices in the Pilotta turned out to be Bodoni's workplace for the rest of his life.

La Pilotta.

The palace of the Pilotta, a vast, forbidding complex, was built in 1583 by the Farnese family, who did not occupy it but used it as a setting for court and government affairs and theatrical extravaganzas. It housed the immense and staggeringly pretentious Farnese theatre and a smaller theatre for the court, as well as barracks, armory, stables, feed stores, and a playing ground for *jeu de paume*, the ancestor of handball and tennis. The scale of the Pilotta was so vast that it could accommodate all this and later house the Archaeological Museum, the Academy of Fine Arts, and the National Gallery.

Bodoni discovered the rooms that were to become his printing office on the ground floor of the west wing of the Pilotta, near where the Ponte della Rochetta (also called the Ponte Verde and now named the Ponte Verdi) crossed the river and led directly to the ducal park and palace. In days to come, if the river were in flood, Bodoni would occasionally find waves lapping at the doors of his studio. His living quarters boasted a fine view across the water to La Rochetta, the 13th-century tower on the other side and, beyond the tower, to the ducal gardens. In an otherwise closely built town, the open sky and spacious view across the water were a pleasant and welcome relief from the exacting, close work of publishing.

When Bodoni arrived, Father Paciaudi was in the process of establishing the library, now the Biblioteca Palatina, which was also housed inside the Pilotta. The happy reunion between Paciaudi, now a mature 58-year-old, and 28-year-old Bodoni was freighted with significance for both of them. Paciaudi was certainly taking a risk by bringing a virtually unknown Italian printer to Parma instead of a surefire Frenchman; Bodoni carried the burden of living up to the expectations of Paciaudi, of Prime Minister Du Tillot, and of the young duke, Don Ferdinando I (referred to as "Don" because King Philip V, the Bourbon king of Spain, was his grandfather, and he himself was an *infante* of Spain).

All three men — Paciaudi, Du Tillot, and Don Ferdinando — were relying on Bodoni to put Parma on the map, and it is worth getting to know them.

Father Paolo Maria Paciaudi was an extraordinarily erudite man with a passion for organizing. When Bodoni knew him in Rome, he was a fiery and fashionable preacher and an archaeologist. After years of excavating and cataloging in both Naples and Rome under the aegis of Cardinal Spinelli, he was invited to Parma in 1761 by Prime Minister Du Tillot. Together the two men worked for educational and ecclesiastical reform, and it was Du Tillot who gave Paciaudi the mandate to re-establish the city's library. (Paciaudi was the first in Italy to use index cards as a means of cataloging books.) He would subsequently become the head librarian, antiquarian, and overseer of archaeological excavations at nearby Veleia.

More important for this story is that Paciaudi had never forgotten the skill of young Giambattista Bodoni at the Propaganda Fide in Rome. What had impressed him most was Bodoni's talent for working with exotic languages. This was a gift that could add glamour to a newly established press.

LÉON GUILLAUME DU TILLOT was born in Bayonne in 1711. The son of a *valet de chambre*, and expected to follow in his father's footsteps, he was a handsome whippet of a man with rapier-like intelligence who made his own way in life and was prepared to leave France if offered the opportunity for advancement. He found work in the household of Don Filippo, Don Ferdinando's father, in Madrid, and accompanied him to Parma when Don Filippo became duke in 1749. Don Filippo quickly made Du Tillot minister of finance, which meant he was effectively in charge of everything. Henri Bédarida describes him as an egalitarian, although always loyal to the sovereigns he served, a man who desired order and regularity but had the ability to adapt, a man who was blessed with an elegant spirit, a happy physiognomy, and a slender silhouette.[79]

Du Tillot had unflagging inventiveness and energy, and he was determined to infuse the city with the spirit of French idealism. He was innovative; he encouraged business, trade, technological reforms, industrial arts, the manufacture of silk, and beekeeping. In 1753 he imported the French architect Ennemond-Alexandre Petitot and the sculptor Jean Baptiste Boudard to freshen Parma's tired face. He was the power behind the reawakening of the University of Parma; he instituted museums and the Academy of Beaux Arts, and he was a religious reformer who made many enemies within the Church with his sweeping ecclesiastical reforms. These reforms included the closing of nonproductive convents and monasteries, and just before Bodoni's arrival in Parma, Du Tillot influenced the duke to sign a decree banishing Jesuits from the city, and that decree was turned into action on 7 February 1768. Unfortunately, Du Tillot also made enemies among the local people, who resented his reforms and above all resented the imposition of so much Frenchification. He had surrounded himself with his compatriots, importing not only Petitot and Boudard but other French workers in place of Italians to take care of the needs of the court. Among these workers were carpet makers, mattress makers, tailors, corset makers, clock makers, carpenters, cabinet makers, metal workers, carriage makers, and gardeners.[80]

Du Tillot first realized the importance of having a press at his command when he wanted to publish a special book as a present for Don Filippo, but had to send it out of the country for publication. No press in Parma in those years was capable of printing a truly elegant book. He also needed a printing office where material could be produced secretly, engaged as he was in a mighty struggle with Rome over issues of ecclesiastical reform.

He set the wheels in motion for the instigation of the press by acquiring supplies of high quality paper and ink, and then he started hunting down good type. In 1758, on seeing a specimen page of Fournier's type, he wrote eagerly about it to Anicet Melot in France. He commented on how beautifully proportioned and elegant Fournier's designs were and wondered if it were possible to acquire some typefaces, including a few rare examples. Melot responded by sending characters "considered by experts to be the best ever made"[81] and insisted that an intelligent compositor who could use them with good taste would produce superior work. That was the catch; skilled compositors were hard to find.

Years passed, and Du Tillot was promoted from finance minister to prime minister, granted the title of *marchese di Felino* [marquis of Felino], and given the lands that accompanied the title. He was often seen in company with the beautiful, literate, and highly intelligent Marchesa Anna Malaspina, the unofficial first lady of the court. Known affectionately as "Annetta," she was the wife of Marchese Giovanni Malaspina della Bastia, a gentleman of the ducal household. She was also the close confidante and mistress of Du Tillot. Her beauty and charm were such that in earlier years she had been summoned to Versailles to distract King Louis XV's attention from Madame de Pompadour. At Parma, "Fiorella Dianeja" (her Arcadian name) was adored by poets, soldiers, and the entire court. "But the prime minister himself was the man whom her beautiful eyes had conquered above all."[82]

Du Tillot was alert to new developments and inventions. Smallpox was a terrible scourge in those days, and after the death of Don Filippo's wife, Louise-Élizabeth of France, from the disease, Du Tillot encouraged the duke to bring Théodore Tronchin, the great Swiss physician and proponent of inoculation, to Parma to inoculate his son, the 13-year-old Ferdinando. It was a wise move; Ferdinando never succumbed to smallpox, but his father, who did not take advantage of Tronchin's skill and Du Tillot's advice, died of it in 1765.[83] The death of Don Filippo and the young age of Don Ferdinando effectively meant that Du Tillot became the most powerful man in the duchy of Parma, Piacenza, and Guastalla. A prestigious court press was now not a whim but an absolute necessity.

In fact, three other presses were already operating in Parma, but they were all dedicated to specific utilitarian purposes. One printed material for the state and for the bishops of Parma and other towns; a second printed material for the mayor; and the third produced scientific and literary texts.[84] None of them aspired to the heights of grandeur that Du Tillot envisioned for the royal press. Although advised by early planners that the printing office could operate perfectly well with just one press, a small selection of type, and a few decorations,[85] Du Tillot was adamant; he wanted far more. But first he sought Paciaudi's counsel in the matter of a perfect, available, intelligent, expert printer who could set up and then run the printing office. It was then that Paciaudi had the brilliant idea of suggesting Giambattista Bodoni.

At the time of Bodoni's arrival in Parma in 1768, Don Ferdinando was 17 years old. On his mother's side, he was the favorite grandson of Louis XV of France, and from an early age he had been educated by French tutors. One of these was Baron Auguste de Keralio, a mathematician and military engineer. Ferdinando himself described him as a truly honest, but excessively severe, man to whom was owed what little value he possessed. The other tutor was Abbé Étienne Bonnot de Condillac, a philosopher, proto-psychologist, sensualist,[86] friend of Rousseau, and key figure in the French Enlightenment. Ferdinando was more interested in what Keralio had to teach him than what the philosopher Condillac espoused; speculation was never Ferdinando's strength, while physics and mechanics remained of interest for the rest of his life.[87] It may have been the young duke's resistance to serious philosphical thought, and his own insistence upon it, that drove Condillac to write his 13-volume *Cours d'Étude pour l'Instruction du Prince de Parme*, which was finally published in its entirety by Bodoni in 1782.

Limp, lame, plump, and squat, the young Don Ferdinando was certainly un-prepossessing. In the early 1770s, Lady Mary Coke described him as having "a very handsome face, fair complexion, fair hair, and dark eyes, good teeth, and something agreeable in his countenance, tho' not a look of sense. His figure bad, very short and thick."[88] Joseph II of Austria described him as being well-mannered, inexperienced, but having no genius and little intelligence, and "is as tiresome as it is possible to be, leaning on my arm and never leaving me alone for a step."[89]

Don Ferdinando spent a great deal of time praying ostentatiously. Marzio Dall'Acqua points out: "He was religious to the point of bigotry, careful to present an external faith, which manifested itself in rites, vestments, collections of relics, trips to various sanctuaries, especially Loretto. Yet his character was also joyful . . . He loved performing in the little theatre at the court in Colorno, and loved celebrating holidays with the countrywomen . . ."[90] Generally regarded as pious to a fault, the purity of his piety has been questioned by some. People in Parma still gossip about him as though he were alive. Gossip, like rumor, knows no bounds; a few say he liked to dress up as a shepherd and head out into the countryside to round up not sheep, but pretty young women.[91] They point out that he had a perfect arrangement. Adjacent to his hunting lodge in the countryside lay a convenient chapel where he could repent of his sins on Sunday mornings after roistering on Saturday nights.

AS THE NEW DIRECTOR of the royal press, Bodoni supervised all aspects of the printing process. He proofread everything; he handled the finances (a task he loathed); he acquired type and paper; he was expected to find apprentices and to direct his workers in such a way that the press would become famous for the beauty, accuracy, and elegance of its printing; and he was entrusted with personally setting the type for works of a secret nature, in a private room with a dedicated printing press.[92] Again with the help of Mariette in Paris, Du Tillot and Bodoni ordered more type from Fournier. This was slow in arriving because it had to be made to order. In the meantime, Bodoni cast some exotic type and decorations using his own punches and matrices brought from Saluzzo, and looked to his father to supply him with more. He also managed to acquire some type from Turin that had belonged to the printer Chays, as well as Hebrew type from Father Tommaso Contin.[93] It was a start.

While they endured the frustrating wait for the delivery of Fournier's type, Du Tillot set about acquiring the presses needed for an important printing office. According to an inventory from December 1770, the printing office owned six magnificent presses, five of them modern; the sixth an antique, but still in fine working order. Du Tillot also wanted to install a foundry on the premises, something he never managed to accomplish. But Bodoni was determined to cast his own type in his own space. He went ahead, setting up a foundry in his second-floor apartment, which was eventually supported by Du Tillot's successor, José De Llano who, renouncing the idea of a government foundry, gave Bodoni full responsibility and freedom for manufacturing type.[94]

Bodoni organized the layout of the printing office. He went to great lengths to arrange the rooms to maximize the amount of light. The book-lined entryway opened into a long corridor with windows where he housed the printing presses, tables for the cases of characters, and a few cupboards. From the ceiling hung a *stenditore*, a sort of clothesline on which to dry printed pages. In the long, light-filled room called *Lo Specchio* [The Mirror], whose length paralleled the *torrente*, he arranged sixteen frames for the compositors and a small desk where they could make corrections. On a shelf above this desk, he laid out French and Latin dictionaries and an atlas.

A little room, next to the well, contained two sinks made of white marble, one of which was used for the cleaning of printer's ink from type, a job involving the use of lye, a highly caustic cleanser made in those days from alkalis leached from wood ash. In the next room, which later became the accountant's territory, he set up two large cupboards, one for roughly bound books, and the other for fresh, white paper. Needing still more storage space, Bodoni laid claim to various storehouses and attics, and would eventually store completed works in a room in the Rochetta and in another room under the arcades of the Pilotta.[95]

At night, he climbed the steps to his modestly furnished apartment on the second floor, where he lived cheek by jowl with the foundry.

Spring sped past. On 10 May 1768, Parma was treated to a visit from Emperor Joseph II (co-regent of Austria with his mother, Maria Theresa, and married to Don Ferdinando's sister, Isabella). He had come to arrange the details of a marriage between his sister Maria Amalia and Don Ferdinando. This important visit caused the enormous buzz of excitement a royal wedding always provokes.

Then it was stinking summer, and still the Fournier type had not arrived. The *torrente* dried up. Flat air, heat, humidity, and legions of mosquitoes assailed Bodoni. His hands sweated as he worked at cutting exotic punches and decorations, and striking matrices in his early efforts to add a wide range of his own type to the ducal arsenal. Du Tillot retreated with the duke to the palace at Colorno. (As Versailles is to Paris, so Colorno is to Parma, but on a much smaller scale.) In so doing, Du Tillot escaped the worst of Parma's heat, but did not escape mosquitoes. In early September, he was struck down with malaria, that dangerous disease with which Bodoni was all too familiar. The prime minister's condition was misdiagnosed and he was given medicine that aggravated his illness so greatly that Adeodato Turchi, a Capuchin monk who later became bishop of Parma, was called in to hear his confession and administer the last rites. Du Tillot surprised everyone by recovering, and by 15 September he was out of danger.

Finally the type from Fournier arrived. It came in six different sizes: Testino, Garamond, Lettura, Silvio, Testo, and Palestina.[96]

Du Tillot and Bodoni quickly assessed what remaining equipment they needed for an establishment that could compete with the other great printing houses of Europe. With the presses already in place and a working arsenal of type at his disposal, Bodoni prepared a list of those minor items that were essential for the smooth running of a printing office. Du Tillot signed an order for them on 6 October 1768, and the order was dispatched. It reads:

We need the following items at the royal printing office:

Two pieces of cloth to put between the outer and inner tympans,[97] the size of a sheet of London paper[98], and two others to put over the tympan, a little wider and longer than the first ones

Ten lengths of rope for hauling the coffin,[99] for securing the platen to the press, and to string up in the printing office in order to spread out the damp sheets

Two medium nails to pull the cords

Four pounds of horsehair to make the ink-balls

One pound of soap to lubricate the coffin rope

Eight pounds of olive oil to lubricate the rails of the press and the nut of its spindle

One copper bucket to draw water from the well

One copper pan to put on the fire, to make paste

A pair of scissors for the press

One pound of iron rods to make the ink-balls

Four sponges to wet the paper

Three brooms

A bucket to put the ash in, and to make lye to wash the formes[100] every time they are lifted from the press

Five pounds of dregs from barrels to put with the ash to make the lye

Five pounds of scrapings of kid skin to make glue and make the friskets and to stick them each time it is needed

Six "weights" of coal to heat the lye

Two brushes for the paste

Six dog skins[101] to make the ink-balls

Six ounces of ordinary thread to sew the ink-balls

Two brushes to clean the formes

Gio: Batta. Bodoni

Please pay attention to the present requirements

Parma 6 ottobre 1768 G. Du Tillot[102]

Everything was in place, but Bodoni needed help. He had the mandate to hire and train apprentices but was not yet acquainted with anyone whom he could trust to do exactly what he wanted. So he sent word to Saluzzo. His brothers Domenico and Giuseppe heeded the call, as did Francesco Costa (brother of Domenico Costa, who had accompanied Bodoni to Rome). They arrived in Parma in the middle of October. How appalled Francesco Bodoni must have been to see his three sons all disappear to Parma. He seems to have pressed his daughter Angela (if not Benedeta too) into service in the family's printing establishment, as can be understood from Angela's letter to Bodoni in October 1768. She told him first how happy she was that he had acquired so much beautiful equipment for the printing house, and went on to say that the family business was in need of another employee, or "sooner or later I will have to take on the task myself." She added that Benedeta's health was good, and that of their father excellent, but fails to mention Mamma. The grape harvest had been scant. She ended with advice to Giambattista and Giuseppe: "Take care of yourselves, and remain always in accord and united like good brothers. Do not annoy each other, love each other always. Never doubt that God will help you more and more. Remember: love me and do not abandon me." In January 1769, Angela watched out for the brothers again, wanting to protect them from opportunists: "If any of our fellow citizens, passing through Parma, come to you seeking favors using the pretext of bringing you our greetings, know that we have not given them any assignment."

Bodoni assigned Domenico, his older brother by four years, the tasks of press-man and compositor. Giuseppe, eight years younger than Bodoni, worked as a compositor, and Costa was another pressman. With their help, Bodoni had the press up and running. A year later almost to the day, Domenico, who did not have Giambattista's robust mental health and suffered from depression, returned to the family business in Saluzzo. He had stood shoulder to shoulder with Bodoni in the challenging early months, but the stress of being away from Saluzzo must have weighed on him. By the time he left, Bodoni had acquired other pressmen and apprentices. His younger brother, Giuseppe, remained by his side for the next thirty years.

Bodoni started printing with the Fournier type. If any of the sorts wore down, he cut new punches and made new type. In this way, he literally became Fournier. It is hard to say where Fournier ends and Bodoni begins, and impossible to overestimate Fournier's influence on him. In time, when there was no original Fournier type remaining, the differences between the two became more pronounced as Bodoni began to put his own stamp on the characters, but the debt to and influence of Fournier is always apparent, more so than the debt to Baskerville. Eventually Bodoni would admit his preference: "Fournier is for me the most excellent example, and by the way Baskerville has done nothing but add to and frame the letters badly. He has become the Borromini of our art: his decorations have ruined precision in the same way the decorations of others have spoiled the architectural majesty of Michelangelo."[103] Here he seems to be accusing Baskerville of putting typographic fig leaves on his work, using unnecessarily strong and unkind words about his erstwhile hero.

Atti Della Solenne Coronazione Fatta In Campidoglio Della Insigne Poetessa D.Na Maria Maddalena Morelli Fernandez. Parma: Bodoni, 1779. Bodoni's type in close imitation of Fournier's.

Pierre-Simon Fournier (1712-1768) is often referred to as Fournier le Jeune, and like Bodoni was born into a printing family. Also like Bodoni, he was a competent wood engraver. In 1737, he invented the first point system for measuring and then naming type sizes, a system that Bodoni would employ in his own work. Fournier was the shining example of a great printer, who was also instrumental in setting up presses for others: he helped Madame de Pompadour establish her own press, and he played the role of advisor in the establishment of printing offices in Sweden and Turin. In 1764, he began publishing a guide to printing, which would cover all aspects of the trade. This became his *Manuel typographique, utile aux gens de lettres et à ceux qui exercent les différentes parties de l'Art de l'Imprimerie* [Typographic manual, useful to men of letters and to those who work in different areas of the printing arts]. He never completed the project, so the net result is a first volume that is indeed a manual for printers, full of sage advice about cutting punches and matrices and casting type, but the second volume (1766) is primarily a reissue of type specimen pages. Bodoni had access to this work, and it fired him with ambition to create his own specimen book (which he would incorrectly call a *manuale*), and to fill it with examples that would surpass even those of Fournier in extent and variety. Producing his own magnificent *Manuale tipografico* became his life's great obsession.

When Bodoni learned of Fournier's death on 8 October 1768, he was deep in

Pierre Simon Fournier (Fournier le Jeune, 1712-1768).

the throes of publishing his first work for the royal press, *I Voti. Canto per la felicemente restituita salute di Sua Eccellenza il signor Don Guglielmo Du Tillot Marchese di Felino, primo Ministro e Segretario di Stato di S.A.R.* [The Offerings. A poem for the happy restitution of the health of his Excellency Guillaume Du Tillot, marquis of Felino, prime Minister and Secretary of State of His Royal Highness.] This publication served many purposes. It pleased Du Tillot because it advertised how important his recovery from malaria was to the court; as a highly significant piece of printing, it delighted the duke and brought attention and praise to Parma; and in using Fournier's characters, Bodoni paid tribute to his great predecessor. It also provided him with an opportunity to demonstrate his skill and to show off some of his own extraordinary little rosettes and garlands. However, nothing about the book yet shouts "Giambattista Bodoni." Fournier's type is evident, as is the influence of Bodoni's father and grandfather. While *I Voti* is an important and highly competent piece of printing, many years had to pass before Bodoni's incomparably spare and elegant style and his impeccable presswork reached their maturity.

Bodoni worked extraordinarily hard during his first few months in Parma. He wasted no time and his hands were never still. In quiet moments, he pulled out gravers and files to create new letters and decorations. He cut punches the way other people knit — to relax while at the same time creating something — but below his window flowed temptation, the murmuring waters of the river, urging him to go outdoors. The city was charming. "Animated

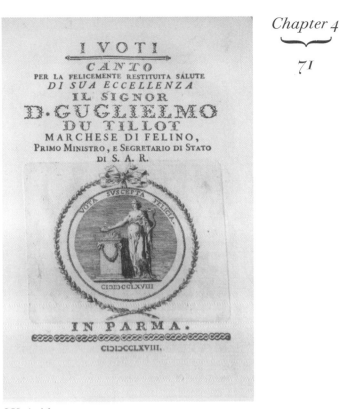

I Voti, title page.

are the conversations; beautiful the walks; restful the holidays; numerous the elegant women. The young people love sincerely, wear their hearts on their sleeves, and are natural in their conversation. Greet them and you will find their eyes are bright, their smiles are jolly, and they enjoy the present without thinking about the future," states Trevisani,[104] but he insists that Bodoni was immune to temptation. "He worked without rest day and night. His constitution, tempered to withstand any effort, did not acknowledge fatigue. It was as though he were in the grips of a fever that did not allow him to rest."[105] Trevisani sounds a familiar refrain, just like those biographers who insist that Bodoni did nothing but work while he was in Rome at the Propaganda Fide press.

Bodoni did spend time outside his printing office. He made a point of visiting Father Paciaudi every day in his apartment in La Rochetta, and he spent time with Petitot, the short, stocky, chatty, self-impressed court architect.[106] In the evenings after work, he began to frequent a bookshop owned by the Faure brothers, Claude and Guillaume, French booksellers (and occasional publishers) who, according to Father Paciaudi, were extremely honest and offered excellent discounts.[107] The bookshop, which carried volumes in five languages, had become a gathering place for the literary élite, and there Bodoni made friends with many whose works he would subsequently publish..

Because the royal printer was a servant of the court, Bodoni moved in literary and artistic rather than court circles, although he could hardly avoid collaborating with the duke. (His status would change in the fullness of time when his fame was so great that important visitors to Parma wanted to meet Bodoni first — and then pay their respects to the duke.) He was well aware of what was going on around him in the court and in the city. After all, he lived and worked in the Pilotta, the buzzing center of Parma activity. Any time he left his office, he entered the stream of people promenading along the banks of the river. If he turned east and walked under the arcades of the Pilotta, he passed the stables where horses and carriages came and went. The arcades led to the enormous courtyard where in the past men had played *pelota*, the game that gave the palace its name. There, all Parma strutted and preened, in thrall to the latest fashions from Paris. Indeed, French floated in the air. A visitor, Abbé Jérôme Richard of Dijon, remarked that in the city of 40,000 people, 4,000 were from France. French was spoken at the court, and the townspeople imitated court speech and ended up speaking a strange mixture of Italian and French. Richard added that almost all the Frenchmen married Parmesan women.[108]

A short walk from the Pilotta took Bodoni past shops, cafés, and the Teatro Ducale. Plays were all the rage, and Du Tillot made sure the townspeople had a steady diet of French drama to enjoy. If Bodoni continued walking away from La Pilotta, he found himself in the ecclesiastical heart of Parma, the beautiful, open space that was the Piazza del Duomo with its Romanesque cathedral and its octagonal baptistry. Once inside the cathedral, his eyes were drawn to the heights of the cupola and from there, or so it seemed, up into the heavens, so extraordinary and daring was Correggio's perspective in his rendering of the Assumption of the Virgin. He would find further evidence of Correggio (c. 1490-1534) in many other buildings in Parma, and would eventually pay his own great tribute to him.

If Bodoni needed refreshment and entertainment, he could enter one of the newly modernized coffee shops that had added card tables and billiard tables to their traditional offerings of beverages and spices; Parma was deeply enthusiastic about billiards, and these popular coffee shops pulled in a clientèle from all classes and broke down social distinctions. Noticing this, Du Tillot saw a chance to further his agenda by insisting that coffee shop owners and innkeepers carry copies of the *Gazzetta di Parma* (Plate 22), the weekly newspaper that had become the official voice of the duchy. (At the time, the *Gazzetta* was printed by Filippo Carmignani, but this task would be turned over to Bodoni in 1772.) The *Gazzetta* had a precise purpose: to introduce the people of Parma to the new culture of the Enlightenment, and the cafés became lively centers where customers of all classes could discuss the changes occurring every day in Parma.[109]

And then there was the Casino Petitot, sited at the east end of the Stradone. Under the Farnese family, the Stradone had been the dull main connector of the city with the military fortress of the Citadella to the south. Du Tillot and Petitot changed the road into an elegant, tree-lined boulevard, reminiscent of those in Paris. The Casino Petitot, a charming architectural extravaganza, drew the eye to it along the length of the boulevard, in the way the Arc du Triomphe draws the eye along the Champs-Élysées in Paris. At the Casino Petitot, the young aristocracy gathered to survey the scene, eat ices, drink lemonade, coffee, or chocolate, and dine while listening to orchestral music being played on the covered terrace. It is tempting to think that Bodoni was invited there by Petitot himself, to relax a little while they discussed the preparation of books they were preparing together for the duke.

Romance does not seem to have played a part in Bodoni's life, which is not to say that he did not have a mistress or a lover. What seems most likely is that he simply did not have the time or inclination for romantic involvement. He might look, but apparently he did not touch.

WHAT DID BODONI eat and drink in Parma? The city had plenty of delights on offer, and had long been a center of gastronomy. Even the twelfth-century baptistry attests to this; one of its pink marble panels is devoted to the sausage-maker and his wares.

The fertile land of the Po plain affords the perfect environment for raising cattle and pigs, and the result is some of the best protein in the world: cheese, including the famous Parmigiano-Reggiano, known as Parmesan in English; the equally famous *prosciutto* [ham], with *culatello* being king; fresh pork, beef, horse (still a favorite on menus in Parma); and anything brought home from the hunt, such as venison, hare, and game birds.

Bodoni would have enjoyed *tortelli*, a local stuffed pasta resembling *ravi-oli* but which uses just a single piece of dough on which the filling is placed

Tortelli d'erbetta.   Anolini in brodo.

before being folded in half and sealed. The most popular filling for *tortelli* is *erbetta* (Swiss chard) with ricotta. Another much loved dish was *anolini in brodo* (said to be the duke's favorite), which was a smaller pasta in the shape of a half moon, stuffed with meat, cheese, and herbs, and served in hot broth, making it a welcome meal on a cold, damp day. *Tortelli* and *anolini* are still enjoyed in Parma today. Oretta Zanini de Vita says of *anolini*: "The *anolini* of Parma are the emblem of a gastronomic civility, a harmonious marriage between popular cooking and bourgeois cuisine that was able to exploit and transform the genuine quality products of its bountiful land."[110] Yes, the delicacies of Parma are all wrapped up in each little half moon.

Other high quality food was available. How much of it Bodoni consumed during his early days in Parma is difficult to assess because of his ambiguous social status. Game birds were popular and included snipe, thrush, turtledove, pigeon, wild duck, and ortolan (a type of bunting). These last were very small and very expensive. Equally sought-after and expensive were freshwater shrimp and fish, brought in from Lake Garda. Frogs starred in *risotto con le rane*.

In a dairy economy like Parma's, people cooked with butter and cream instead of the olive oil to which Bodoni had become accustomed in Rome. In addition to hard cheese such as Parmigiano, then called "*formaggio di Lodi*," a range of soft cheeses from the nearby mountains was available, including gorgonzola and the wildly delicious *stracchino*.

Some of the fruit and vegetables that Bodoni consumed are no longer found in the markets, although efforts are being made to bring them back. Then, as now, artichokes, cardoons, and asparagus were always available. Apples and pears were popular, and people in Parma were wild about conserving fruit with sugar, vinegar, or spirits. Their appetite for ice cream and sorbet knew no bounds.

Bodoni's Parma diet was based almost entirely on protein and pasta, and differed greatly from his Roman diet with its abundance of olive oil and fresh vegetables. This would have dire consequences for him later in life. However, his digestion was no doubt aided (or at least he thought it was) by the sparkling wines of the region, dark red Lambrusco and pale yellow Malvasia. The climatic conditions in which the local wines were made imparted amazing fizz, and the populace always had an unwavering belief in the curative powers of bubbles.

AND SO BODONI came to the end of his first year in Parma. He had much for which to be grateful. He had landed on his feet; he had a patron, Don Ferdinando, to underwrite his printing; he had the encouragement of Guillaume Du Tillot and Father Paciaudi; his brothers were at hand to support him; he could be proud of the fact that he had set up the royal press and had already published *I Voti*; and he had been entrusted with a challenging new commission: to produce a slim, elegant guide to a large, impressively virile, marble monument called *Ara Amicitiae*.

The duke and Du Tillot had decided to commemorate Emperor Joseph II's momentous visit to Parma. They chose Petitot to design *Ara Amicitiae*, and they called on Father Paciaudi to write a description of its symbolic meaning and inscriptions. Naturally, Parma's new printing office would publish the resulting volume, and Paciaudi's description of the monument offered Bodoni a perfect opportunity to show off his typographic skills. In the nine-page folio volume he included engravings by Bossi, Baratti, and Ravenet, and divided Paciaudi's French and Italian text into two columns, with Italian in italics on the left, French in Roman on the right. He interspersed this with Latin inscriptions from the monument in Roman capitals. Bodoni had plenty of time to work on the volume throughout the winter; its publication was timed to coincide with the installation of the monument on 7 June 1769.

With Don Ferdinando and Du Tillot pleased that their dream of a royal press for Parma was finally being realized, Bodoni was well placed to face the extraordinary demands of 1769.

OB . FELICISSIMVM .
IMPERATORIS . SEMPER . AVG .
IOSEPHI . II . ADVENTVM .
ARA . AMICITIAE .
IVSSV . FERDINANDI . II .
DEVOTA . CONSECRATAQVE . EST

AD . PERPETVITATEM
NOMINIS ,
IMP . IOSEPHI . II .
MAX . PII . INVICTI
QVOD
PRISTINAM
BENEVOLENTIAM
NOVIS . MERITIS
PRAESENSQ . CVMVLARIT
FERDINANDVS . I . H . I .
PARM . PLAC . VAST . DVX
MVTVO . AMORE
MONVMENTVM . HOC .
LOCARI . DICARIQVE
SANCIVIT .

CIↃIↃCCLXVIIII .

Scala di   1   2   3   4   5   6 Piedi del Re.

Ara Amicitiae.

Saluzzo mia amata patria.

PLATE 19 *Manuale tipografico,* 1788. Bodoni's tribute to his birthplace is printed in Papale, the last and largest of the typefaces in the book. The first and smallest, Parmigianina, pays tribute to his adopted city of Parma.

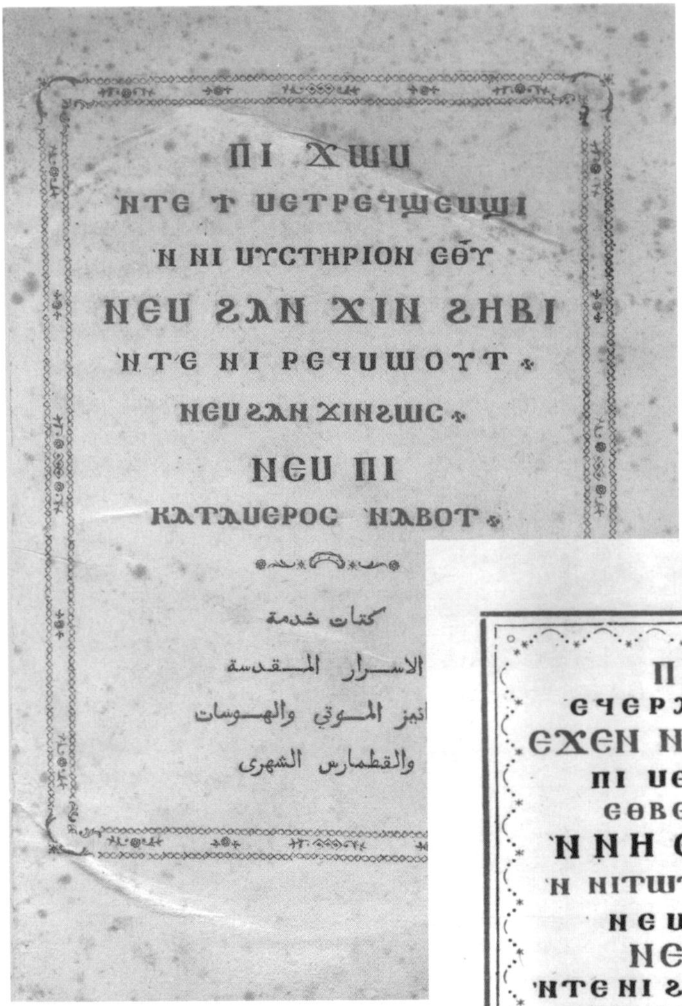

PLATE 20 Frontispiece for *Pontificale copto-arabo* without Bodoni's name.

PLATE 21 Frontispiece for *Pontificale copto-arabo* with Bodoni's name.

GAZZETTA DI PARMA.

MARTEDI' 4. AGOSTO 1772.

PETERSBOURG 7. *Luglio*.

L Generale Feld-Marefcial-
lo Conte Pietro Aleffan-
drowitz Romanzow ha
ricevuto dal Gran-Vifir
Mouffun-Oglou il Rati-
ficamento degli Articoli
dell'Armiftizio conchiufo il 30. Maggio a
tenore della copia reciprocamente da lui
fpeditagli, ed è conceputo ne' feguenti
termini.

Sul principio vedefi in lingua Ara-
ba tale efpreffione: »Con fiducia nell'ajuto di Dio in-
» divifibile, nella fua foftanza, a cui
» nulla può uguagliarfi, e che ha creato
» il tutto.

» L' Imperatore, per beneplacito
» dell'Altiffimo, e della fua eterna Gra-
» zia, il più graziofo, il più potente,
» il più giufto, mio graziofiffimo Signo-
» re, dotato d'imperiali preminenze, e
» d'amore verfo l'uman genere, ftabilito
» al Divina fervigia della fanta Città
» della Mecca, e deftinato colla più
» grande potenza, e con moltitudine di
» Popolazioni a fignoreggiare fopra Ter-
» re, e Mari, il quale tra' giuftiffimi
» Sultani è il più Saggio, tra' rifpetta-
» biliffimi Regnanti l'Eletto, ed il più
» rinomato, ed eccelfo Dominante dello

» ftipite più fublime del mondo. E così
» tutti gli Schiavi, ed abitatori delle
» Provincie porgono a Lui ringrazia-
» menti per la minima grazia loro di-
» moftrata: cui a tenore dell'innato fuo
» Imperiale amore per l'umanità, e fic-
» come l'Univerfo n'è ftato teftimonio,
» hanno penetrato nel cuore le angu-
» ftie, e miferie de' Sudditi a Lui con-
» fidati, ed il quale, fe foffe poffibile
» di efporre minutamente alla noftra
» corta, veduta gli avvenimenti, e le
» cofe fuccedute, che appartengono all'
» occulta Sapienza Divina; moftrerebbe
» agli occhi de' faggi, e de' prudenti,
» che per alcune contingenze, ed ofcu-
» re cagioni venne a rompere l'amici-
» zia già conchiufa tra l'alto, e fempre
» durevole Impero Ottomano, e quel
» di Ruffia, e che in fequela fcoppiò,
» e alimentoffi per alcuni anni il fuoco
» della Guerra collo fpargimento di tan-
» to fangue umano da ambe le parti.
» Or quantunque ciò fia accaduto fe-
» condo i preordinati Decreti dell'Onni-
» potente Creatore, tuttavia il profegui-
» mento della Guerra, e la nimiftà de-
» gli Abitanti dell'una, e dell'altra par-
» te ha cagionato gli eftremi torbidi,
» ed aperto l'adito a molte defolazioni.
» Per lo che il più celebre tra' grandi
» Principi, che credono in GESU', l'E-

PLATE 22 Bodoni took over the printing of the *Gazzetta di Parma* on 4 August, 1772. This is his layout for the front page. (Even without Bodoni's help, the *Gazzetta* still prospers as Parma's daily newspaper.)

ALL' IMMORTALE
IPERIDE FOCEO
VIGILANTISSIMO
VICE-CUSTODE
DELLA
COLONIA PARMENSE
PER AVER FATTO ASCRIVERE ALLA MEDESIMA
ALCIPPO PERSEJO

Eccelso Vate, di sudore aspergo
    Anch'io quel calle, onde alla Gloria vassi;
    E l'ardua meta, a cui mi spingo, ed ergo,
    Già poco lungi dal mio sguardo stassi.

Quindi l'opra, e l'ingegno affino, e tergo;
    Quindi prendo vigor, e affretto i passi;
    E là, dov'hanno i chiari nomi albergo,
    Spero, che alfine il nome mio vedrassi.

IPERIDE *, se il vanto è troppo audace,
    Pensa, che dentro all'alma io serbo impresso
    Quanto il tuo labbro in mio favor non tace.

Pieno de' detti tuoi, merto perdono,
    Se ardisco immaginar d'esser quel desso,
    Che tu dici; ch'io bramo; e che non sono.

* Nome Arcadico di S. E. il Signor Conte AURELIO TERRAROSSA BERNIERI, Gentiluomo di Camera di S. A. R. con Esercizio, Vice-Presidente del Magistrato degli Studj, e R. Conservatore del Collegio de' Nobili, Cavaliere molto coltissimo ed umanissimo, il quale spontaneamente fece ascrivere alla Colonia Parmense GIAMBATISTA BODONI Direttore della R. Tipografia, e Socio della R. Accademia delle Belle Arti, sotto il nome di *Alcippo Persejo*.

DALLA REALE STAMPERIA PARMENSE

1781

PLATE 23 *All'Immortale Iperide Foceo* (1782) is a poster printed by Bodoni to thank Aurelio Bernieri Terrarossa, his fellow Arcadian, for championing his entry into the academy.

ΣΟΥΙΔΑΣ

ΠΕΡΙ ΤΟΥ ΒΙΟΥ ΤΕ

ΚΑΙ ΤΩΝ ΣΥΓΓΡΑΜΜΑΤΩΝ ΤΟΥ

ΚΑΛΛΙΜΑΧΟΥ

Καλλίμαχος, υἱὸς Βάττου καὶ Μεσά-
τμας, Κυρηναῖος, γραμματικός, μα-
θητὴς Ἑρμοκράτους τοῦ Ἰασέως, γραμ-
ματικοῦ· γαμετὴν ἐσχηκὼς τὴν Εὐφρά-
του τοῦ Συρακουσίου θυγατέρα. ἀδελ-
φῆς δὲ αὐτοῦ παῖς ἦν ὁ νέος Καλλίμα-

PLATE 24 Bodoni published Callimachus's hymns and epigrams in 1792 in celebration of the marriage of the duke and duchess of Parma's eldest daughter, Carolina Teresa di Borbone to Maximilian of Saxony.

33

those words, a ray of moonshine stream-
ing through a cranny of the ruin abore
shone directly on the lock they sought
—Oh! transport! said *Isabella*, here
is the trap-door! and taking out the key,
she touched the spring, which starting
aside, discovered an iron ring. Lift up
the door, said the Princess. The stranger obeyed; and beneath appeared some
stone steps descending into a vault
totally darck. We must go down here,
said *Isabella*: Follow me; dark and dismal as it is, we cannot miss our way;
it leads directly to the church of St. *Ni-
colas*—but perhaps, added the Princess modestly, you have no reason to
leave the castle, nor have I farther occasion for your service; in a few minutes I shall be safe from *Manfred*'s rage
—only let me know to whom I am so
much obliged. I will never quit you,
said the stranger eagerly, until I have

PLATE 25 Sample page from *The Castle of
Otranto* including at least three typographical
errors.

PLATE 26 Ghitta presented a copy of *La Réligion Vengée* (1795) to Queen Marie Clothilde
on the Bodonis' triumphal visit to Turin in
1798.

LA RELIGION VENGÉE

CHANT PREMIER.

De l'esprit de Dieu même immortelle clarté
Je t'invoque aujourd'hui, puissante Vérité,
Toi qui, du haut des cieux ici bas descendue,
Toujours victorieuse et toujours combattue,
Loin du peuple et des grands aimes à te cacher,
Pour te montrer sans voile à qui veut te chercher,
Viens remplir mon esprit de ta splendeur divine,
Viens des erreurs du monde éclairer l'origine;
Dis-moi comment l'orgueil pénétra dans les cieux,
Arma l'ange rebelle et l'homme audacieux,
Comment la volupté, sa sœur et sa complice,
De la Religion ébranla l'édifice;
De ces monstres ligués peins toutes les fureurs,
Fais voir dans leur accord la source des erreurs;
Et du monde ébloui par leurs fausses maximes,
Viens chasser à la fois les doutes et les crimes:

SIRE

 E arpe de' Bardi ac-
compagnarono un dì
le armi di Carlomagno, allor-
chè dalle rive Aquitaniche,

PLATE 27 Vincenzo Monti's address to Napoleon at the beginning of *Il Bardo della Selva Nera* (1806), showing one of seven headpieces previously used by Bodoni in the *Epithalamia* (1775).

THÉATRE

COMPLET

DE

JEAN RACINE

———

TOME PREMIER.

A PARME

·········

DE L'IMPRIMERIE BODONI

~

MDCCCXIII.

PLATE 28 *Théatre Complet de Jean Racine* was the last book printed by Bodoni, and was on the press on 30 November 1813, the day of his death.

Descrizione delle Feste . . . Fireworks at Colorno.

5
The Duchess and Du Tillot

The marriage in 1769 between Philip's son Ferdinand and Maria Amalia consolidated the Bourbon-Habsburg alliance, ensuring political stability for three decades. These tortuous political conditions and diplomatic relations provided Bodoni with important ties to the Vatican, to Spain, to the Hapsburgs and, in the early 19th century, to France.

STEPHAN FÜSSEL

PARMA WAS bubbling with excitement. The decision had been made: Don Ferdinando, the 18-year-old duke, was to marry 23-year-old Archduchess Maria Amalia, the eighth of the sixteen children of Empress Maria Theresa of Austria.

Emotionally, Maria Amalia was damaged goods. She had fallen in love with Karl Augustus of Zweibrücken and desperately wanted to marry him. However, her mother had more ambitious plans for her. The empress was determined to strengthen the allegiance between the Hapsburgs and the French and Spanish branches of the Bourbon family. She had her eye on Europe's three most eligible bachelors, the Bourbon cousins: Ferdinando IV of Naples; the dauphin Louis of France; and Ferdinando I of Parma. She farmed Maria Amalia out to the duke of Parma; Maria Carolina to King Ferdinand IV of Naples; and her youngest daughter, the ill-starred Antoine, went to the dauphin of France to become Marie Antoinette.

All Maria Theresa's daughters were trained in obedience, and they knew their mother's will was ironclad. The empress made sure that the primary text of their upbringing was *Les Aventures de Télémaque*. This book was written in the late 1600s by the French theologian François Fénelon for the duke of Burgundy, son of the then dauphin, to teach him (successfully) the virtues of obedience and self-discipline. She hoped it would have the same effect on her daughters. It was the same book with which Bodoni would have dealings late in his life.

The pairing with Parma did not sit well with the "ugly, astute, wily, intriguing, dominating, vindictive, sensual, heedless of etiquette, extravagant, and fun-loving" Maria Amalia.[111] Nor did the pairing please Guillaume Du Tillot, who distrusted an alliance with Austria. He had lobbied hard for Don Ferdinando to marry Beatrice d'Este of Modena, his favorite of several candidates, in a union that would strengthen and consolidate the two Bourbon duchies. Maria Amalia soon learned about Du Tillot's preference, and she held it against him from the moment she arrived in Parma.

The details of the marriage contract were negotiated in the autumn of 1768, and the wedding was planned for January 1769. However, Pope Clement XIII refused to grant a dispensation, in part because of Du Tillot's anti-ecclesiastical reforms. The pope's death in February and the subsequent investiture of Clement XIV in May solved this problem, and the dispensation was granted.[112]

Once the contract was signed, Vienna celebrated with banquets, audiences, spectacles, and fireworks, and the celebrations were followed by a proxy wedding. Maria Theresa escorted her daughter to the altar, while Maria Amalia's brother Ferdinand stood in for Don Ferdinando who awaited her in Parma. Then, accompanied by 50 carriages full of her possessions, Maria Amalia left Vienna for Parma. En route, at Mantua, she met up with her eldest brother, Joseph II, the emperor and co-regent of Austria. (Joseph had enjoyed his visit to Parma in 1768, and had written favorably about it to his mother, an act which may have helped to consolidate plans for the royal wedding.) There was no love lost between brother and sister, and together they spent four rather uncomfortable days.[113] By this time, Don Ferdinando had become impatient to meet his bride. He hurried to Mantua, where he dined with Joseph and Maria Amalia, and then headed straight back home. Maria Amalia recognized immediately that she had nothing in common with the mild, dumpy, and stupefyingly religious duke with his extravagantly good manners and pious conversation. What a contrast he made with her dashing Karl Augustus of Zweibrücken! However, she was clever enough to acknowledge that the duke afforded her something useful: a character she could mold to her will. He in turn must have had certain qualms about the arrogant but undeniably lively archduchess.

This is the couple around whom Bodoni's life revolved for the next 33 years.

ON 19 JULY 1769, Maria Amalia left Mantua for her solemn state entry into the duchy of Parma. At Cassalmaggiore, the members of the Austrian court who had accompanied her thus far, returned to Vienna. That evening, she crossed the river Po on a barge, and travelled the few remaining miles to the palace of Colorno. She received a warm welcome from many of her new subjects, was treated to a pastoral recitation in the Royal Theatre, and presented with a slim volume, *Pastorale recitata nel R. Teatro di Colorno in festeggiamento dell'arrivo di S.A.R.l'Arciducessa Maria Amalia nostra graziosissima Sovrana* [A pastoral recited in the Royal Theatre of Colorno in celebration of the arrival of her Royal Highness the Archduchess Maria Amalia, our most gracious sovereign.] This was her first exposure to Bodoni's work, and she did not forget it.

The royal wedding was celebrated at Colorno on 27 July. Finally, on 24 August, Ferdinando and Maria Amalia made their way in a huge procession from Colorno to the cathedral in Parma, cheered along the way by jubilant throngs craning their necks to catch a glimpse of their new duchess. Even though Du Tillot was not enthusiastic about the choice of Maria Amalia for Ferdinando's bride, he threw himself into organizing an enormous celebration in the royal gardens. The festivities continued into the first ten days of September. It was a bittersweet celebration for Du Tillot who by then thoroughly disapproved of the duchess, but a wonderful opportunity for him to display Parma's bright face to the invited dignitaries of Europe. He organized a tournament; a Chinese fair; an Arcadian idyll presented by the leading Arcadians of Parma; and performances of plays and the first performance of *Le Feste d'Apollo,* an opera by Gluck, whom Maria

Lucrezia Agujari being augmented by her admirer, the Parmesan composer Giuseppe Colla, who later became her husband. (N.B. the play on words; "colla" means glue.)

Amalia had known in Vienna, where she had performed in two of his operas. In *Le Feste d'Apollo,* the part of Arcinia was performed by a local and international favorite, the coloratura soprano Lucrezia Agujari, "La Bastardella."

Planning these events required all Du Tillot's formidable organizational skill, and he insisted on recording the results in the most beautiful way possible. To this end, he gathered together Bodoni, Petitot, and Benigno Bossi, the renowned engraver, and exhorted them to produce albums that would astonish everyone with their magnificence. The first and most important of these was *Descrizione delle Feste celebrate in Parma l'anno MDC-CLXIX per le auguste nozze di S.A.R. l'Infante Don Ferdinando colla R. Arcid. Maria Amalia* [Description of the festivities celebrated in Parma in 1769 for the august wedding of His Royal Highness the Infante Don Ferdinando with the Royal Duchess Maria Amalia.] The volume was published in folio, and H.C. Brooks, the eminent cataloger of Bodoni's works, describes it as being exquisitely beautiful and perhaps the most attractive of all Bodoni's books for the elegance of its illustrations. The other three volumes, published in quarto, were *Eco e Narciso; Le Feste d'Apollo;* and *Le Pastorelle d'Arcadia.*

The volumes immediately attracted the attention of a wide audience,

The Chinese Fair. The supposedly Chinese figure on the right bears a distinct resemblance to Petitot himself.

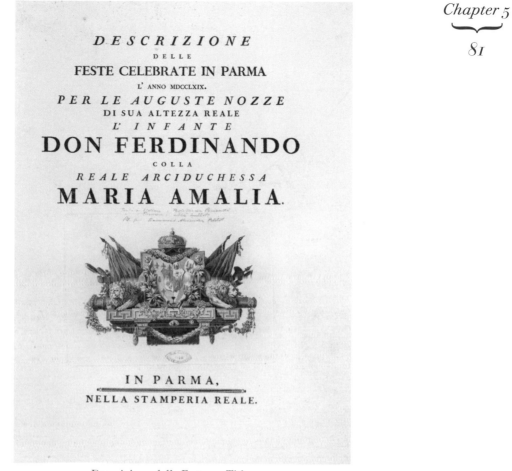

Descrizione delle Feste . . . Title page

and letters of congratulation began to pour in. *Descrizione delle Feste . . .* in particular received praise from many quarters. After receiving her copy, Marie Antoinette wrote to Maria Amalia: "The dauphin and I have looked at the beautiful book with much interest . . . the prints are very well made . . . Italy, as the good Metastasio often repeats to me, is ever the home of the arts."[114] Welcome praise came from that most urbane and knowledgeable of critics, Pierre Jean Mariette in Paris. In his letter to Father Paciaudi he said: "I did not expect, I confess, to see such a perfectly executed book, in all its parts, issue from a fledgling press . . . I want to tell you in one word that no other work of its kind has caused me so much satisfaction. I consider it to be a masterpiece."[115] It is still considered a masterpiece today.

Shortly after the publication of *Descrizione delle Feste . . . ,* Petitot drew

L'Auteur des Figures à la Grecque

Ennemond Petitot, (1727-1801). Self-portrait in *Mascarade à la Grecque.*

and Bossi engraved an album of engravings of characters *à la grecque* in a parody of images they found in the prime minister's closet. Calling it *Mascarade à la Grecque,*[116] Bossi presented the album to Du Tillot, and in his dedication took a jab at the recent fashion and folly for making everything appear Greek. The last image in this charming parody is a self-portrait of Petitot. His right hand rests on his pride and joy, the *Descrizione delle Feste...,* the same volume that can be seen at his feet in the portrait of him in the color section.

Unfortunately, despite the enthusiastic reception Maria Amalia received at first in Parma, and despite her accomplishments as a singer and artist, members of the court were soon offended by her outrageous behavior. They thought her loud, uncivilized, extravagant, and entirely unsuited to be a duchess of anywhere, least of all Parma. She, for her part, found them stuffy, humorless, and constricted by etiquette. She continually flew in the face of convention by ignoring the court and consorting with the common people or leaping on a horse and galloping all over the countryside. To Du Tillot's alarm, she was often found in the company of her guards and groomsmen.[117]

Problems between the newly married duke and duchess surfaced immediately. For three months, Ferdinando was impotent, despite letters filled with encouragement and advice from his grandfather, King Louis XV of France. Fortunately, thanks to mysterious interventions from Dr. Camuti, Ferdinando's chief doctor, these matters were resolved. Maria Amalia wasted no time in informing her lady-in-waiting, Marchesa Anna Malaspina della Bastia, of the news, and Ferdinando crowed proudly to the Baron de la Houze that he had been "perfectly happy twice in a row" and that he believed the duchess was already pregnant.[118] Maria Amalia gave birth to their first child, Carolina, on 22 November 1770.

This happy event presented Bodoni with the opportunity to print a poem of celebration written by Count Della Torre di Rezzonico. Bodoni's skill at printing so impressed Maria Amalia that in 1772 she commissioned him to print a book expressly for her in German Fraktur (that is, German gothic black letter) entitled *Sieben Gebeten einer Schwangern Frauen um glückliche Entbindung* [Seven prayers for a pregnant woman for her happy delivery].

After the demands of 1769, 1770 was a quiet year at the press, if not at the court. Among other visitors to Parma, Leopold Mozart blew in on a musical tour with his 14-year old son, Wolfgang Amadeus. The older Mozart was entertained by La Bastardella and amazed by her prodigious vocal range. The lull at the press gave Bodoni time to enrich his type collection.

Hand-stamped proofs of metal type ornaments for *Fregi e Majuscole* with Bodoni's handwritten identification at head.

He cut more punches, struck more matrices, cast more type. He began to train local apprentices to take the place of his older brother Domenico who had returned to Saluzzo in October 1769. Among the workers he hired over a span of several years were Leonardo Freddi from Corniglio, the Amoretti brothers from nearby San Pancrazio, Giacomo Boregana, and after 1795, Luigi Pezzanelli. He was overjoyed when Jean George Handwerck arrived from Lyons to take over the business side of the press. Handwerck turned out to be a most loyal accountant as well as a true friend. It was a relief to hand over the financial reins to such a man.

Bodoni was thinking small in 1770. He had come up with the idea of producing a little specimen book to display his growing collection of decorations, frames, and capital letters. Such specimen books had been preceded by single-page specimen sheets ever since the late 1400s. The first surviving complex sheet, that is, one advertising more than a single typeface, printed by Erhard Ratdolt in Augsburg in 1486, was an astonishing piece of work. Ratdolt eschewed the traditional German gothic black letter and instead advertised fourteen typefaces he had brought back to Germany from Venice, including one in Greek.[119] Gradually, as printing became more sophisticated and printers started acquiring large numbers of typefaces, entire books of specimens were produced. These albums reached their full flowering in the Neo-Classical period, and it is safe to say that Bodoni's enormous *Manuale tipografico* of 1818 was the greatest specimen of them all.

But for his first little specimen book, Bodoni leant heavily on examples he found in Fournier's *Manuel typographique*, stressing that while the characters were derived from Fournier's, they were not an exact imitation.[120]

He cut hundreds of punches for detailed decorations, frames, *culs-de-lampe* (ornaments placed at the end of chapters), and capital letters. It is useful to remember here that it takes a skilled punchcutter between four and six hours to complete a single punch. The result of Bodoni's labors, *Fregi e majuscole*, was published in quarto in 1771. In this, his first specimen book, he took the design of the title page straight from Fournier's *Manuel*, making sure his name was displayed larger than any other words on the page. He wrote a rambling introduction, dedicated to "careful and diligent typographers," in which he managed to include a short history of printing; a challenge to his readers to find better printing in all of Italy; and gracious thanks to his patron, Ferdinando, whom he compared to Louis XI (1423-1483), the king who had welcomed and supported the nascent printing arts in France. Yes, *Fregi e majuscole* was little in size but large in ambition. Bodoni sent it all over Europe as a gift and an advertisement. Europe took note, and the book's success led to his being invited by Count Firmian, governor of Lombardy,

Fregi e majuscole. Title page.

to direct the royal press in Milan. This was the first of many invitations Bodoni received to move to other cities. De Lama states that Bodoni refused this one because he had already developed a great affection for his adopted city.[121]

Back at the court, Maria Amalia, in the mistaken belief that she and the duke were rulers of the duchy, had already locked horns with the de facto ruler, Du Tillot. She still burned with resentment at his opposition to her marriage; for his part, Du Tillot recognized that he had been right in opposing it. All his legendary charm and diplomacy could not persuade her to conform. She vowed to do everything in her power to rid Parma of its prime minister, and she started by alienating her husband against him. This was not difficult because Ferdinando was already concerned about some of Du Tillot's religious reforms, particularly the closing of non-productive monasteries and convents, as well as the expulsion of the Jesuits from Parma, even though he himself had agreed to it. Word of the enmity between the duchess and the prime minister reached the ear of Louis XV in France. The king, who had great respect for Du Tillot, tried to intervene, writing to Ferdinando on 1 November 1769: "Du Tillot is an honest man, whom your father cherished and in whom he had confidence in the administration of your little states. The minister has enlightened zeal for your interests. His respect for the memory of your father and your mother, and his love for you, may make you uncomfortable sometimes and may look like prying, but your glory, your glory without his own personal ambition, is the only motive that animates his zeal. Every man has drawbacks; but he who has more uses and attachment than drawbacks is a precious minister for princes. This is how it is with Du Tillot for you."[122]

Not even his grandfather's words could soothe the growing animosity; not even the efforts of the marquis of Chauvelin, a special envoy from Louis XV, were able to rein in Maria Amalia's wild impulses and pour water on the fires of Ferdinando's religious mania; not even Choiseul, the prime minister of France, could encourage religious moderation in the duke with his words: "When you are a prince, you cannot without ridicule be a monk."[123] And nothing could make Maria Amalia conform.

Word about her intransigence reached her mother in Vienna, and the empress immediately wrote a letter excoriating her daughter. She insisted that Maria Amalia strive for a perfect harmony between herself and her husband. She advised her against dominating him and taking hold of the reins of the state, and she instructed her daughter not to oppose the prime minister, of whom she had a favorable opinion. Maria Amalia was maddened by her mother's interfering injunctions, and immediately wrote a diatribe containing 21 points repudiating her mother's advice. She insisted that neither she nor her husband were respected by the French as rulers. As duchess of Parma she had a perfect right to give orders to members of the court. Above all, she utterly rejected interventions by intermediaries from the Bourbon courts of France and Spain. This letter brought about a freeze in the correspondence between the empress and her daughter, a rift that thawed only slightly in 1773 on the birth of Ludovico, Ferdinando and Maria Amalia's second child, their son and heir.

Maria Amalia spent money wildly, more money than the court could afford. She kept more than 50 horses in her stables, and made her apartments an extension of her kennels. Six or seven dogs stretched out on her bed; one day she complained that her greyhound had almost bitten off her finger.[124] When she was bored, she played blind man's bluff with the lesser members of her staff. About her, Élizabeth Vigée Le Brun, the celebrated French artist, commented: "She is much older than our queen [Marie Antoinette], and she is neither beautiful nor gracious . . . This princess rides her horses every day. Her way of life and her manners are those of a man. All in all, I didn't find her pleasing, even though she received me quite kindly."[125]

In the court itself, Maria Amalia was suspicious of her chief lady-in-waiting, Anna Malaspina, because she was Du Tillot's confidante. The duchess eventually refused to allow Anna Malaspina into the ducal apartments, took away her keys, and insisted that she was nothing but a servant. When Du Tillot named Anna Malaspina the head of household for the duke's baby daughter Carolina, Maria Amalia was enraged. On 21 July 1771, the marchesa was stripped of her retinue, and temporarily removed to a house in the country.

DU TILLOT'S DAYS were numbered. Growing anger in ecclesiastical circles was joined by a huge swell of anti-French sentiment, particularly among the people of Piacenza. (Piacenza was one of the three towns that made up the duchy of Parma, along with Guastalla.) They had become resentful at having to pay taxes that appeared to be spent only on the city of Parma, and began protesting and stirring up trouble, discord that Maria Amalia was happy to encourage, and which seeped into all corners of the duchy.

Du Tillot wrote to the king of France and the king of Spain asking for permission to retire. The duke, in a letter clearly prompted by his wife, also wrote to the kings, asking them to recall Du Tillot. The kings, distrusting Maria Amalia and having nothing but admiration for Du Tillot, refused these requests. Instead, they sent envoys to Parma to try to calm the situation. But the situation had gone too far, and the envoys were helpless; they could do nothing but report back to the kings about a state of affairs they perceived as out of hand. The people cried out for the assassination of Du Tillot. He was even accused of wanting to poison the duchess. Finally, the kings granted, but then revoked, his dismissal. "The duchess, humiliated and angry at her plans being overthrown, retired to Sala [Sala Baganza, her preferred residence in the countryside]. She resolved in a move worthy of Lysistrata not to return to the duke in Colorno while Du Tillot was still there."[126] The duke rushed to Sala and tried to persuade her to return to his arms. She refused, and the duke returned to Colorno, where "solitude and idleness forced him to look elsewhere for those distractions the duchess had denied him. The rustic sex of Colorno served his interests. 'And yet he only wanted to be good; but it seems that the duchess wanted him to be bad.'"[127]

Three months of misery ensued for Du Tillot. Smears were written about him, death threats issued, acidly satirical songs sung in the streets, and finally he was put under house arrest at his home in Colorno. Even there the humiliation continued, including signs on his door reading "House for rent. House for sale. Death to Du Tillot and his lackeys."[128] Finally he was given permission to leave. Vainly he asked to see the duke to say goodbye. At first permission was granted, but suddenly withdrawn after the duchess learned of the proposed meeting.

Guillaume Du Tillot escaped from Parma under cover of night on 19 November 1771. He made his way overland to Madrid, where he was warmly welcomed by the king of Spain, and then proceeded to France where he received an equally enthusiastic reception. He took up residence in Paris, and on 13 December 1774, three years after his ignominious departure from Parma, died at his home of a stroke.

In a letter to Count Algarotti in 1762, at a time when he was extremely effective and much appreciated by Don Filippo, Du Tillot predicted his own downfall: "[My life] is more turbulent [than yours] and is so filled with public business that I do not perhaps have the fortune to do useful things. However, I have done what I could for the public advantage; it is an idol to which I sacrifice everything. I love this country as I love my homeland. I have instigated many initiatives and some succeeded, but I have had to combat a sort of indolence, in a state with limited ability. I need a great deal of patience, and after many years I have made some progress, but little that is appreciable. I must not be discouraged; but I die in the struggle. What a life, Monsieur!"[129]

The well-furnished press. *Die Wol-eingerichtete Buchdruckerey* (1733).

6

Bodoni at Work

Typography is divided into three distinct parts: cutting, casting the type, and printing. Each one of these parts has specialists: he who cuts is an engraver, he who casts is a founder, and he who prints is a printer. Only he who brings together these three qualities can be called a typographer.

FOURNIER LE JEUNE

The practice of typography if it be followed faithfully, is hard work — full of petty restrictions, full of drudgery, and not greatly rewarded as men now count rewards . . . But in the light of history, and of art, and of knowledge, and of man's achievement, it is as interesting a work as exists.

DANIEL BERKELEY UPDIKE

. . . by typographer, I mean such a one, who by his own judgement, from solid reasoning within himself, can either perform, or direct others to perform from the beginning to the end, all the handy-works and physical operations relating to typographie.

JOSEPH MOXON

I N B ODONI's day, the definition of typographer was much broader and referred to someone who could do everything: design a letter, cut the punch, strike the matrix, cast the letter, set it, and print it. Bodoni was indubitably a typographer in Fournier and Moxon's terms, and this is the sense in which the word is used in this book when describing him. Nowadays, the word "typographer" refers to a person who arranges type for the purpose of printing.

It is worth bearing in mind that Bodoni had employees who could prepare the steel for the punches as well as trained men such as the Amoretti brothers who were capable of cutting them and striking matrices as necessary; he had compositors; and his brother Giuseppe ran the foundry. But he was the brain, the *primum mobile,* behind everything, the designer who strove for perfection who was capable of performing every function in the printing process. He made sure that his instructions were followed, literally, to the letter. He thought endlessly about style, typeface, size, spacing, color and quality of paper, and blackness of ink (which he acquired from Fratelli Rocchi in Venice and then doctored a bit to suit his exacting standards).[130] His four guiding principles were uniformity, neatness, good taste, and charm. He made the initial decisions, constantly cut punches himself, supervised and approved the efforts of others, and had the final word. To the minds of many in his own day as in ours, Bodoni was *il sommo tipografo* [the greatest typographer].

By the 1770s, Bodoni was in the grips of an obsession to enlarge his typographic arsenal and to outdo Fournier. He amassed thousands of punches, and toiled lovingly over this work until the end of his life. As mentioned already, it takes a skilled punch cutter approximately five hours to cut just one medium-sized punch. As a measure of how skilled and speedy Bodoni was at the task, J.G.C. Adler, the great orientalist, commented after a visit to the press that Bodoni had a huge capacity for cutting and was able to finish a new, moderately easy alphabet in two to three days.

Despite the conflicts seething around him, Bodoni continued to work calmly and steadily in his premises on the banks of the Parma. He was then, and would remain for the rest of his life, immune to political crises, being too busy to take sides or to involve himself in political machinations. However, he was greatly saddened by the fall of Du Tillot, the man who had dreamed of a great cultural center on the banks of the Parma, and who had worked so zealously with Bodoni to establish a printing office to rival those in the rest of Europe. He also missed his daily visits to Father Paciaudi, who because of his francophilia and close friendship with Du Tillot, was under house arrest in the Theatine convent in Parma. On Paciaudi's release in February 1772, he was allowed to return to his work at the library and was understandably overjoyed to see how the press was prospering under the direction of his protégé. During that year, Bodoni published plays, inscriptions, and dissertations, and was entrusted with the publication of Parma's newspaper, *La Gazzetta di Parma*. The first edition under his aegis appeared on 4 August 1772. He was also called upon to publish public announcements, one of which, attempting to curb crime on the streets, declared that anyone failing to carry a light while walking around the city during nighttime hours would be subject to incarceration.

By 1772, the political situation in Parma had calmed down, although the duchess had taken a dislike to the new Prime Minister, José de Llano. He had been sent to Parma by Carlos III, the Bourbon king of Spain, at the time of the fall of Du Tillot, but nothing the Bourbon family initiated would please the duchess. Not surprisingly, Llano's tenure was short-lived. Despite resistance from the kings of Spain and France, the duke and duchess succeeded in having him removed from office. Llano was the last foreign prime minister of Parma. He was succeeded in 1773 by Giuseppe Sacco, who limply presided over a period of counter reformation in which almost all of Du Tillot's political achievements were reversed. The duke and duchess considered themselves finally in control of the duchy.

BY 1773 THE ROYAL PRESS was producing a wide variety of items including plays, poems, inscriptions, essays, presentation books, and a two-page decorated missive to accompany a gift of type that Bodoni had sent to Giovanni Cristofano Amaduzzi, the new superintendent of the Propaganda Fide. Bodoni never lost touch with his connections in Rome and would have been acquainted with Amaduzzi when they were both young men studying at La Sapienza.

Rome, the Propaganda Fide, and exotic typefaces were much on Bodoni's mind. The duchess had given birth to a son, Ludovico, in July 1773, an event that offered Bodoni the perfect opportunity to create a gorgeous presentation book for the baby's baptism, *Pel solenne battestismo di S.A.R. Ludovico Principe Primogenito di Parma . . .* (published on 18 April 1774). In it he displayed, in quarto, twenty of his newly cut exotic faces, and confirmed his position as a frontrunner among European typographers. At the same time, it gave him an opportunity to show his gratitude for his education at the Propaganda Fide and to celebrate the memory of Cardinal Spinelli. As usual, he had fun congratulating himself, even while thanking others. He wrote in his introduction: "Having exposed to the public my specimen of Latin type, adorned with as many unusual decorations and adornments as lovers of perfect printing could possibly desire, I decided to make punches and matrices for 20 exotic typefaces and to cast them with the same accuracy . . . To bring my enterprise to its desired end, I did not have to beg for help from abroad . . . everything was provided for me by the munificence of his Royal Highness [the duke of Parma], who can be justly called father of letters. The sumptuousness of his library . . . has provided me with reliable examples from which to draw and then cut and cast so many different faces."

Finally, with a rare dose of modesty, he launched himself into paroxysms of praise for the Propaganda Fide and Cardinal Spinelli: ". . . there I learned what little I know; there were born in me the first ideas to cut and to cast; there rose up in me fondness for this kind of type, and this kind of study, which encouraged me to undertake the most difficult designs, and to prevail with strength over all the most serious challenges. I do not believe I am able to show myself more grateful for the kindness received than to record it here, in the face of the public."

As well as *Pel solenne battestismo . . .*, the press produced at least fourteen publications in 1774, including poems, plays, and announcements. It is hard to be precise about the exact number. Brooks's monumental effort to catalog all the works printed by Bodoni has surprisingly few holes in it, but inevitably some ephemera — broadsheets, invitations, and announcements — are missing. One of the publications that Brooks lists for 1774 is *Il Figlio del Gran Turco*, a comedy with music for use in the royal theatre of Colorno. Its author? None other than Don Ferdinando himself.

ANTON RAPHAEL MENGS, the renowned artist, whom Bodoni would have known during his time in Rome, arrived in Parma in 1775. He had come to look, and look again, at his hero Correggio's frescoes in the Cathedral of Santa Maria Assunta and in the Church of San Giovanni Evangelista. These frescoes are literally breathtaking, the daring of the perspective in the cupolas making viewers on the floor of the churches gasp and feel as though they, too, are breaking earthly bounds and flying heavenward with the Virgin and with Saint John the Evangelist.

Anton Raphael Mengs (1728-1779). Self-portrait.

Mengs had another mission. Word had reached him that there were more frescoes by Correggio located in a secret room, the Camera di San Paolo, in a convent in the center of Parma. He carried with him a letter of safe conduct from Nicolás De Azara, a Spanish diplomat in Rome, requesting that Prime Minister De Llano seek permission for Mengs to enter the convent, which had been closed to the public for nearly two hundred years. The request was granted.

The approach to the eleventh-century Benedictine convent of San Paolo is through an impressive gateway and down a long, straight path between two buildings. The Camera di San Paolo is found in the heart of the convent; it has no windows, no daylight penetrates it, so Mengs would have examined it by torchlight and candlelight. What he saw was sensational.

By 1519, the convent had become a literary and artistic center under the leadership of its abbess, Giovanna di Piacenza, a cultivated, enlightened noblewoman. As well as providing an environment where ideas of the day were discussed, Giovanna sought to improve the fabric of the convent, and this included having two rooms completely decorated with frescoes. The first, painted by Alessandro Araldi (1460-1520), depicted classical and biblical scenes in the traditional renaissance manner. Although Araldi's work was highly competent, the abbess chose a different painter for the second room, young Antonio Allegri da Correggio. Correggio accepted the challenge, avoiding anything to do with biblical matters and focussing instead on the myth of Diana and the hunt. He created a kind of vaulted pergola, divided into wedges decorated with bouquets and garlands. Each wedge contained an oval image of *putti* and dogs on a sky-blue background and, in one image, the severed head of a deer. Below the *putti,* in monochrome *trompe l'oeil* niches, stand classical figures. A large fireplace at one side of the room is surmounted by a portrait of Diana herself, with flowing robes and flowing hair, adorned with her sign, the moon diadem. She is seated in a horse-drawn chariot, and her left index finger points at the horse's rear end; much is speculated about the significance of this gesture. Is she, in fact, mocking the Catholic Church? She gazes penetratingly at the viewer.

This mysterious room is what Mengs examined by flickering candlelight. This vision, this memory, and this moment would later have repercussions for Bodoni.

Most of the 25 works published by the royal press in 1775 were relatively short, and included poems, plays, announcements, another commission from the duchess (this time a prayer book containing the Mass for the Dead), and Bodoni's only significant medical imprint, *Anatomici summi septemdecim tabulae quas nunc primum edit atque explicat iisque alias addit de structura mammorum et de tunica testis vaginali* by Giovanni Domenico Santorini (1681-circa 1737). Published posthumously, the volume contains 17 plates by Giovanni Battista Piazetta, engraved by Florentia Marcella, and examines such intriguing subjects as the *risorius* muscle (the insincere smile muscle), the organs of smell and hearing, and the *plexus pudendalis venosus,* now often referred to as the Santorini labyrinth.

The year also included the publication of what is justly called the masterpiece of Bodoni's early works. It was published in celebration of the wedding of Carlo Emanuele, the prince of Piedmont (the same prince who had expressed a desire to see Bodoni before he set off for the Court of Parma) and Maria Adelaide Clothilde, sister of the king of France. What a perfect opportunity for Bodoni to create the most extravagantly beautiful and extensive polyglot book the world had ever seen!

It took a team to complete the monumental *Epithalamia exoticis linguis reddita* [Wedding ode rendered in foreign languages]. Its 125 pages contained 139 illustrations (etchings, capital letters, and *culs-de-lampe*). Three artists worked

INCLYTA . REGVM . PROGENIES
ET . ALTERA . GENTIS . SVBALPINAE . SPES
CAROLE . EMMANVEL . FERDINANDE
PRINCEPS . PEDEMONTII
CIVITATES
QVAE . IN . PATRIS . IMPERIO . SVNT
CONNVBIO . TVO . FELICISSIMO
DOCTISONIS . EPITHALAMIIS . PLAVDENTES
EXCIPE
EISQVE . TVO . NVMINE . FAVE
MAIORVM . TVORVM . IMAGINES
VRBIVMQVE . NOSTRARVM . MEMORABILIA
TE . MAGNIS . EDITVM . REGIBVS
STRENVISQVE . POPVLIS . COLVMEN . FVTVRVM
PORTENDVNT
HOC . QVIDQVID . EST . OPERAE . AC . LABORIS
EFFINGENDVM . CVRAVIT
TIBIQVE . SACRVM . INSCRIPTVMQVE
VOLVIT
IOHANNES . BAPTISTA . BODONIVS . SALVTIENSIS
REGIAE . PARMENSI . TYPOGRAPHIAE
PRAEFECTVS .

MARIAE . ADELAIDIS . CLOTHILDIS
LVDOVICI . XVI . FRANCORVM . REGIS
SVAVISSIMAE . SORORIS
CAROLO . EMMANVELI . FERDINANDO
SVBALPINAE . GALLIAE . PRINCIPI
NVPTVM . DATAE
ALLOBROGES . QVOS . PRAESENTIA . SVA . BEAVIT
PRAETERVECTAE
ET . AD . TAVRINOS . PROPERANTIS
ADVENTVM . VERE . FELICISSIMVM
BEATOSQVE . HYMENAEOS
NOVO . ARTIS . TYPOGRAPHICAE . MOLIMINE
GRATVLATVR
IOHANNES . BAPTISTA . BODONIVS . SALVTIENSIS

DATE . LAETITIAM . POPVLI
PLEXISQVE . MYRTO . COROLLIS
REDIMITE . TRAMITES . LARESQVE
ET . DVM . AMOR . QVATIT . TAEDAS
CONNVBIALE . OCCINITE . CARMEN
DEXTERVM . VOBIS . OMEN . PORTENDVNT
AVGVSTAE . CLOTHILDIS
MORES . INGENIVM . CHARITES .

Carlo Emmanuele and Marie Clothilde.

on designing and etching portraits and coats-of-arms. Four authors (including Father Paciaudi) wrote the text, and Count Rezzonico was trotted out again to write a Latin poem, this time running to twenty pages. Bodoni worked hardest of all, preparing good wishes to the royal couple in 26 different languages, each page bearing the name of a different city in Piedmont and an illustrated allegory of the city. All this he designed with "optical harmony" (Fournier's phrase. Allen Hutt, in another example of the synesthesia of type and music, refers to Fournier himself as "the Mozart of typography."[131])

Epithalamia exoticis linguis reddita was a grand success, particularly in Turin. Writing from that city on 2 October 1775, Father Paciaudi stated: "The book has aroused admiration here. It is sought out with avidity . . . and all the foreign visitors try to take it back across the mountains."[132] Carlo Emanuele was so delighted with his wedding present that he rewarded Bodoni with a gift of gold coins enclosed in a golden casket made in Paris.

Following publication, Bodoni was deluged with orders for type from distant printers who wanted to advertise that their offices could offer works printed

Epithalamia . . . Title page

Epithalamia . . . in honor of Saluzzo.

Bodoni's sketches
for exotic type.

with type cast by Bodoni.[133] Trevisani points out that Bodoni's fascination with producing exotic type was no mere caprice. It responded to a real need. Codices and early books in foreign languages were continually arriving from Asia and the Near East; scholars desperately needed printed copies of these works in order to study them.

Admiration was not the only thing with which Bodoni was deluged that year. On 6 November, right outside the printworks, "an awesome flood of the Parma *torrente* smashed two of the arches of the bridge, one wood and one stone. The tobacco factory next door was also damaged."[134]

EVEN THE DEATH OF HIS FATHER could not deflect Bodoni from his work in Parma. His brother Domenico broke the news gently and eloquently on 2 January 1776:

Dearest Brothers, we are without our father. Oh Holy God, why did it not please you to let us keep him for a few more days? . . . He left this vale of misery at 2 o'clock in the morning on the first day of this year, after three days of a slight illness in which he hardly went to bed . . . My tears fall and mix with the ink while I tell you about the circumstances of his passage to eternity; the sadness which oppresses my spirit makes my hands weak and trembly . . . God will console you and all of us.

Leonardo Farinelli, director emeritus of the Biblioteca Palatina and Bodoni Museum, who has spent years scrutinizing the Bodoni correspondence, points out that he has found no trace of acknowledgement on Bodoni's part of the death of his father.[135]

The next few years saw the publication of plenty of material for the court, but nothing on nearly as grand a scale as the publications celebrating the marriages of the duke of Parma and of the prince of Piedmont. He did, however, produce a fascinating specimen book, *Specimen ineditae et hexaplaris Bibliorum versionis syro-estranghelai . . .* which contains the beginning of Psalm I in six columns: Greek; Syro-Estranghelo; Latin from the Septuagint in Roman letters; Hebrew; Peschito (old Syriac used by the early Christians); and the Latin translation of the Peschito in italics. Edited by Johannes Bern, it bears a dedication to P.G. Granieri.

Specimen ineditae et hexaplaris Bibliorum versionis syro-estranghelae . . .

Meanwhile, the duchess continued to bear children and the duke continued to pray. Du Tillot's reforms were slowly eroded or eliminated, and Father Paciaudi was sent to Turin, from where he wrote letters to Bodoni complaining about the cold and the scarcity of good books. Bodoni desperately needed a challenge. By great good fortune, another patron arrived in his life, a *deus ex machina* just when he needed one.

This avatar was the Spanish diplomat José Nicolás de Azara.

José Nicolás de Azara

7
José Nicolás de Azara

Essentially and exquisitely a diplomat, a mediator . . . his deadly enemies were ignorance, superstition, and the fanaticism owed to ecclesiastic oppression.

ANGELO CIAVARELLA

NICOLÁS DE AZARA, the Spanish diplomat, was in love with books. His library in Rome contained 20,000 volumes, and of these, 3,000 were rare editions from the fifteenth and sixteenth centuries. Every Wednesday evening, he invited the city's literary élite to gather at the Palazzo Monaldeschi, the home of the Spanish embassy in the Piazza di Spagna, to discuss the latest books and cultural events, and to be persuaded that literature, art, and science were the key to greater tolerance that might generate a new public spirit. Azara's guests were welcome to admire his large collection of paintings, classical antiquities, and Japanese porcelain.[136] Among the guests were two of his early protégés, the artist Anton Raphael Mengs and the classicist Johann Joachim Winckelmann, with whom he indulged in conversation about their mutual passion for classical antiquities. Caught up in the contemporary archeological frenzy, Azara began undertaking excavations himself and made important discoveries. At the time of his transfer to Paris in 1798, he was able to ship 70 classical sculptures to Carlos IV, the king of Spain.[137]

Azara had been sent to Rome in 1765, the year before Bodoni left the city. The Spanish embassy stood cheek by jowl with the Propaganda Fide, and with Azara's connections in the world of books and classical antiquities, it is more than likely that he and Bodoni first met through the auspices of Cardinal Spinelli some time during 1765.

Born in the small town of Barbuñales, in Aragon, in northeastern Spain, Azara was an excellent student. He left home to study at the University of Salamanca, which was founded in 1218 and is the oldest university in Spain. After a brilliant academic career, he started work in the Secretariat of the State in 1760, and in 1765 was sent to Rome where he remained for the next 32 years. His business acumen was such that he was soon traveling to Parma and Paris on diplomatic and trade missions. He rose steadily in the ranks: agent general, plenipotentiary minister, counsellor of state, and eventually Spanish ambassador to Rome. A pacifist and philosopher but a fierce anti-Jesuit, a man of great culture and intelligence, he was his country's perfect representative, always loyal to Spain but completely at home in Rome.

Bodoni and Azara became good friends in November 1773 during one of Azara's missions to Parma,[138] and they began a correspondence that lasted for nearly 30 years. Azara was extraordinarily knowledgeable about printing, and much of their correspondence is concerned with the minutiae of type. Even so, he was a lively and engaging letter writer. Almost all his letters to Bodoni have been saved; unfortunately, Bodoni's to him have disappeared, although many of his rough drafts are available, particularly from the later years of their correspondence. Azara writes in a jaunty, tumbling Italian. Bodoni's prose is ornate, Latinate, and prolix; he is capable of writing twenty-line sentences and only succumbing occasionally and surprisingly to paragraphing.

In Bodoni, Azara felt he had found not only a protégé and soulmate but the perfect typographer, a man whose taste for type and design could be melded with his. He wanted to own Bodoni. Again and again he tried to persuade him to move to Rome. He nagged his friend, accusing him of wasting his talents in a backwater like Parma. He insisted that Bodoni should print nothing but important books, classical books.

He had a point. Bodoni spent most of his time printing for the prime minister; the office of the Annona; the supreme magistrate; the office of the commune; the royal household; the revenue office; the academy; the library, the Faure bookstore; and the entire community. He produced invitations, tickets, announcements, injunctions, notices — all kinds of texts on all sorts of paper. He published books for himself and reproduced books for others. He printed for the duke and for his ministers, for other printers, for poets, and for teachers at the university and the academies. Above all, he was called upon to produce broadsheets to mark festivals, baptisms, weddings, births, funerals, restorations to health, and the taking of holy orders.[139]

Azara kept insisting in letters such as this one from 19 January 1791 that Bodoni print nothing but major works and do so in a city (Rome) that would stimulate his ingenuity: "For the love of God, I exhort you to resist all the miserable little printings of miserable little books of miserable poetry that are proposed to you. They are only embarrassments that will impede you from making your way towards the glory of classical works. You should not let yourself be overcome by the vanity of authors who will base their entire reputations on the fact that they were printed by Bodoni." Azara continually enticed Bodoni with offers of liberty, comfortable lodgings and a press in the Palazzo Monaldeschi, decent food, and enduring friendship, but Bodoni never had the courage to make his home anywhere but Parma. He was perfectly content in the calm waters of the smaller city, and offered as his excuse for not moving the parallel with Archimedes, the great mathematician and inventor, who in the middle of the sacking of Syracuse, remained tranquil and kept working at a mathematical problem while the harbor was in flames. Bodoni seems to have forgotten that Archimedes was shortly thereafter run through by a Roman sword

The first extant letter from Azara to Bodoni is dated 29 August 1776. Bodoni had sent a copy of the *Epithalamia* to him, and Azara responded with gratitude, calling it a masterwork of typographic beauty. He was so moved that he asked Bodoni if he could procure some Greek and Hebrew type for the king of Spain's library in Madrid, whose director was setting up a new and magnificent printing office. He then asked Bodoni if he would publish for him the written works of his artist friend Mengs, saying, "You will make a good midwife for this humble birth." Mengs was the favorite painter of Carlos III, who had designated him the first painter at the Spanish court.

Bodoni accepted the challenge, realizing that if Azara were pleased with the results he would reward him with more commissions. *Opere di Antonio Raf-*

faello Mengs was published in 1780, after lengthy considerations about paper and the details of its printing. Azara was, indeed, pleased with the results, and presented a copy to Carlos III, who in turn was so impressed by Bodoni's skill that he awarded him the title of Typographer to the Royal Household and presented him with an annual pension (a pension that was kept in place by his son, Carlos IV). The title and the constant nudging of Azara to broaden his horizons convinced Bodoni to strike out on his own, but it was hard for him to do so. He had to find a decent stretch of time. However, in 1783, in honor of his friend Giuseppe Lovera's nomination as Bishop of Saluzzo, he managed to publish, on his own account, the small but highly decorated volume, *Gestorum ab Episcopis Salutiensibus . . .* The title page information in Latin boasts his name, followed by words that inform the reader that he is Typographer to the King of Spain and Prefect of the Royal Press of Parma.

Nonetheless, he was still working for the duke, and when in 1782 he heard that Emperor Paul I of Russia (son of Catherine the Great) and his wife were planning a visit to Parma, he recognized an ideal opportunity to show off his skills with Russian type. He quickly put aside his other work, and in just a few weeks had produced *Essai de caracteres Russes gravés et fondus par Jean Baptiste Bodoni Typographe de S.M. le Roi d'Espagne . . .* a congratulatory folio publication in Russian and Latin. Only a few copies were published, and it remains among Bodoni's rarest and most sought-after works. In one sense, it is yet another of his specimen books. The "counts of the north" were stunned by the beauty of the work, marveling that Russian characters of such exquisite neatness, made in Italy no less, should so far surpass the work of all the presses of Russia.[140]

Sample page from *Essai de caracteres Russes . . .*

Bodoni and Azara continued to

communicate, and tucked in among all the details of publication were occasional, intriguing glimpses into their lives. In Bodoni's letter written in November 1783 comes the first mention of his having an eye for the opposite sex. Until this moment, his life appears to have been spent entirely in the company of men, but here, after telling Azara that the duke had left for Pisa and Naples taking with him a retinue of knights and gentlemen, he mentions, right at the end of the letter, that also in the suite was Mademoiselle Trombara, the favorite lady-in-waiting, "who for many years I have had the pleasure of knowing; she's no Venus, but is not lacking in spirit."

The death of Father Paciaudi on 1 February 1785 was a sad blow for both men, but particularly for Bodoni for whom Paciaudi had been such an inspiration and loyal friend. Together in their correspondence, Bodoni and Azara grieved the loss of their "dear man," and Bodoni would later pay tribute to the cleric who had plucked him from obscurity and brought him to fame at the court of Parma.

In April 1785, Bodoni wrote: "Last winter I had the misfortune to slip on the ice, but did not fall to the ground because I grabbed hold of a wooden table which by good fortune I saw beside me." Bodoni had to retire to bed for weeks, presumably because the accident had injured his back. The pain kept recurring, and he complained, "I cannot on any account sit in a chair. I write these few quick lines with difficulty, standing on my feet." This painful injury may have signaled the beginning of his troubles with sciatica.

Because Bodoni kept working on fulfilling orders for "silly sonnets" and other lightweight items, Azara persisted in nagging him to move to Rome, writing on 18 May 1785: "I repeat that you should come to Rome and set up a press in this palace where I have already prepared a beautiful apartment for you, separated from the rest of the building, and extremely convenient for working and printing whenever you want to without being subject to any political or economic annoyance." He simply could not understand Bodoni's hesitation, but he must have been somewhat mollified by two of Bodoni's elegant productions. The first was *Upomnema Parmense in Adventu Gustavi III*, printed in celebration of the king of Sweden's visit to Parma, and the second, *Anacreontis Teii Odaria*, printed in Greek miniscule, was dedicated to Azara himself.

The king of Sweden was just one of the important visitors who showed up at the press. Another was the young English botanist and founder of the Linnean Society, Sir James Edward Smith, who visited in 1786 and wrote in his three-volume *A Sketch of a Tour on the Continent* that a great attraction in Parma was the press directed by Signor Bodoni, a man who had carried typography to a height of perfection never before achieved. Smith added that nothing could exceed Bodoni's courtesy in showing him and his companion beautiful examples of his work, offering them several copies, and demonstrating for them how to cut and polish type. He also noted that Bodoni desperately wanted to acquire a tiny file made only in Sheffield, and promised to find one for him as soon as he returned to England.[141]

That same year, Bodoni threw Azara a sop. He sent him a copy of *Gli amori pastorali di Dafni e di Cloe . . .* by Longus. The book was financed by 56 bibliophiles, and the title page makes no mention of the royal press. The publication information states simply "*Crisopoli*" (the ancient name for Parma) and "*Impresso co'caratteri bodoniani*" [Printed with Bodoni's type]. Azara was delighted with the gift and became even more determined to uproot Bodoni from Parma. In his letter of 20 September 1786, he reminded Bodoni that ". . . the best men of this country and many foreigners come to eat with me, and they have all looked at your Longus with wonder. The name Didot was trotted out by several Frenchmen, but I confronted them with the Longus, and had the satisfaction of seeing the protectors of that poor artisan blush." This Didot was the Frenchman, François-Ambroise Didot (1730-1804), Bodoni's typographic contemporary and fierce competitor.

During 1787, Bodoni was working obsessively on his first extensive specimen book, which would become the *Manuale tipografico* of 1788, and in the same year he published another specimen book, *Serie di Majuscole e caratteri cancellereschi.* (The *majuscole* are capital letters, and the *caratteri cancellereschi* are letters in chancery script, which was developed for the Vatican in the fifteenth century.) He certainly had no intention of moving to Rome while he was in the throes of creating these important works. Azara was irritated by the insupportable delay, and on 17 January 1787 wrote: "We need to finish this business [the manual] but I am convinced that while you are in Parma, nothing will be concluded. Think therefore of making an escape to Rome on any pretext, and here we will finish everything in a few days. If you need a pretext to make this little trip, say that the Pope was the impetus . . . Enough already of indecision. Let us resolve on a departure date. As for the current work at your press, your brother can handle that, and you will have nothing to think about except finishing the manual. I repeat, you must finish this work because life passes by too quickly."

Bodoni apparently took this message to heart because on 31 January Azara wrote: "I am aware of your intention to leave Parma, and I am thinking about how we can effect this . . . although I cannot do it as quickly as I wish. Even I need to choose the right moment, and at present I have a few little clouds on the horizon, which I hope will easily be dispersed . . . My feeling is that unless you come to Rome and we talk through our business, nothing will ever be concluded." Azara must have dealt with the little clouds, because on 28 February, he described a plan of action. He had already written to Spain asking the king to bring Bodoni to Madrid to make improvements in the royal press, saying first that he needed to discuss the matter with Bodoni in Rome. He explained: "In this way, you will have a license to leave Parma with decorum and with the duke's permission. I will appear ignorant of the deal, which will seem to come directly from Spain, so don't tell anyone. Take the necessary time to settle your affairs, and then we will see each other here." On 14 March, he added: "Without your escaping from that hole, nothing can be done." Again, on 11 April, he complained about the delay, but this time with an edge of bitterness: "My head spins at the immensity of little printing jobs you have undertaken. Do you not have the strength to turn down this plague of poetry that inundates you? . . . Reserve yourself for greater things. Otherwise old age will surprise you, still caught up in things of little glory."

It was true, Bodoni *was* printing endless little nothings for the court — he had to if he wanted the duke's support — but he was at the same time working steadily, day after day, night after night, cutting punches and readying type for the publication of the *Manuale tipografico* of 1788. He was convinced this was where his true glory lay, and while Azara understood Bodoni's desire to complete the book, he was still convinced that Bodoni's time would be better spent in Rome fulfilling his (Azara's) commissions with the glorious type already in hand.

On each page of the *Manuale,* Bodoni presents a description of a different city in Italy for each typeface, but the pagination makes a strange jump from page 70 to page 72. A mystery surrounds this missing page and its missing city. (See James Mosley's detective work in Appendix IV.) But Parma is there, of course, in all its glory and the description reveals, at least in part, Bodoni's reluctance to move to Rome: "The City of Parma has a good bishop's palace, a strong citadel, a famous university, and a distinguished public library. The cathedral is magnificent; the palace of the Pilotta is vast and well built; the great theatre is the most beautiful in all Europe. The Academy of Beaux Arts is renowned, and the most splendid work executed by the painter Antonio Allegri, called Correggio, is housed there. Parma also has a fine college for the education of noble youths and for pages to the royal family."

In April 1787, Bodoni suddenly wrote to Azara that he was planning a trip to Florence, Rome, and Naples in the middle of June, returning to Parma in September, but this did not occur because of one of those protracted bouts of gout to which he was becoming ever more prone. However, things improved to the point where Azara could write on 4 July: ". . . good news about your health and the continuation of your Herculean labors, which, thank God, I see are coming to a satisfactory end. It seems as though the Manuale has taken a thousand years." He wrote again on 12 October: "What are you up to? It's a thousand years since I've had your news . . . The blessed Manuale approaches its end? I desire this more than anything in the world, even more now that hope begins to rise in me that Spain may acquire some of your works . . . Finish the Manuale and we will immediately make plans. But first you must come to my house in Rome. You cannot deny that you need freedom to breathe after so much work, and once you are here, God will show the way."

Benjamin Franklin.

By this point in time, Bodoni's fame had spread as far as America where, as Passerini says, he had a fervent admirer in the great Benjamin Franklin, himself a master printer, and whose praise was worth the praise of a thousand others. Somehow or other Franklin had acquired works printed by Bodoni, works he admired so much that he wrote him a very gracious letter, in English. When it arrived, one of Bodoni's friends excitedly snatched it from his hands and rushed with it straight to the duke. Don Ferdinando was so overjoyed to see his press praised by such an eminence that he took it upon himself to translate the letter before returning the original to Bodoni. Passerini continues: "I can't publish this letter, because it is impossible to unearth it from a thousand others among which the inimitable Bodoni has buried it.[142] I will give another instead, which by chance fell into my hands."[143] (This second letter from Franklin is still available in the Bodoni collection for all to see and hold.)

It was sent from Philadelphia, dated 14 October 1787. Franklin opened with the words: "Sir, I have had the very great pleasure of receiving and perusing your excellent *Essai des Characteres* [sic] *de l'Imprimerie* [Essay on Type]. It is one of the most beautiful that Art has hitherto produced." The letter so delighted Bodoni that he eventually forwarded it to Azara, who responded on 12 March

Fan letter from Benjamin
Franklin.

1788, saying: "Franklin's letter, which I am returning, gave me great pleasure. He did well to admire you."

Admiration, yes, at least in the opening paragraph, but the rest of the letter hardly reeks of it. Franklin had written in English again (a language Bodoni never learned) when he was perfectly capable of writing in French, the *lingua franca* he would correctly assume that Bodoni understood. In the remainder of the letter, he vaunted his own printing knowledge, saying, "I do not presume to criticize . . ." and then proceeded to do precisely that, taking Bodoni to task for his choice of the form of certain letters.

The river of competitiveness runs deep among printers.

At last Bodoni sent proofs of the first 50 Latin characters of the 1788 *Manuale* to Azara, who was highly impressed by them, even though he had a few suggestions to make in his letter of 2 January 1788. He claimed that Bodoni was making typographic history, and then asked him for the first time about printing a volume of Horace for him.

Azara was right; Bodoni was indeed making publication history because the publication of the 1788 *Manuale* marked the transition from Old Style to Modern. "Here at last was presented a new order of type, which came to be called Modern Roman," writes Henry Lewis Bullen,[144] "the chief characteristic of which is a new kind of serif, cut flat and placed at right angles with the letter proper, and of the same thickness as the minor lines of the letters . . . while the main lines were much heavier than in the old style letters . . . This pronounced contrast of the lines in the letters gives a vivacity to the Bodoni types that is not found in the monotone effect of the conventional old style Roman designs." The printing of Horace for Azara became a typographic milestone for Bodoni, and is considered one of his greatest achievements because, even though it is classified as Modern, it is admired for its classical beauty, balance, and purity of form.

In his next letter (30 January 1788), Azara again brought up the topic of Didot, asking why Bodoni paid him any notice. Then he launched into a diatribe about the French: "The French believe that outside of Paris, there is no taste, and they are not convinced that we even know how to eat or drink. Their vanity is based on nothing but fashion."

Bodoni was panic-stricken when on 13 February Azara wrote that he was having difficulty writing because of a bandaged arm, the result of having been bled that morning due to several attacks of dizziness and the frequent spitting of blood. Bodoni responded that he enjoyed neither peace nor rest since hearing about Azara's illness; melancholy days were followed by murky and restless nights; he was inconsolable. Apparently, nothing could more effectively galvanize Bodoni into going to Rome than news that Azara was ill. Suddenly, he realized that Azara was mortal and that his open-ended invitation to Rome might one day come to nothing.

Bodoni set a date, and Azara wrote: "The hope you have given me of seeing you in Rome this May has given me so much pleasure that I cannot describe it. I shall expect you at my house, where you will have bed, board, and full liberty, not to mention books and well-read friends, who are anxious to make your acquaintance." But once again, Bodoni's plans were scuttled by ill health. Still, Azara would not accept this as an excuse to remain at home; instead he insisted that Bodoni had the perfect reason to claim the need for a change of air: "I implore you to set out the moment that your illness allows you to get out of bed. I have already told you a thousand times that in my house you will always find a bed prepared and every convenience, much more than you would find in any inn . . . Leave Parma immediately and come to Rome where friendship awaits you with open arms."

"Where are we on the trip to Rome?" Azara asked on 30 April. "Your bed is ready and waiting." At last, on 4 June, he noted that they agreed about the details of Bodoni's trip, and was waiting to hear the exact date so that he could obtain a pass for the Porta del Popolo, Bodoni's point of entry into Rome. By 2 July, Azara was again concerned about Bodoni's health because he had not heard from him, and on 16 July, despite his impatience to embrace him, Azara was concerned that the scorching heat in Rome would not be good for him. For two weeks the temperature had constantly been over 90 degrees in the shade and was likely to stay that way until the middle of August. Then he took another swipe at that "poor devil" Didot, saying, "Didot is a printer, and you are a typographer."

On 6 August, Azara wrote how pleased he was to receive from Bodoni twelve examples of Ennio Quirino Visconti's dissertation, *Osservazioni di Ennio Quirino Visconti su due Musaici antichi istoriati*, a work containing exquisite engravings by Bossi and Cecchini and much valued by scholars and lovers of beautiful editions. Azara then mentioned that *Il Sommo Ierarca* (the Pope) had already praised it at great length. Then he returned to his main theme: "It seems to be taking a thousand years for the weather to cool enough so that you can make your journey and I can embrace you."

Bodoni finally went to Rome.

While he was away, his brother Giuseppe in Parma took it upon himself to write to their brother Domenico in Saluzzo. Angela responded on 14 October 1788, telling Giuseppe that his letter to Domenico had pulled him out of his depression. She added that she always tried to cook meals that he enjoyed, and that she coped with his melancholy and her own illnesses by always believing in the ability of good weather to improve their health.

A gap naturally occurs in Azara's letters because he and Bodoni could communicate face to face, but there are other sources relating Bodoni's travels. De Lama reports that he broke his journey to Rome twice: once in Bologna, where he was welcomed by two eminent cardinals, and then in Florence, where he was greeted by Grand Duke Leopold I. When he finally reached Rome and alighted in the Piazza di Spagna, everything was ready for his much-anticipated arrival. After an absence of 22 years, Bodoni had returned to the Piazza di Spagna, no longer a lowly apprentice but an eminent typographer, the darling of diplomats and cardinals.

De Lama continues: "On his arrival, all the most distinguished Romans, foreigners, scholars, and artists competed to meet him, to study him themselves, to caress him, and to honor him. Not a few famous cardinals, struck by his beautiful manners, his knowledge, and his eloquence, and desiring to possess him as an ornament to Rome, proposed that he establish himself there. In the same way, Cavalier Azara (knowing well how much Bodoni loved glory) tempted him with a flattering offer to set up a press and to have him immediately reproduce in folio four classic authors, each in three languages — Greek, Latin, and Italian."[145]

Heady stuff, even for one already accustomed to glory.

BODONI HIMSELF described his audience with Pope Pius VI, a pope much interested in arts and letters. Writing from Rome in 1788 to his brother Giuseppe, who was keeping things running smoothly at the press during his absence, he said:

Pope Pius VI.

You will be impatient to hear about how I was received by the Holy Father. This morning I had the honor of kneeling at his feet. From the ticket I enclose, you will see that I was informed by his staff of the day and hour when I should appear at the Quirinale. At the entrance to the Pontifical Chamber, one kneels; half way through the room, one kneels again; and right next to the little table where the Primate sits, one kneels a third time. As he had his feet under the table, I kissed his hand, and then he made me rise and held me in conversation for an hour and a half. Then he dismissed me with the papal benediction, and I kissed his hand again. As I left the ante-camera, Monsignor Pignatelli told me that it had been eons since the Holy Father had granted such a long audience, but I had been instructed ahead of time to wait until the Pope dismissed me himself. Cavalier Azara accompanied me to the Quirinale Palace in his own carriage and livery . . . The Pope spoke to me with great affability and sweetness, and read to me the letter from the duke that I had delivered myself . . . In sum, I will always remember this day as the most propitious and happy of my life, such was the comfort that I experienced at the feet of the Holy Father.

Bodoni took the opportunity of his visit to Rome to do some sightseeing farther south. He wrote to Azara from Naples, calling it "this most tumultuous of metropolises," saying that he intended to return to the banks of the Tiber in the coming week, and begging Azara to procure another entry pass for him. His impression of Naples was powerful; it was a madhouse after placid little Parma. "But for lack of time and my scant talent, I would give you a graphic description of this dizzying land, where it is impossible for anyone who is accustomed to quiet and tranquility to stay for any length of time. I limit myself to assuring you that all the proposed works for reviving the Arts and Letters here are in perfect chaos. It is in vain to try to make this nation emerge from a state of inertia and ignorance . . . Tomorrow I will go to Caserta to see friends and acquaintances, and Thursday I will make a trip to Pompeii."

Bodoni set off in the company of Abbé Alberto Fortis (1741-1803), a renowned naturalist. They visited the lovely beaches at Miseno, Pozzuoli, and Baiae; gazed at the frescoes in Herculaneum; and picked their way carefully through the ash at Pompeii. Among the many honors he received on returning to Naples, was being summoned to the court there to visit Queen Maria Carolina (a younger sister of Maria Amalia, duchess of Parma) who already knew Bodoni and was aware of his increasing fame as a typographer. However, Bodoni was just about to leave the city, so he sent his apologies, saying that he already had his boots on and the carriage was waiting. The queen would not be deterred: "Come as you are," she gushed. "You, you alone do I wish to see again."[146] Bodoni went to see her.

Bodoni spent a total of two months away from Parma, and his trip was a resounding success. Back in Saluzzo his sister Angela was boiling with resentment that he had not taken the time to visit the family. On 9 January 1789 she set up a bitter wail to Giuseppe: "We have not had any news from you for ages, not even about Giovanni's trip and whether it went well or not. Since he was already on the road he could have made a sidestep to his fatherland. It's possible that he forgot both his house and his fatherland because the accommodation was not beautiful enough . . . My consolation would be to see him before Death takes us from this world."

The correspondence between Azara and Bodoni picked up again with Bodoni's thank-you letter. As usual, he spends a great deal of time making excuses for not having written sooner:

Since my happy return to my old residence I have thought many times of sending you my most fulsome thanks for the kind welcome and partiality you demonstrated to me during my brief stay in that most opulent metropolis. But I had scarcely arrived on the banks of the Parma when I had to take up again all the business

Queen Maria Carolina of Naples.

that had run aground while I was on my Italian peregrinations, and deal with those essential works that overwhelm me each year as we approach Christmas. This was the sole reason why I was not able to thank you before. But now you have given me a greater impulse to write, and thanks to the courtesy of your letter of the 16th, I can no longer refrain from my obligation to renew my already many times iterated protests of sincere and wide-ranging gratitude that will forever be engraved in my spirit and my heart.

He continues with this theme a few days later, but this time doling out a few details of his journey home:

Surrounded by a multitude of friends and acquaintances I can scarcely lift my head to let you know about my arrival in Parma last Thursday at about 10 o'clock at night. The journey from Rome to Bologna was fast, but the narrowness of the confines in which we traveled with the Spanish mail was so uncomfortable that I could not continue the journey. I remained for four days resting in Felsina [the ancient name for Bologna], where melancholy crept over my spirit . . . Yesterday I had my first ministerial audience, and now I am awaiting the order to throw myself at the feet of his Royal Highness . . . I won't write at length because I know how much you are oppressed with letters, and I will be consoled if I receive a few lines from you once a month. I won't repeat my extensive and sincere thanks for all the acts of kindness and fondness you demonstrated to me during my stay in Rome because I know I am unable to do this duty with dignity, and because I know that you do not like and do not wish useless verbal expressions. I will merely say that while I breathe, I will be yours eternally and immutably, Bodoni.

Azara responds immediately:

Your letter gave me incredible pleasure, because I had been anxiously awaiting the news of your arrival, having heard nothing since your departure. Thank God you are safely home. I can just imagine the crowd of friends and of matters to attend to that you faced after more than a two-month absence from a place that after so many years you call your own. What I can assure you is that the pleasure caused by your arrival in Parma is nowhere nearly as great as the displeasure caused by your departure from Rome. I feel like a widower without you in my house. But let's not talk about the past; let us rather rejoice in the hope of seeing each other again in more tranquility.

In a letter of 3 December 1788 Azara reiterated his interest in publishing the Horace, completely at his own expense. In a postscript he mentioned having received a letter from the duke about plans he (the duke) had made with Bodoni to counterfeit the English New Testament, swearing Bodoni to secrecy. Then Azara cried out: "Can it be possible that Bodoni seeks glory in copying others, in making contraband?"[147] In his subsequent letter, written right at the end of 1788, Azara came down hard on this idea, claiming it unworthy of his friend.

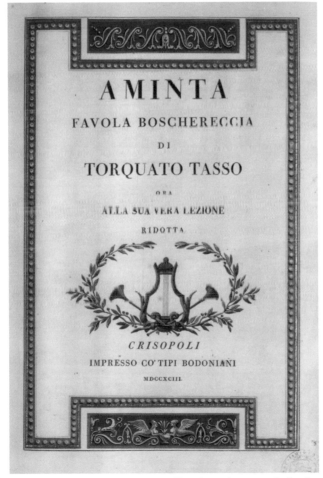

Aminta. Title page of the unique illuminated copy made for the wedding of Marchesa Anna Malaspina's niece.

BODONI WAS ENERGIZED by his trip to Rome, and on his return home launched himself into publishing two sumptuous presentation volumes. The first was *In funere Caroli III Hispan. Regis,* a collection of orations declaimed at the funeral of Don Ferdinando's uncle, the king of Spain. Bodoni worked closely with Azara on this volume, which was printed in both folio and quarto, and illustrated with engravings by Morghen and Volpato. The second impressive piece of work was Tasso's *Aminta,* published in celebration of the wedding of Marchesa Anna Malaspina's niece, and dedicated by Bodoni to the lovely marchesa herself, who had always regarded him and his work with the greatest favor.

It is difficult to gauge the effect on Bodoni of his trip to Rome, apart from the fact that it energized him in a direction that would have appealed to Azara. It would certainly have fed his need for adulation, but he clearly felt a sense of relief on returning to Parma after the noise and chaos of Rome and Naples. In addition, he now had a far more compelling reason to remain in the city he now called home.

Cherchez la femme.

Sant'Andrea, the tiny twelfth-century church in Parma where Bodoni
and Margherita Dall'Aglio were married.

8

Margherita Dall'Aglio

Marry someone like your mother: good-humored and not too tall.

CARLO BODONI

F OR SOME TIME, Bodoni had been subject to hints from his family that it
was time to marry. His uncle Carlo in Rome was particularly insistent.
He began as early as August 1780, by which time Bodoni was 40 years old,
suggesting that Giambattista and Giuseppe start taking an interest in women
and marriage. It appears that Bodoni did not take kindly to his uncle's nagging
and refrained from responding. On 26 May 1781 Carlo wrote again in a distinctly
minatory tone, implying that Bodoni could make himself sick and turn to debauchery if he did not heed his uncle's advice:

Don't accuse me of pestering you if I write again; I do this merely from the natural affection in my warm breast which wants to fuel and reheat the frigid humors of your breast towards me. Those humors, that bile, increasing in your stomach can ascend from the pancreatic juice to the trachea, obstructing your breath and slowing down the sistole and diastole that control the beating of your heart, and via the trachea jugular find their secret way to the brain, there making the pia mater *membrane somewhat vulnerable, and blocking your imagination from the vast multitude of grand and weighty duties you have, and then slicing through your intellect in its most delicate part and driving you into a world of debauchery. Should this ever happen, everything for you is over.*

Having delivered himself of this nasty threat, Carlo, who had a sideline in herbal medicine, set about prescribing remedies for all that might ail Bodoni.

My son, your fame has already spread throughout the whole world. You have acquired it at the cost of so much sweat, so try not lose it too soon. If ever you are troubled by headaches, neck aches, or chest aches, do not be tempted to fall under the surgeon's knife; instead, by leading a life of temperance you will be cured of all troubles. If you have a headache, make a decoction of carnation flowers and leaves, and add sugar; drink this decoction for five or six days, and the headache will go away. If you have a sore throat as a result of too much talking, chew on a bit of mace, and if this doesn't help, simmer the mace in plain water for half an hour until it dissolves and the water darkens. Add sugar, and gargle so that the mixture passes over the inflammation and throat ulcers, if you have them, and all other afflictions of the throat. Should you suffer any discomfort of the chest, which is the most precious "chest" you can possibly possess, do not take anything but coffee or tea with goat's milk, and if this makes you nauseated try a decoction of these three herbs, artemisia, hyssop, and licorice with sugar as a simple drink or else as a syrup . . .

If, God forbid, you suffer from kidney stones that prevent you from urinating, try strawberries, having first rinsed them in a good white wine, and sprinkle fine sugar on top. It is true, if you make decoctions from the roots and leaves of borage and licorice, they will cure you perfectly.

Carlo continued to pester Bodoni about his need for a companion in the house. Several times he mentioned that the woman with whom he lived in Rome took very good care of him. On Christmas Day 1790, he suggested that Bodoni invite one of his sisters to come to Parma and put his house in order. "It would do you a lot of good." Then he boldly suggested that Bodoni could achieve the greatest happiness were he to find a woman, "not too rich but good-humored" and, like his mother, not too tall, someone who would take care of him when he was sick.

He continued: "And the good Lord will bless you with children. I beg you to fulfill what I am writing about. I want you to live happily, but I don't want to annoy you any longer with my words."

Bodoni was indeed in need of loving care. He had become subject to serious attacks of sciatica and gout, and he was beginning to feel his age. In February 1790, the month in which he celebrated his fiftieth birthday, he wrote to Azara: "I am getting old, and if I don't hurry up and give the public a few more examples of my typographic valor, posterity will reproach me for publishing mere nothings . . ."

Even before he received the nudge from his uncle, Bodoni had clearly been thinking about making a nest

Margherita Dall'Aglio (1758-1841).

and, like the bower bird, had worked to make his home attractive to a potential mate. On 27 June 1788, he wrote to his friend Giuseppe Lucatelli (an artist who would later paint his portrait) about improvements in his living quarters, saying that he had extra rooms at his disposal, and that his apartment now resembled more a Sybarite's than a misanthrope's or philosopher's.

At 50 years old, Bodoni was a popular catch. He was well acquainted with Parma's literary, musical, and artistic sets, and was surrounded by a bevy of aspiring wives, among them Ninetta, Manon, Ghitta, La Boselli, and La Guarnieri.[148] Manon (Trombara), possibly the Mademoiselle Trombara mentioned in Bodoni's November 1783 letter to Azara, had a young cousin, Margherita Dall'Aglio (Ghitta), and it was on her that Bodoni's particular gaze had fallen some time before his trip to Rome. Unfortunately, she was engaged to someone else. Bodoni was undaunted.

Paola Margherita Dall'Aglio was born in Parma in the parish of Santa Cristina on 27 February 1758 (the same month that eighteen-year-old Giambattista Bodoni was arriving in Rome). She was one of four children of Filippo Dall'Aglio and Paola Trombara, both of whom came from distinguished local families. She was baptized the day after her birth, and her godparents were Count Scipione Ventura and Marchesa Paola Tagliaferri Verugola. Her father's family was known for its distinguished military officers; her mother's family was replete with artists, musicians, and architects. Ghitta (Bodoni's preferred name for her) was a singularly intelligent and competent young woman, with curly brown hair and sparkling eyes. She spoke French and Italian fluently and eloquently, and learned English quickly when called upon to do so. As added bonuses, she played the guitar, wrote poetry and, according to Carlo Bodoni's strictures, was good-humored and small in stature, like Bodoni's mother. Probably introduced to each other by her cousin Manon Trombara, she and Bodoni became fast friends. By the time Bodoni left Parma on his trip to Rome, their relationship had developed into something more than friendship — but there was still the problem of her existing fiancé.

Ghitta felt the need to be cautious, but that did not prevent her from writing to Bodoni while he was in Rome. In her first letter, written on 4 August 1788, she admitted that there was no news about her wedding, and stated: ". . . the rooster [her fiancé] crows, but the hen pretends not to hear his voice. Whether the marriage will take place, I do not know." She then promised to let Bodoni know when there was any news, complained that the hours after lunch were extremely boring since his departure, and hoped that the Roman and Florentine women would not make him forget her and Manon. For propriety's sake, the letter is signed "Ghitta, and Manon Trombara."

She wrote again in tandem with Manon on 18 September 1788, letting Bodoni know that the wedding was still uncertain, and that she needed to spend time in necessary reflection "for fear of unhappy consequences." She then added some news of a sensational nature about the highwaymen who had attacked the Turin mail. (She had a vested interest in this mail coach since it was the means by which her letters were sent to Bodoni in Rome.) The men had been arrested, and their punishment meted out; they were hanged and quartered at the site where the crime had taken place, their bodies left there as deterrent to others who might have similar designs on the postal service.

By 9 October 1788, Ghitta had gained enough confidence to write without Manon at her elbow. She reiterated that there was no news regarding her wedding, and that it merited further mature reflection. In signing off, she begged Bodoni to remain her friend "because nothing interests me more than this." Then she begged him to forgive her awful handwriting. (Ghitta's handwriting is large, easy to read, but sloppy and blobby if she is writing in a hurry.)

On 24 October, she wrote expressing concern at not having heard from Bodoni and again worrying that the alluring Roman women and the lively Neapolitans had made him forget her and Manon. She declared how much she was looking forward to seeing him again and assured him of her attachment to him.

It would take another two years of mature reflection on Ghitta's part and of persistence on Bodoni's before they took steps to marry. Perhaps the rooster was tenacious; perhaps Ghitta was under pressure from her parents to wed her fiancé; she was probably worried about the eighteen-year age difference between her and Bodoni and anxious (with good reason) about his health. In July 1790, Bodoni suffered a particularly debilitating siege of sciatica and took himself off to Bagni di Lucca to try to relieve the pain. Ghitta wrote to him there in response to a letter she had received, expressing her prayers and good wishes for his health.

She wrote again a few days later, saying, "Nothing hurts me more than to know you are still suffering. I hope the baths will restore you to perfect health, something I desire with all my heart." She then admitted to being delighted to learn that he was bored at Bagni di Lucca, and went on to comment, "I was told that when Signor Mallarne learned you wanted to go to Bagni, he counseled you to visit the baths near here instead." Indeed, Ghitta would have much preferred to have Bodoni at nearby Monticelli or Salsamaggiore rather than 200 kilometers away in Tuscany. She may have been unaware that Bodoni had made plans to reunite in Bagni di Lucca with Nicolás de Azara. As early as April of that year, Azara had told Bodoni of his wish to visit the baths; he repeated this intention in early June, adding that he hoped to see Bodoni either there or in Parma. In his letter of 16 June, he noted with pleasure that Bodoni had decided to join him. "We shall talk about everything at the baths," he exulted.

Six months later, Ghitta had completed her mature and extended reflection, and in February 1791, Bodoni informed Azara that he was about to be married. Azara responded on 2 March, saying: "I am happy to hear about your intention to marry. Never having had this vocation myself . . . I know that at a certain age it is necessary to make a match, not as a caprice but upon reflection. So I wish you every happiness in your new state." And Azara sent Bodoni a gift. The draft of Bodoni's response is interesting. It is headed "Parma, 1791," and in it he thanks his friend for the gift of a "most elegant" portrait ring, and continues: "In the future I will have in front of my eyes this almost breathing, living image of a person whom I love above any other in this world." He goes on to say that Death will sever the thread of his life before he takes from his finger this precious memory of Azara's affection for him.

Bodoni also informed his siblings about his upcoming marriage, and asked Domenico to acquire for him a statement from Saluzzo stating that he was free to marry. (One cannot help wondering whether he would have informed them had he not needed the statement.) On 16 February, Angela responded to the request, but first she felt called upon to make Bodoni feel guilty for writing so infrequently: "On receiving into his hands your most welcome letter after such a long series of years, Domenico was so surprised and happy on reading it that I noticed his hands trembling madly with joy." She then addressed the matter in hand: "Domenico will send you the paper . . . now that you have resolved to set up house. Make sure that you choose a woman worthy of your merit, one who does not make you uneasy or disturb your spirit. Make a decision you will not regret later." And finally she added: "We wish you every joy, blessing, prosperity, and happiness."

Domenico then wrote to Bodoni on 15 March, informing him that he had sent off the papers, and expressing the hope that just because Bodoni was getting married, he would not forget his blood relatives. He then confessed to his brother that he himself had decided not to marry and procreate, "thus annihilating the human species from my 'song,'" but hoped that Bodoni's wife would "print many good subjects," and that Bodoni would bring her to Saluzzo to visit the family.

On 19 March 1791, 51-year-old Giambattista Bodoni married 33-year-old Margherita Dall'Aglio in the tiny twelfth-century church of Sant'Andrea in Parma.

The newlyweds set up home in Bodoni's apartment above the printworks, and by all accounts, they adored each other. They were disappointed not to have children but were resigned to the fact, and if anyone were bold enough to enquire why he and Ghitta were childless, Bodoni wittily responded: *Gli alberi piemontese non allignano nel suolo parmigiano.* [The trees of Piedmont do not take root in the soil of Parma.] Ghitta turned her maternal instincts towards helping to care for her two motherless nephews, and later on she belonged to the Societé Maternelle in Parma, which supported poor mothers and their newborn babies. With a young, energetic, and loving wife by his side, Bodoni's life took a huge turn for the better. Not only did Ghitta take over the reins of the household and cater to Bodoni's every need, she helped him respond to the enormous number of letters he received from customers, booksellers, paper providers, friends, and admirers. Fully capable of taking the initiative, she did not lean on her husband, as can be seen from Le Chevalier de Souza's letter of 28 August 1798, in which he says, "I have never been married and I have no knowledge of household affairs. But I believe that a woman should not always be represented by her husband . . . I note with pleasure that you have exerted your prerogative, and have written to me in your own hand."

Ghitta launched herself into the business side of the press, dealt with all the correspondence, while welcoming the steady stream of curious visitors hoping to see the printing establishment and its famous typographer. She began to study English in earnest so she could help her husband deal with orders from the British Isles. As her English improved, she started receiving letters in that language from admiring friends, mostly men, lauding her merits (perhaps trying to break through the portcullis to enter the castle of the great man himself). One of her most faithful English correspondents and admirers was a nobleman named Henry Thomson. He wrote to her in amusing fashion from Bologna in May 1794: "In the name of Bacchus, how well you write English, my dear Mrs Bodoni . . . you deserve great praise; and if I was at Parma I'd give you a sugar plumb [sic]." Later in the same letter, Thomson refers to Ghitta's clapping Chi Chi on his back and spitting in his mouth if he was surly; Chi Chi was presumably her little dog, but Chi Chi was not the Bodoni's only dog. A sonnet by Domenico Testa rejoices in the fact that Bodoni's missing dog, his dear Lili, had been found. It ends with the words "I am Bodoni's dog. Nobody touch me."

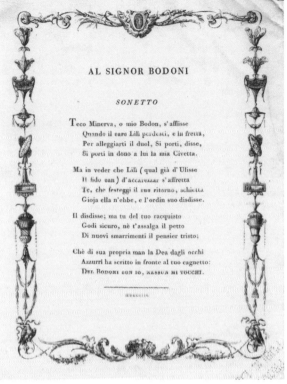

Teco Minerva, o mio Bodoni . . .

Another friend who encouraged Ghitta's efforts at English, Salvatore Mammaioni, himself a student of the language, wrote to her in English from Rome on 21 January 1797, saying: "You need not be, in the least, embarrassed writing in English. It is clear you understand the language very well, & only want exercise in this particular; nor is it therefore to be wonder'd at if you encounter difficulty to express your sentiments with ease and propriety. But let not this deter you from writing; nay, write as much as you can, and I assure you that you will soon write very correctly & with facility."

As well as composing letters, Ghitta enjoyed writing light verse that was "sparkling with brio and revealing of her feelings and her personality."[149] She often wrote under her Arcadian name, Cloride Tanagria. After their marriage, Bodoni became the favorite subject of her verse, referred to as Alcippo, his Arcadian name.

> *. . . ma in lingue mille ben vorrei l'affetto*
> *poter spiegar, che ho per Alcippo in petto.*
>
> [I would love to be able to explain in a thousand languages
> the affection I hold in my breast for Alcippo.]

By 1791, Bodoni's fame and visibility had increased to the point that whenever he and Ghitta took a break from work and strolled through Parma arm in arm, people would point and say: "Look, there goes Bodoni!"[150] Together they gathered around them a circle of literary and musical friends. The undated drawing, *Conversazione in Casa Bodoni* (attributed to Antonio Pasini; see front endpaper), cleverly illustrates the atmosphere at one of their Friday afternoon literary gatherings. This particular gathering included, from left to right, a slightly surly-looking Bodoni embosomed in conversation with Giuseppe De Lama (who later became his biographer); the poet Vincenzo Jacobacci; Gaetano Ziliani, a master papermaker and loyal supplier to Bodoni; Count Giovanni Bonaventura Porta; Margherita, looking curly and cute with her guitar; and, gazing raptly at her, the composer Ferdinando Paër. Behind them stand the handsome manservant, Dalmastro, and Giambattista Zambiagi, Bodoni's right hand at the press. (It is notable that Bodoni's brother Giuseppe is not included in the picture. Perhaps as a foundry man and typesetter, he was considered a second-class citizen, someone with even less status than Dalmastro. Or perhaps he was just too busy at the press to break away.)

These regular Friday afternoon *conversazioni* at the Bodonis' were the highpoint of the week, a time for relaxing, making music, and talking with like-minded friends. Writing from Florence on 28 August 1801, De Lama stressed how much he was looking forward to returning to Parma and the *conversazioni*, and asks: "Does one ever forget the instants that friendship and gaiety embellish?" It is a relief to know that, at least on Friday afternoons, Bodoni took a little time off for fun.

Detail of Rosaspina's engraving of decorations in the Camera di San Paolo.

9

The Private Press & the Amoretti and Didot Débacles

As a literary man, I condemn his editions, as a typographer I admire them.

FIRMIN DIDOT

THE YEAR of his marriage, 1791, was deeply significant for Bodoni in many ways. The year before, Azara had tried a new tactic to bring him to Rome permanently. He bypassed the typographer himself and went directly to Don Ferdinando, requesting permission for Bodoni to set up a press in the Spanish legation. This proposal did not sit well with the duke since he was happily reaping the benefits of having a famous typographer associated with his court. And with reason; Bodoni continued to attract more and more visitors to Parma each year, and with visitors came income to enrich the city's coffers. The duke was well aware that Bodoni received invitations to move away and was anxious not to lose him. As recently as 1789, on a trip to Lombardy, Bodoni had been invited, not for the first time, to direct the royal press in Milan.

Don Ferdinando decided on a compromise: instead of allowing Bodoni to go to Rome, he gave him permission to set up a private press alongside the royal press. In this way, the typographer would have the freedom to print whatever he wished in the city he called home while still directing the royal press. The last thing Bodoni wanted, having recently married a woman rooted to her city, was to leave Parma on Azara's whim; after all, the diplomat could be transferred to another country or be recalled to Spain at any moment, leaving Bodoni high and dry. In addition, Bodoni felt a certain loyalty to the duke, having already worked for him for 22 years. He appreciated the stability of the sinecure, even though he grumbled that he was never properly rewarded or appreciated for his efforts.

As soon as he had permission to open his own press, Bodoni set to work with a vengeance. At his own expense, he commissioned two up-to-date presses and established them in a room on the second floor, next to his foundry. He chose his own workers and paid their wages himself. Bodoni now had three enterprises under his direction: the royal press, his private press, and his foundry. The last supplied type to the first two and provided Bodoni with a source of income from the sale of type to other cities and individuals.

Even though he did not make the move to Rome, Bodoni's career finally took off in the direction Azara had been encouraging.

First off the private press was the Horace for Azara, printed in folio using the blackest ink on the whitest paper, and sporting huge margins. This volume marked the moment when the true Bodoni style, referred to as "Modern," the type we recognize today as "Bodoni," burst upon the scene. Its title page contained absolutely no ornamentation, and was elegant in the simplicity of one initial Q. and the words HORATII FLACCI OPERA stacked one below the other. Publication information at the foot of the page declared the book to have been published IN AEDIBUS PALATINIS (inside the Palatina) and printed using TYPIS BODONIANIS. The Horace was a banner that announced the new Bodoni, the uncompromising Neoclassicist — uncompromising, that is, in the quality of his type and his exquisite production values. Where he fell down (as Azara was only too quick to point out) was in the correctness of the text itself. He desperately needed a "Grim Reader," a final proofreader completely new to the text for whom the obvious errors would jump out. By the time a book came to the press, Bodoni was already tiring of it; he was already planning his next work. He did not take into account that, no matter how beautifully printed, a text containing multiple errors lost credibility. His failure to pay sufficient attention to proofreading would come back to haunt him.

Q.

HORATII

FLACCI

OPERA

PARMAE
IN AEDIBVS PALATINIS
CIƆ IƆ CC LXXXXI
TYPIS BODONIANIS.

Horace, title page.

Azara took Bodoni to task on 10 August 1791 after Bodoni sent him a copy of the *Anacreonte* in the smaller of the two new editions he printed that year. Azara started gently: "It is a true masterpiece of printing in this genre." Then he gets going: "Your errors cause me pain. They are a defect that ruins the beauty of your undertakings . . . they are a terrible, indelible blot on your productions. The other day, my abbés found no less than eight serious errors in a few pages . . . You know the history of what Estienne, Aldus, Plantin, and other great printers had to do to merit immortality. You who outdo them all in beauty, why do you not aspire to outdo them in correctness?"

When Azara finally received three boxes of the Horace, he was again dismayed. The book had been going back and forth between them for years, and Azara who underwrote the publication had every reason to expect a flawless production. He complained: "To my great regret I see in the preface that the errors are still there in spite of my having pointed them out . . . They completely disgrace the edition." Then he started ranting again about Bodoni's resistance to moving to Rome. "I cannot think without great sorrow about your obstinacy in burying yourself in that cave where you do not find, and will never find, the least encouragement or help." Bodoni must have been able to correct matters because by March 1792 Azara was satisfied enough to tell Bodoni how thrilled he was with the current craze for the Horace, and how he hoped it would continue to expand. In May, he shouted: "Hooray for Callimachus! The world has never seen such a production. This book and the Horace mark an epoch in the annals of typography and will bring ultimate posterity to Bodoni's name."

The Horace, which had driven Azara to despair and then to exultation, became the central cause of friction in 1791 between Bodoni and his two assistants, the Amoretti brothers, Pancrazio (1732-1816) and Giacomo (1738-1820). The two men came from a family of well-established metalworkers who ran a foundry in San Pancrazio, a small town just seven kilometers outside Parma. By 1770, the firm had already fulfilled commissions for Du Tillot, and in 1774 Bodoni hired the two brothers to remake some moulds for him, using steel. The originals had been prepared in brass by a clockmaker, but the brass had lost its precision over time.[151] Bodoni was delighted with the Amorettis' steel moulds, and recognizing in particular the skill of Giacomo, invited them to become his apprentices. Their first jobs were to refine and polish punches and counterpunches, while their young and talented nephew, the indefatigable Don Andrea (1758-1807), acted as a go-between, carrying material and tools between San Pancrazio and

Parma. It was not long before he was working with his uncles at the Bodoni printworks, and he turned out to be the most talented and ambitious of the lot.

At first, the relationship between Bodoni and the Amorettis was cordial, and Bodoni's brother Giuseppe enjoyed socializing with them. As the years went by, years in which they spent time working beside the master and observing his extraordinary accuracy in carving letters, the Amorettis became skilled punchcutters themselves. In the same way that it was difficult to distinguish Bodoni from Fournier during his early years in

Don Andrea Amoretti (1758-1807).

Parma, so it became challenging by 1791 to differentiate Bodoni's work from that of the Amorettis. While the exact cause of the sudden rupture in their relationship has never been disclosed, commentators such as Campanini, Passerini, and Trevisani agree that when Bodoni first opened his private press and published the Horace, the Amorettis expected their work to be acknowledged. As already mentioned, the title page of the Horace bore the words "TYPIS BODONIANIS" and their names were nowhere to be seen.

Bodoni, in turn, had reason to resent the Amorettis. He had learned that certain of his early proofs, full of errors, were circulating in Paris and bringing discredit to his press. He soon suspected that he had been betrayed by someone close to him, someone who had saved his discards and disseminated them. It was easy for him to suspect an Amoretti or two or three, but impossible to prove his case.[152]

Resentment and betrayal were at the heart of the matter of the Bodoni/Amoretti rupture, and the rift was never healed. Bodoni lost his most competent assistants, but soon gained two more, in whom he had the utmost trust, Luigi Orsi, who remained with him until the end of his life, and Zefferino Campanini. The Amorettis returned to San Pancrazio where they set up their own printing house under the direction of Don Andrea. They celebrated its opening by printing a sonnet dedicated to the duke of Parma. At last they could print the words *"co'caratteri de' fratelli Amoretti"* or *"Tipis Amoretti"* at the foot of their title pages.

Their work was of a high quality, clearly resembled the work of Bodoni, and was more affordable. It was appreciated by its customers and sold well, but that elusive spark of genius was missing.

Most of the works Bodoni printed in 1791 were issued from the royal press, but this soon began to change. As his fame spread, he began attracting work for the private press from outside Italy. James Edwards, a bookseller in London, commissioned him to publish a new edition of Horace Walpole's *The Castle of Otranto*, generally regarded as the first ever gothic novel. On receiving the book, Edwards

wrote to Bodoni, saying he found it to be the most beautiful possible book in English (albeit error-ridden) (Plate 25). With the success of that publication and then Viscount Hampden's *Britannia, Lathmon, Villa Bromhamensis*, Bodoni's fame began spreading in England. Baskerville had died in 1775, and it was time for a new typographic hero, someone who could give the Didots in France a run for their money.

France, too, was paying attention to the Italian upstart. Although French collectors of fine printing were loyal to their own, they could not help but admire the quality of Bodoni's work. In June 1791, Bodoni received an enthusiastic letter from a young bibliophile in Paris, Antoine-Auguste Renouard, who

Amoretti, *Saggio* . . . title page.

claimed that his attention had been captured by Bodoni's brilliant success in the typographic arts, and that he was determined to collect all Bodoni's beautiful editions. A businessman, Renouard finally gave in to his bibliophilia, opened his own press and bookstore in 1797, became a champion of Bodoni, defended him against invidious criticism, and stocked his books with pride.

Chauvinism being what it is, a keen and sometimes acrimonious competition began between the Didot family in Paris and Bodoni in Parma. This was not the first rivalry between the Didots and a non-French printer. In a letter from Paris to William Strachan on 4 December 1781, Benjamin Franklin pointed out that there was a "strong emulation" between the beautiful printing of Madrid and Paris, saying: "Here a M. Didot *le jeune* has a Passion for the Art. He has executed several charming Editions. But the 'Salust' [sic] and the 'Don Quixote' of Madrid are thought to excel them."[153] By Madrid, Franklin is referring to the great Spanish printer, Joachim Ibarra (1725-1785), whose Sallust of 1772 remains one of the triumphs of eighteenth-century printing. According to D.B. Updike, Didot was less than generous in his praise of Ibarra, using both his name and Baskerville's "as pegs on which to hang laurels in honour of his excellent papa!"

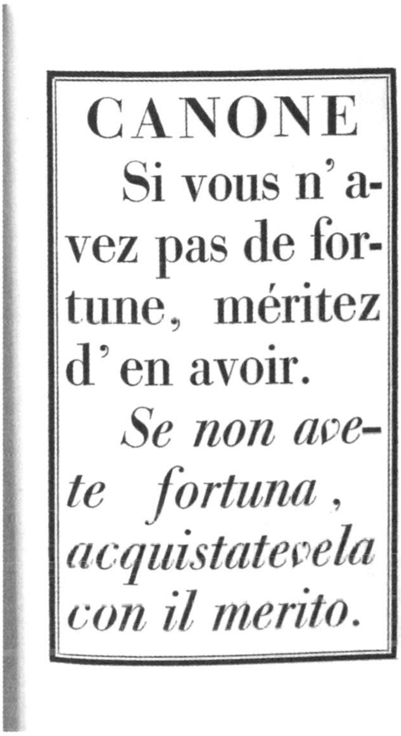

CANONE
Si vous n' a-
vez pas de for-
tune, méritez
d' en avoir.
*Se non ave-
te fortuna,
acquistatevela
con il merito.*

CANONE

Quousque tandem
abutêre, Catilina,
patientiâ nostrâ ?
quamdiu etiam fu-
*ror iste tuus nos e-
ludet? quem ad fi-*
M. T. CICERO
ARPINAS ORATOR.

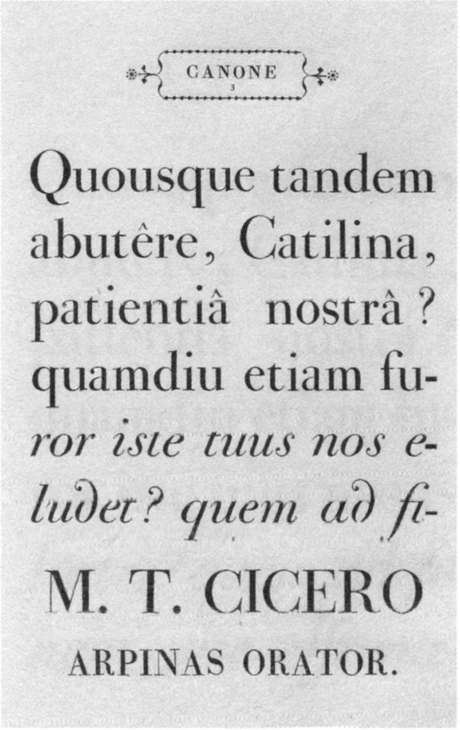

Amoretti, Canono.   Bodoni, Canone.

By contrast, in 1774 Bodoni gave praise where it was due, referring to ". . . the stupendous Sallust not long since printed with so much *finitezza* at Madrid."[154]

The Didots were typographic heirs to the Fournier family, with four generations of Didots operating printworks in France. In the second generation, François-Ambroise Didot (1730-1804) reorganized the sizing of typefaces by their type body height, creating the "didot point system," a measurement which was eventually taken up throughout Europe. But it was his sons, Pierre (1760-1853) and Firmin (1764-1836), who caused Bodoni particular anguish. In their desire to maintain France's primacy in the printing world, they went to extreme lengths to discredit him. Even though they could not find fault with the beauty of his printing, they managed to find his Achilles' heel (the same heel that Azara was so concerned about) in the inaccuracies of his texts. Why they were quite so vindictive remains a mystery, but James Mosley puts forward the theory that, as high-minded French republicans, the Didots prided themselves on being "rightful legatees of the sober

BRITANNIA,
LATHMON,
VILLA
BROMHAMENSIS.

PARMAE
IN AEDIBVS PALATINIS
TYPIS BODONIANIS
CIƆ IƆ CC XCII.

Britannia, Lathmon, Villa Bromhamensis. Title page.

but morally impressive Roman heritage." He points out that their intellectual abilities were formidable (and they knew it), and that their family reunions must have resembled a meeting of the Royal Society.[155] That a nobody operating out of a little Italian city with an autocratic regime could challenge their supremacy, and France's, was more than they could abide. They felt compelled to lash out.

In the preface to his 1798 edition of Virgil, Pierre Didot slammed Bodoni for the number of errors that appeared in Bodoni's luxurious 1793 edition, and cruelly listed them one by one for all to see, adding: "It seems as though the grandeur of the characters renders the errors more evident . . . the sheer number of them dishonors this work, which claims in its preface that it is a masterpiece of art and a most correct edition."

Bodoni was cut to the quick. Knowing that Azara would always champion him in the face of the Didots (even though Azara might agree with them about the number of errors), he fired off a letter to him in Paris on 17 June 1798. "I have already received word about Didot's Virgil and I know he has condemned our edition, claiming to have found many errors. I cannot respond to this accusation until I have seen the book." Bodoni then expressed to Azara his conviction that the copy Pierre Didot had in his hands was an uncorrected proof, and to confirm this he had written to Renouard, the Parisian bookseller, about his suspicion. After a scrupulous reading of the copy he owned, Renouard had replied, saying that he had found just one minor error, the substitution of *par* for *per*.

At this point, notes of envy and cringing modesty creep into Bodoni's letter to Azara. "By now you will have seen the Didots' magnificent printing house, which no doubt surpasses mine in size and in the number of presses and operators; but in my series of punches and matrices I can . . . catch up with them. I know they have advantages in terms of paper, in the abundance of assistants to be found in Paris, and in the opulence of the country in which they live. But I am content in my delightful situation, and I will continue to make a few little things from time to time . . . until I arrive peacefully at the *ultima linea rerum* [the finish line]." Lest we forget, the little things Bodoni was working on from time to time, and which would indeed keep him occupied for the rest of his life, were the punches and matrices for his monumental *Manuale tipografico*.

Firmin Didot picked up the cudgels in 1799, in a letter written in response to an article by a certain P.H.M, in the *Magazine Enciclopédique*: "Bodoni's reputation is fixed; without doubt, his books hold one of the first places in the libraries of booklovers, but they will be excluded from those of scholars . . . It is time, Citizen, that men of letters unite against negligent printers who believe they have done everything if they have used beautiful characters and lovely paper, even as they consider that correcting the texts is a mere bagatelle . . . As a literary man, I condemn his editions, as a typographer I admire them."[156]

Eventually hostilities between the rivals simmered down, and by 1801, Firmin Didot was able to write to Luigi Lamberti, the classical scholar: "If you see Signor Bodoni, give him my compliments and tell him that, even though we had a little dispute in which he was the aggressor, I have nevertheless always done him justice, and if I ever find anyone denigrating him, he will have no partisan warmer than me."[157]

As far as Bodoni was concerned, matters may have simmered down, but he never forgot the hurt. And unfortunately for him, printing errors do not just disappear; they remain in place, always lurking within the text to surprise and annoy the reader.

WITH THE PRIVATE PRESS securely established and his domestic life in an eminently satisfactory state, Bodoni became hugely productive in 1792. In all, between the two presses he published 41 different items, twice as many as the year before. Alongside a steady stream of sonnets and panegyrics printed for the royal press, Bodoni kept steadily producing classics at the private press, where he felt free to experiment with formats and typefaces. In celebration of the marriage of the duke and duchess of Parma's eldest daughter Carolina Teresa di Borbone to Maximilian of Saxony, he published Callimachus's hymns and epigrams in four different editions, trying out various typefaces in different sizes and using a wide range of paper and parchment. To advertise the Callimachus, he put out a five-page flyer in French, *Jean Baptiste Bodoni au Lecteur*, aimed at attracting foreign buyers. Then, never missing an opportunity to insinuate himself into the highest realm of the Church, Bodoni sent the Horace and a copy of the Callimachus to Pope Pius VI (Plate 24). The Pope rewarded him with a letter of thanks and two medals. Bodoni immediately typeset the Pope's letter, and printed a few copies of it in folio. These copies are now rare and highly prized.

One publication in 1791 must have given him particular pleasure: *Alla ornatissima Signora Paola Margherita Bodoni Arcade in Roma col nome di Cloride Tanagria*. This was an eighteen-page ode, written by Count Bernieri to celebrate Ghitta's entry into Arcadia as Cloride Tanagria. Bodoni himself had been welcomed as an Arcadian in 1782, and given the Arcadian name Alcippo

Perseio. He celebrated the event by printing a large poster in black and red as a thank-you to his sponsor (Plate 23).

As married Arcadians Cloride and Alcippo, the Bodonis climbed to a higher rung of the social ladder.

Juggling work at the two presses was no mean feat. Bodoni had the responsibility for the expenses of his private press, and he sank a great deal of his own money into stocking it. On 14 April 1795, he complained to Azara: "I am continuing to work on my typographic enterprises with indefatigable ardor, and at incredible expense." He continued: "I await with true impatience the return of calm and tranquility, having received from Paris and London considerable orders to fulfill as soon as peace appears. God knows if I will enjoy the fruit of my arduous labor . . . but I am as steadfast as a rock in the sea, and as inflexible as an alpine oak, and I move ahead fearlessly without allowing myself to be intimidated by the baying of hungry dogs."

Since the 1780s, Bodoni had been working to the accompaniment of the rattle of revolution in France. News from France was always dire. Incidents leading to revolution mounted up one by one: the storming of the Bastille and of the Tuileries; the Great Fear; the suppression of religious orders, the abolition of the *parlements*; food riots in Paris; and then on 21 September 1792, the abolition of the monarchy and the proclamation of the First French Republic. This led to the guillotining of King Louis XVI on 21 January 1793; Queen Marie Antoinette, the duchess of Parma's sister, followed him to the guillotine on 16 October. Jean-Loup de Virieu Beauvoir, the minister plenipotentiary from Parma, declared that the queen's behavior at the end never betrayed for a moment her great soul or her Hapsburg blood.[158]

Despite the roaring of revolution in France and its aftershocks in Italy, Bodoni put out 50 publications during 1793. Year by year, his production grew and his reputation spread. Local and foreign dignitaries crowded to his studio, including in 1792 Prince Augustus Frederick of England, the nineteen-year old son of George III. Bodoni also had a heartwarming visit from Frederick Hervey, earl of Bristol and bishop of Derry. So successful was the visit that the earl made Bodoni a promise. Should Azara ever cease to be Bodoni's patron, he would step in. Bodoni, always with an eye to funding his endeavors, was so gratified by this promise that he printed a volume of poems by the earl's favorite poet, Thomas Gray.[159] The publication information declares simply "Printed by Bodoni," and the dedication is written in English. For the dedication Bodoni must have leaned on Ghitta for help, and she in turn would have looked for corrections from her English friends.

The dedication reads:

> *To the most noble, and most illustrious Frederick Hervey earl of Bristol and bishop of Derry an enlightened lover of letters, a generous patron of the arts, and a passionate admirer of the poet.*
>
> *My Lord, I shall ever remember with pleasure the instruction I receiv'd from your Lordship's most learned conversation during the short time you staid at Parma to admire the inimitable works of the divine Corregio.* [sic]
>
> *But I feel with the deepest impression of gratitude your spontaneous offer to be my Augustus, should cruel Fate deprive me of my Moecenas* [sic]*, the Chevalier Azzara* [sic]*, who was then dangerously ill.*
>
> *May Heaven preserve for many, many Years the precious life of my most liberal Protector!*
>
> *In the mean time, to your Lordship I consecrate this slender production of my press as a mark of Respect, Veneration and profound Gratitude . . .*

Fortunately, Azara recovered from his illness and Bodoni did not have to call on the earl for help; but the promise of the insurance would have comforted Bodoni.

Despite Bodoni's industry and initiative, the times were not entirely favorable for the creation of a new printing establishment; from the beginning of 1794, war interrupted commerce with France, and hence with Britain and the rest of Europe. Bodoni became discouraged when sales slumped and he found himself overstaffed. Inevitably, other printers in the duchy envied Bodoni's sinecure at the royal press and, believing him to be a rich darling of the court, went out of their way to make life difficult for him. He found it harder and harder to acquire

Pietro Miliani (1744-1817).

good paper, and had it not been for his good friend, the papermaker Gaetano Ziliani, he would have been left high and dry. Eventually, he struck up a business relationship with Pietro Miliani, a papermaker at Fabriano in the Marche, who produced paper of the highest quality. Unfortunately, Fabriano was 262 kilometers from Parma, which meant tariffs and shipping costs, but Bodoni was determined to use only the best paper, and he and Pietro Miliani enhanced each other's reputations for many years.

A stunning example of their cooperation was the 1800 publication in folio of *Pitture di Antonio Allegri detto il Correggio esistenti nel Monistero di San Paolo.* On 18 December 1790, Azara had written to Bodoni that the duke of Parma and Count Ventura had approved a project to have Correggio's frescoes in the Camera di San Paolo engraved; they would have the paintings copied and would send the copies to Rome for engraving by Morghen and Volpato. Azara wrote again to Bodoni on 2 February 1791, fearing nothing was moving on the project since he knew that the only person in Parma who did anything was Bodoni. Years passed and still nothing happened, but in 1795 the Camera di San Paolo was again opened for inspection, this time by four "gallant gentlemen."[160] These men were the painter Gaetano Callani; Professor Biagio Martini; the Portuguese artist, Francesco Vieira; and Bodoni's good friend, the engraver Francesco Rosaspina. At eight o'clock on the morning of 16 June, the four men slipped quietly into the convent and made their way to the secret room. They stepped from darkness into what seemed like a brilliantly illuminated cave. Aladdin himself could not have been more astonished. It was not until eight o'clock the same evening that they left the Camera di San Paolo, having spent twelve hours feverishly writing and

drawing. Vieira had managed to complete a total of 26 drawings, Martini completed seven, while Rosaspina set himself the task of drawing Diana. At last the project to have the frescoes engraved could move forward.

Azara was unhappy when Rosaspina rather than Morghen was chosen to do the engraving. Morghen was unavailable; then at the height of his powers, he was working on an engraving of Leonardo's *Last Supper.* In a letter of 5 December 1795 to Bodoni, Azara stated: "I tell you frankly that the engraver is not up to the task. I can't talk about the artist [Vieira] because I need to see

Francesco Rosaspina (1762-1841).

what he can do. Engraving has been carried to a point of perfection today, of which we had no idea a few years ago, and I can say that if Morghen is in the third rank, Rosaspina is in the tenth." He continued in the same vein on 9 January 1796, this time attacking not only Vieira but all Portuguese painters: "It is impossible that a painter, much less a Portuguese painter, could do twenty paintings in a morning and even more difficult to copy a Correggio while being true to its character."

Rather sheepishly, at the end of a voluminous letter of 8 December 1797 to Azara, Bodoni admitted that he was about to publish his book about Correggio's paintings in the Camera di San Paolo with engravings by Rosaspina. He added that the text would be in Italian, French, and Spanish. The book was finally published in 1800, and Bodoni printed some copies with the engravings in sanguine; the rest were in black. Brooks rightfully considers it to be a most beautiful book.

Details of Rosaspina's engravings of decorations
in the Camera di San Paolo.

Punches for a large size of Bodoni's chancery italic type.

IO

Gout and a Grape Seed

Thro' every joint the thrilling anguish pours, and gnaws, and burns, and tortures, and devours.

LUCIAN

It feels like walking on my eyeballs.

REV. SYDNEY SMITH

"ALL MY ARDUOUS WORK and incredible efforts have dimmed my eyesight, and I have to wear glasses," Bodoni wrote to Azara on 7 October 1794. "Nevertheless, I raise my hands to heaven, thanking the true giver of health for having accorded me so much vigor and will to pursue my work in spite of all the impediments and deadlocks that we are suffering in every corner of Europe. I am confident that my work will again be sought after in the future by lovers of beautiful typography." He wrote again about health matters on 14 April 1795 in a letter of manifold subjects and stunning length. "My health is pretty good. Pray God this lasts. I feel from time to time a slight attack of gout, but I keep myself well purged and this dissipates its morbid effects." The purge he refers to is probably colchicine, a cathartic used for millennia in the treatment of gout and rheumatism, and still administered to those suffering from gout flares. Its plant source is the autumn crocus, and Bodoni's fan, Benjamin Franklin, another sufferer from the painful disease, is known to have imported autumn crocus corms to the United States after his stint in France.

Bodoni continued in the same, long overdue, letter: "What pains me more is that I have become rather stout, which I attribute to the sedentary life I am obliged to lead, remaining from morning to night curved over my table without ever being able to get away for a couple of hours. I have more than twenty people working on my account in various departments, but if I take a break, they remain idle."

On the one hand, Bodoni thanked God for his good health; on the other hand, he was clearly suffering. Throughout the 1790s, his life was accompanied by the low drone of sciatica and the occasional screaming agony of gout, and as he confessed to Azara, he had gained weight. The food he enjoyed in Parma, a diet rich in protein particularly in winter when vegetables were scarce, and dominated by *salumi* (cold cuts), game, and dairy products, certainly contributed to this gain. To offset the lack of fresh vegetables, friends sometimes sent gifts to Bodoni and Ghitta from places as far away as Genoa, gifts such as the 24 artichokes, six cauliflowers, and fresh peas ("the most beautiful I could find") they received from their friend Francesco Baroni. On the other hand, another friend, the Irish Dominican John Hyacinth Clarke then staying in Zibello, wrote to Ghitta on 17 September 1799, saying: "Finding myself now in a place where there's nothing delicate or pleasing for lovely ladies . . . I am constrained to turn to a type of food, very ordinary but I believe appreciated by people in Parma, and being of good quality in these parts. This is a dish which I heard praised in that capital, and not often available in the city. I am taking the liberty of sending you a sample." This gift must have been the prized *culatello di Zibello* (dried cured ham, whose name means "little backside"), which was hardly advisable for Bodoni's health, particularly as it and other cold cuts were sometimes eaten with another local specialty, *torta fritta* (dough deep-fried in lard).

It is easy to point to food, drink, and Bodoni's sedentary life — the usual culprits — as causes for his illness in an age when the swollen, swaddled foot of a fat man became the emblem of gout. However, there was a more sinister contributor to his condition.

"Lead is a cold poison," wrote Ulrich Ellenbog as early as 1473, "for it maketh heaviness and tightness of the chest, burdeneth the limbs and ofttimes lameth them as often one seeth in foundries where men do work with large masses and the vital inward members become burdened therefrom."[161] Bodoni's foundry with its molten lead for the casting of characters was located cheek by jowl with his living quarters, and its noxious vapors streamed into his apartment. He became a strong candidate for gout as a result of lead poisoning (Saturnine gout). Lead poisoning inhibits the excretion of salts formed by the accumulation of uric acid; these salt crystals settle in the joints and cause gout's inflammation and excruciating pain. The first joint to suffer is usually the big toe. Throughout the centuries the disease seems to have taken particular aim at literary, artistic, and political luminaries: Leonardo da Vinci, Galileo, Martin Luther, Joseph Conrad ("the horror, the horror"), Karl Marx, Benjamin Disraeli, King George IV, Thomas Jefferson, Benjamin Franklin, and Bodoni himself were all sufferers.

Bodoni published *Del coraggio nelle malattie* [Courage in Illness] in 1792, a treatise by Giuseppe Pasta, a physician from Bergamo. The section on gout offered Bodoni scant comfort. It started off: "If it is true that gout has no remedy, it is also true that courage is the unique refuge for its sufferers."[162] The good doctor, leaning on Thomas Sydenham, also recommended rest and tranquility. Bodoni showed plenty of courage, but rest and tranquility were tough pills to swallow for someone who lived to work.

Bodoni's brother Giuseppe, who spent his life working in Bodoni's foundry and handling lead letters as he typeset, managed to escape the ravages of gout, only to suffer mightily from another effect of working with lead: chronic asthma, caused by the "pestiferous exhalations" coming from molten lead and antimony. He also suffered from hernias and terribly calloused hands, the result of heaving around cases of lead characters, punches, and matrices, and performing other heavy tasks entailed in running a foundry.[163]

In early 1796, Bodoni experienced a nasty accident, the results of which were to plague him for many years. "I haven't been able to write because my eyes have been constantly running," he wrote to Azara on 1 February. "This is because of a grape seed which accidentally flew up into my nasal passages a few weeks ago. It is my misfortune to have been unable to expel it so far, in spite of sneezing with much force. The experts tell me this accident will not have dire consequences; in time the seed will dissolve or grow smaller, and will leave its niche. At first, this unthinkable accident filled me with black melancholy but then I quickly remembered the case of Anacreon, to whom the same mishap occurred."

A friend had presented Bodoni with a basket of beautiful grapes. While hurrying home with them, he delightedly popped one into his mouth, but as he chewed, he coughed, and the seed flew up into the whorls of his nose and settled comfortably in. This particular grape seed must have had a carapace of steel. It remained in Bodoni's nose for years, failing to macerate, making it difficult for him to breathe and causing splitting headaches.

He was still complaining about it to Azara on 27 February 1799: "I am suffering from an eye infection, which worries me a great deal. I suppose it derives from that damned grape seed which has been lodged in my nose for five years now, and which, it seems, I must endure until I head off into eternity." In the same letter, he complained about a ferocious attack of gout and mentioned a painful operation on a toenail which prevented him from walking. On top of all that, he was also suffering from a terrible sore throat, which made him anticipate Lent by a few days (that is, he had to give up eating) and only slowly was he able to swallow a little broth. Also in the same letter, Bodoni complained about the frigid temperatures, which had added to the misery of his "already fat and heavy body," had frozen his ink solid, and contributed to the three-month siege of gout.

In 1805, Bodoni, who distrusted doctors on principle, decided in desperation to try a "cure" for gout proposed by a Frenchman, M. Cadet de Veaux. Bodoni wrote about this terrible experience to Luigi Lamberti, the Greek scholar and editor: "In the space of twelve hours I drank 36 pints of scalding hot water, and every three hours I guzzled another nine-ounce glassful. I started at ten o'clock in the morning, and did not eat anything all day. At eleven o'clock that evening, I arose, but while I was eating a little something, I passed out, and had to return to bed. I sweated so much that I drenched the mattress. You have no idea how much this experiment exhausted me."[164] Indeed, all that water must have been quite a surprise for his kidneys; people drank very little water in the eighteenth century because they knew it might carry disease. The Cadet de Veaux cure might well have done him good with today's purified water.

The grape seed continued to be an irritation. In a charming letter written to Ghitta from Genoa on 30 November 1811, the writer Francesco Baroni told her that he had received a present of a box of Spanish tobacco and, recalling the grape seed, decided to send some of it to Bodoni in the hope that it might help expel the seed. He was also sending seven rare books to amuse Bodoni after a hard day's work and added that he was including a length of dress fabric for her in the latest mode, as well as a coffee service made of wood from a fig tree. He reckoned that a wooden coffee service was a good thing because the wood was so light, and one could hold the cup of coffee without getting burned. Baroni explained to her that he had packed everything in a box, which he begged her to open immediately and withdraw the fresh flowers he had laid on top of everything, flowers which were not available in cold Parma in November. She should then put them quickly into water and after two or three hours, they would look freshly picked. What delight this letter and package from Genoa must have provided for the Bodonis during Parma's dark November days.

BODONI WAS SERIOUSLY ILL during 1811, so ill that he penned his own epitaph on 28 March.[165]

Giace in questa fossa breve
Di Bodoni il corpo greve.
Viase lieto, e faticato;
Dagli amici, e Grandi amato.
Soffrà morbo podagroso:
Or suo spirto ha in Ciel riposo,
Digli Vale, *o pellegrino*
E prosequi il tuo camino.

[Here lies in this little grave the heavy body of Bodoni.
He lived happily and worked hard,
he was loved by his friends and illustrious people,
and he suffered from gout.
Now his spirit rests in heaven.
Say farewell, o pilgrim, and continue on your way.]

Despite his physical problems, which included increasing deafness and a persistent cough, Bodoni always managed to impress visitors by what appeared to be his vigorous good health, even when he was ill. In 1812, just a year before he died, at a time when he was confined to bed, he was visited by Napoleon's emissary, Count de Saint Vallier. This meeting surprised and delighted Bodoni, and when he expressed his gratitude for the visit, Saint Vallier responded: "Monsieur Bodoni, if you have so much fire in you when you are ill, what must you be like when you are well?"[166]

Portrait of Correggio designed for Bodoni by Asioli.

II

Two Thefts and a Fire

By 5 a.m. the characters had been sold to a smelter, and by 7 a.m. more than a hundred pounds had been melted and sold for the lead. At 11 a.m. the same day, the police found the wife of one of the robbers with a saucepan on the fire, stirring while the rest melted.

GIAMBATTISTA BODONI

O N 2 JUNE 1795, between one and two o'clock in the morning, a young boy squeezed through the iron bars protecting the windows of Bodoni's private press. Working with accomplices who lurked below on the riverbank, he collected cases of type that Bodoni had prepared over many years and planned to use in a specimen book of exotic fonts. The boy then lowered the cases down to the men below, and they disappeared with them into the night.

Bodoni had zealously guarded these fonts in his living quarters for several years, but had recently moved them to the press to begin work on the specimen book. Word of the move must have reached the thieves, who wrongly assumed that the type was made of silver. Writing to Azara on 25 July, Bodoni described what happened after the theft: "By 5 a.m. the characters had been sold to a smelter, and by 7 a.m. more than a hundred pounds had been melted and sold for the lead. At 11 a.m. the same day, the police found the wife of one of the robbers with a saucepan on the fire, stirring while the rest melted." The letters had already fused and were unserviceable.

This was an expensive loss for Bodoni. As he reported to Azara, the collection represented "the many and various exotic characters that I had thrown with great expense and patience in my more energetic and robust years . . . I do not flatter myself that I have enough health, life, energy, and free time to redo the work that cost me so much arduous effort." But even in the face of his loss, Bodoni managed to remain magnanimous. (He could afford to because he still retained the matrices.) He prayed for the thieves, who had been swiftly apprehended, and went so far as to provide funds for the mother of one of them[167] – presumably the small boy who went through the window.

Wholesale thievery was rife. Napoleon set the example by invading and looting Italy, stealing its finest paintings and sculptures. On 27 July 1798, Azara wrote to Bodoni from Paris: "As I write this, carriages carrying the masterpieces stolen from Italy are passing beneath my window. They are being carried with a majesty that rivals the triumph of Paulus Emilius. Tomorrow, the anniversary of the fall of Robespierre, the Directory will assemble at the Champs de Mars to receive them with the greatest pomp imaginable. I will be there with the diplomatic corps, and you can just imagine what thoughts will be passing through my head." Parma was not immune to this looting and suffered the loss of many great paintings, but fortunately the greatest of its treasures were Correggio's frescoes on the walls and domes of its sacred buildings, and they could not be removed.

In 1801, at a time when Bodoni was regarded as a wealthy man, he suffered a second robbery. On the night of 26 December, he and Ghitta went to the Teatro Reale for the opening night of *La Giulietta,* "a semi-serious drama in two acts . . . with poetry by Gaetano Rossi of Venice [and] new music expressly composed by Giuseppe Farinelli . . . dances composed and directed by Pietro Angiolini."[168] It was a gala event, attended by Parma's élite, with everyone decked in the latest fashions and sparkling with jewels. The Bodonis sat in their box on the first level with friends, listening to the opening act. Unfortunately, Bodoni was feeling unwell and ill at ease; he was tired from the aftereffects of a heavy cold that had kept him at home for several weeks, and he found himself irrationally irritated by the sinister faces of two men in the orchestra stalls, men who kept glancing at him. He became overwhelmingly anxious, and decided to return home. Loyal Ghitta accompanied him. When they arrived at La Pilotta, they climbed the stairs to their apartment and found the door wide open. Clothes and linens were scattered all over the floor; wardrobes were smashed; money and silver had been stolen from locked drawers. All the Bodonis' precious goods were missing: gold and silver medals, clocks, cameos, jewels, silverware, and other items, some of them received from kings and princes, others bought with Bodoni's own money. Although this was a huge monetary loss, he was relieved to find that, even though the robbers had penetrated the furthest reaches of the apartment, they had not stolen his collection of punches and matrices. These thieves, who had unlocked the front door with counterfeit keys, were looking for treasures that carried more monetary value than steel and copper.[169]

Word of the theft buzzed around Parma. The duke ordered a hunt for the thieves and allowed searchers into even the most private quarters of his palace; the ministers of France, Spain, and Italy all flew into action; Bodoni was compelled to compile a list of every item that had been stolen. The list was published (not by Bodoni) and disseminated throughout the city and the outlying villages. Four suspects, sighted at an inn outside the Porta San Michele, were believed to be Frenchmen between the ages of 25 and 30, handsome, well-dressed, of medium height, wearing hats with cockades. One of them was chewing tobacco.

They were arrested, and turned out to be members of a larger gang, which included eight men and one woman (the fence), according to a notification posted by the Supreme Council of Criminal Justice. Their punishments included imprisonment and exile. Bodoni was happy to write to Azara on 4 March 1802 that most of the stolen goods had been recovered; they had been found in three different locations along the Via Emilia, just outside Parma.

A year later, almost to the day, Bodoni and Ghitta came close to losing everything they possessed at La Pilotta. About eight o'clock that December evening, Bodoni was seated at home, writing a letter. Ghitta was standing beside the fireplace in the front room, welcoming Federico Cavriani, the distinguished author and translator of Ovid's *Amores,* the second edition of which Bodoni had just published. She led the visitor to Bodoni's study, and Bodoni rose to greet him. Noticing that Cavriani was shivering with cold, he took him back to the fireside in the front room, but unknowingly left a lighted match on his writing table. By sheer luck, he suddenly decided to show Cavriani a certain book, and returned to his study to fetch it. He found the room full of smoke, and flames had begun to devour the piles of correspondence on his desk and to lick at the window frames and adjacent shelves. Like a madman, Bodoni leapt to his desk and flung everything onto the floor, stamped on the papers, and suffocated the fire.

"If I had waited two more minutes," he wrote to his friend the engraver, Francesco Rosaspina, "the entire room where I keep my punches, matrices, paper, and precious things, would have gone up in flames."

This detailed description of the event in Giuseppe De Lama's *Vita del Cavaliere Giambattista Bodoni* bears the sound of Ghitta's voice. She was beside De Lama as he wrote her husband's biography, recalling what she could and censuring what she felt was unnecessary. In this instance, she herself witnessed the fire and Bodoni's feral courage, and the event must have shaken her to the core.

List of the stolen goods.

Il Pozzetto, Bodoni's country house
in San Prospero.

12

1798 · The Triumphal Return,
and Life on the Farm

Bodoni fu qui; se non cononsci ancora, a lui ti prostra, ed il gran Genio adora.
[Bodoni was here; if you don't yet know him, bow down to him, and worship his
great genius.]

EVASIO LEONE

*Poco prima di raggiungere il paese di S. Prospero si diparte a sinistra della
via Emilia una sinuosa stradetta che porta a questa villa.*
[On the left side of the Via Emilia, shortly before you arrive in San Prospero, a
sinuous little street leads to this villa.]

LODOVICO GAMBARA

REVOLUTION in France and America; counterrevolution; Jacobinism;
Napoleon's arrival on the scene; the subjection of Italy by French forces;
stirrings of nationalism (Italy at the time was still a loose collection
of kingdoms, duchies, republics, and papal states); renewed war; and rising
resentment against the French for conscripting Italian soldiers and raising
taxes all formed the background to Bodoni's life for the next few years. True to

form, he remained apolitical and loyal to Parma and its duke, saying in a letter to Azara on 8 December 1797: "I have decided to remain a tranquil and peaceful spectator to the huge convulsions and incredible metamorphoses which they say must happen in our peninsula." Yet again he went on to remind Azara of his similarity to Archimedes who continued to work on geometrical problems during the slaughter at Syracuse. "Just so will I carry on preparing the most refined editions of Latin, Greek, and Italian classics for the few but intelligent bibliophiles throughout the cultured parts of Europe."

Azara replied on 25 January 1798: "We are now at the critical moment in which the fate of Rome will be decided . . ." It was also the moment when Azara's own fate was decided. In April, he received the news from Spain that he had been made ambassador to France, and was to leave Rome for Paris immediately. "It is not possible to explain the torment in my head at being severed from this beloved country, at leaving all my friends, setting up house in Paris, and having to leave behind in my Roman house so many things that are the delight of my life. Enough! This is too bitter to talk about." This sad separation from Rome, however, opened up an opportunity for Bodoni and Azara to see each other again.

At the end of April, Azara set off on the long journey to Paris. He had informed Bodoni of his intention to make a brief stop in Parma to visit him and Ghitta. Overjoyed by the news, Bodoni was unable to wait patiently until Azara's arrival. Instead, he hastened to Reggio, about 30 kilometers south of the city, met the ambassador there, and accompanied him to Parma. When Azara departed on 5 May for Turin, with a stop in Milan, Bodoni decided to surprise him again. He had already planned a return to his homeland in Piedmont for the first time in 30 years; intercepting Azara in Milan would coincide neatly with those plans.

Together with Ghitta, Giuseppe De Lama, and Jean George Handwerck (the longtime treasurer of the royal press), Bodoni set off on the triumphal return to his fatherland. In Milan, he successfully surprised Azara by appearing when least expected. Azara then introduced him to important officials in Milan, all of whom were eager to spend time with the great typographer, lionizing him as he discussed the printing arts.[170]

Bodoni's group accompanied Azara from Milan to Turin, making a sightseeing stop along the way at the ancient city of Vercelli. The entire entourage arrived in Turin on 9 May, and there, after many festive occasions to which they were both invited, the friends parted ways. Azara was leaving Italy forever, and the two friends were never to see one another again.

Giuseppe De Lama later wrote a long letter to a friend, describing to the fullest Bodoni's return to Piedmont.[171] What follows is a brief paraphrase of his letter.

After Azara's departure, Bodoni and Ghitta continued to be overwhelmed by the hospitality of admirers in Turin vying to entertain them, so much so that Ghitta became indisposed and had to retire to her room for a couple of days. Everyone wanted to meet the great typographer, including his early admirer Carlo Emmanuele IV, who granted him an audience. (Until 1796, Carlo Emanuele had been known as the prince of Piedmont, but was now also styled the king of Sardinia.) Bodoni presented him with a copy of the handsome folio edition of the *De Imitatione Christi* by Thomas à Kempis. Thirteen minutes later, Ghitta was granted an audience with the queen, and presented her with Bodoni's beautiful printing of Count de Bernis's tedious poem *La Réligion Vengée* (Plate 26). (The queen may have had some connection with the count.) Four minutes after that, Bodoni and Ghitta each emerged from their audiences, delighted by their conversations with the king and queen.[172] They fled back to their lodgings and fell on their lunch, their hunger sharpened by the long morning of social engagements and adulation. Chatting about their audiences, Bodoni recounted that the king had asked if he had children, and he had responded that in these unfortunate times it was better not to have any. The king replied that he thanked heaven he was also without them. "And then," said Bodoni, "thanking me for the Thomas à Kempis, he turned his eyes to the sky and exclaimed, 'Ah, this is a book I need to read to give me courage!'"[173]

The celebrations in Turin continued for another week. Finally, on 25 May, Bodoni and his entourage set off for Saluzzo. Along the way they encountered messenger after messenger from the count of Verzolo, imploring them to stay at his palace. By seven o'clock that evening they could perceive the town of Saluzzo spread out above them on the misty hillside. Bodoni was overwhelmed with emotion, and tears ran down his face. At half past seven, preceded by horses and carriages, they entered Saluzzo and made their way to the Palazzo Verzolo.

The townspeople were desperate to lay eyes on their local hero; everyone, everywhere, at every level of society, paid tribute to him and his "amiable consort." The couple was feted without cease, and Bodoni was often overwhelmed by his feelings. At a reception given by the community on the day of Pentecost, he was entertained with a pageant, speeches, and a song. Responding as a citizen of Saluzzo, Bodoni swore that he adored his birthplace and intended to present the city with copies of all his works as an everlasting memorial to his love for it, a promise that he later fulfilled.

On 30 May, Bodoni was honored at the town hall where, again overwhelmed by adulation, he jubilantly contested the biblical claim, "A prophet hath no honor in his own country." The next day, he warmly thanked the count of Verzolo for his hospitality and left his hometown for good.

Disappointingly, what De Lama fails to describe is the time Bodoni spent with his sisters Angela and Benedeta and his brother Domenico. He certainly did not ignore them because it is evident from letters between Angela and Ghitta that the sisters-in-law met each other and became good friends. It is, of course, possible that the family felt slighted by the fact that Bodoni did not stay with them (or perhaps they were relieved).

Before leaving Saluzzo, Bodoni received a letter from Handwerck, which must have warmed his heart and Ghitta's, encouraging them to think fondly of their return to peaceful Parma after all the exigencies of the trip. "Your Delmastro, full of attention for you, is preparing your apartment very carefully," wrote the treasurer. "You will find everything changed for the better."

AFTER THE COOL, FRESH AIR OF SALUZZO, the humid miasma of Parma's summer heat was more than Chitta could bear. Living literally within the printing house in the heat of summer was a nightmare. Her husband's typographic empire had flowed over into their living quarters. He stored his treasures and his best paper in the closets of their apartment; the crashing and banging of the press one flight downstairs disturbed their peace; and they were constantly assailed by fumes of molten lead and antimony wafting from the foundry. In addition, Bodoni's appetite for work, plus an unending stream of visitors, to whom Ghitta was unfailingly gracious, left them with little spare time. They needed a refuge. She found one, and she persuaded Bodoni to spend his savings on it.

Bodoni traveled the three miles to San Prospero to see what Ghitta had found. His first sight after turning off the Via Emilia and making his way down a snaky road was of a decrepit, tumbledown hovel on one level, with two unequally pitched roofs and a crude front porch. This building was the remains of a rest stop for pilgrims as they traveled along the Via Emilia.[174] Fortunately, this was not the property Ghitta wanted him to buy. A few hundred yards further down the path, he came to a small farm. The property was bordered on one side by a clear stream, overhung by weeping willows. Through luxuriant foliage, Bodoni caught a glimpse of a square, unpretentious, two-story house, set in the midst of a flourishing garden. He tasted the water from a natural spring and found it delicious.

Il Pozzetto [the well] was one of two little farms purchased by Bodoni and Ghitta, according to a deed dated 7 August 1798. The properties, previously owned by two Lateran canons, were described as Le Berline [the stocks] and Il Pozzetto.[175] Bodoni and Ghitta decided to occupy the latter, and set about restoring the main house while retaining its original stone walls. As Angelo Ciavarella points out, the house became a metaphor for Bodoni's work: "Bodoni's house has a plain and elegant aspect; it is a faithful transposition of his art, of his taste, in a habitation. The architect of the printed page, clean, bright, fundamental is in the same manner the architect of a comfortable, linear, fundamental house."[176]

IN NOVEMBER 1800, Bodoni wrote to Azara that, even though his health was not exactly robust, he had profited greatly from autumn walks at his little suburban farm, walks that kept his blood moving vigorously. Il Pozzetto provided him with much pleasure, and he enjoyed playing at being a farmer, planting trees, raising ducks and chickens, and breathing the fresh country air. However, as time went on and work piled up, he did not allow himself to spend much time there. By September 1801, he was complaining to Azara that he was 60 years old and had never had a chance to reap the rewards of his incredible labors. He then added that the place was overrun by "a mob of little nephews of my wife, orphaned at the tender age of seven and eight." Another factor prevented him from going to Il Pozzetto on a regular basis. The purchase had presented him with financial challenges and, weighed down by taxes, mortgages, and the cost of renovation, he could not afford to buy a carriage in which to travel from La Pilotta in Parma to Il Pozzetto in San Prospero. For a sedentary man of his age, suffering from gout and sciatica, those three miles on foot or horseback must have been daunting.

13
A Letter from Jean George Handwerck

Oh happy day! I have just seen Azara.   HANDWERCK

AFTER 31 YEARS of service to Bodoni, running the business side of the royal press, Jean George Handwerck deemed it time to retire and to reestablish connections with the family he had left so long ago. Before returning to Frankfurt where his relatives lived, he decided to travel in France. Bodoni was naturally distressed to lose such a loyal friend and co-worker but was prepared to do anything he could to pave Handwerck's way. He wrote at once to Azara in Paris, asking the diplomat to receive his friend with kindness.

Handwerck went first to see friends in Lyons, where he had resided before coming to Parma, and then traveled on to Paris. "Quite frankly," he admitted to Bodoni in his letter of 24 July 1801, "without flattery, I can tell you that all the printers and bookstores that I frequented in Lyons prefer you to Didot. I find the same thing here in Paris."

Handwerck's enthusiasm about his visit to Azara was boundless. He told Bodoni how he set off in a carriage for the ambassador's residence, which he described as being on one floor at the end of a long courtyard. Two rooms preceded the study, which was a square room lined with bookcases filled with leather-bound volumes. In the middle of the room stood a round writing table. Azara was seated at the table, wearing a blue coat with a yellow waistcoat, black breeches, gray hose, and shoes with buckles. He wore no wig, and what little hair he had was shaved. He had put on weight but looked in perfect health.

Azara welcomed Handwerck to the residence, and they began a long conversation. Here is Handwerck's word by word recollection of it. He speaks formally at first.

"I take the liberty of presenting you with my humble respects, while I am at the same time flattered to present you with a letter from my friend Bodoni of Parma."

"Please sit down." *An armchair was directly in front of him. I started reading your letter to him, and when I came to the part about the trip we made in his company four years ago, he stopped me, saying,*

"Yes, I remember that trip, and I remember you too." *I was extremely touched by his gracious recollection. I continued to read the letter. When I neared the end and reached the place where you say you can't wait for the happy moment of seeing him again in Italy, he said:*

"I do hope to see Italy again."

"May God accomplish your wish very soon, not just for Bodoni's sake but for that of all your friends in Italy." *When I finished reading the letter, he placed it next to him on the table.*

"Is it your first time in Paris?"

"Yes, Excellency."

"Will you stay here for a while?"

"That is my plan."

"You will see many beautiful things. What is Bodoni doing these days?"

"He works day and night to finish his *Manuale tipografico.*"

"This has been promised for a long time."

"Excellency, he is more determined than ever to finish it now. He has put aside everything else to work exclusively on the *Manuale tipografico.*"

"When do you think it will be published?"

"By the end of this year or the beginning of next, unless an illness puts him out of commission and prolongs the entire execution." [Handwerck was off by seventeen years.]

"A certain rivalry makes it necessary to place something important in front of the eyes of the literary world, and his *Manuale* would be the primary object with which to combat Didot. Didot is a printer; Bodoni a typographer. There are Frenchmen who ignorantly prefer Didot; but the palm of victory always goes to Bodoni . . . Bodoni never wanted to leave Parma."

"He has always loved tranquility and sweet peace, which he can find nowhere other than Parma. Today more than ever he needs this, now that he is advancing in age."

"He's not old yet."

"No, Excellency, he is not old yet. He must be 60 now, but a man who has worked as hard as he has for so many years must feel his strength diminishing."

"How is the duke?"

"When I left Parma, he was in excellent health, but the duchess was obliged to remain in bed because of a slight indisposition as the result of a cut on her foot. The princess is in a convent."

"She's a very pretty princess."

"Yes, Excellency. She is in the convent of the Ursulines. The duke goes to see her two or three times a week. Everyone in Parma wants the duke to remain in power. May God grant this wish. Everyone profits from a prince who is so gracious and so charitable and so good"

"I did everything I could for that country."

At that point, Azara started to write something, and Handwerck decided it was time to leave. Before he did so, he asked Azara for the favor of a permit of residence, which Azara graciously granted.

Handwerck remained in Paris for two happy months, delighting in the beauty of the city and its many interesting inhabitants. Then he headed east, stopping in Metz and Majeuse along the way. He commented happily on the ease with which one could travel around France, and how inexpensive it was. He finally wrote to Bodoni from Frankfurt on 11 February 1803, a letter full of nostalgia for Parma and complaints about Frankfurt and its rich inhabitants who cared only about money and not a whit about literature and the beaux arts. "I feel all the pain of the distance that separates us," he mourned. "Only the hope of seeing you again consoles me . . ."

Bodoni, too, must have keenly felt the loss of such a friend, but worse losses were yet to come.

Médéric Louis Élie Moreau de Saint-Méry,
Adminitsrator General of Parma

14

The Death of a Duke,
the Presentation of a Medal, and
the Death of a Diplomat

The death of a prince must be the result of extraordinary causes.

MOREAU DE SAINT-MÉRY

"YOU HAVE NO DOUBT been inundated by a flood of letters announcing the most unfortunate event that could ever befall this unhappy place," wrote Bodoni to Azara on 19 October 1802. He was referring to the death of the duke of Parma ten days earlier. "I want to weave here an exact description of this tragic and unexpected fatal blow, even if I risk carrying vases to Samos, owls to Athens, and crocodiles to Egypt."

Then Bodoni launched into the tale of the death of 51-year-old Don Ferdinando, his employer and protector for 33 years. He described how, early on the morning of 6 October, the duke had eaten a "light" meal at the convent of Saint Alessandro: *anolini in brodo*, his favorite dish, followed by a few slices of pork shoulder, and some white wine. Taking leave of the nuns, he traveled to the bishop's palace where he lunched with Bishop Turchi. There he consumed polenta made with milk and served with *uccelli* [birds, probably songbirds or pigeon]. Among other serious meats, he then tucked into *cotechino di Modena*. Gillian Riley describes this regional delicacy as a boiling sausage made from glutinous bits of pig, very rich and fatty, salted, usually flavored with cinnamon and black pepper, stuffed into the skin of a pig's trotter and leg, and traditionally served with *mostarda di frutta*, fruits preserved in a mustardy syrup.

Onlookers at the bishop's palace noticed that the duke was not his usual jolly self.

Immediately after lunch, he left the convent and set out for the Abbey of Fontevivo, just twelve kilometers from Parma. As he climbed into the coach he began to groan and complained that he was not feeling well; however, he proceeded with the journey. On arrival, he greeted his hosts and a gathering of people who had convened at the abbey for a dramatic presentation. When he learned he was expected to attend the event, he asked anxiously how long it would last and was told an hour. Again, people remarked that he looked unwell. The presentation over, everyone retired to the refectory where the duke sat down at the long table. He asked what soup was being served, and was told that it was broth with *vermicelli di Genova*. He had barely tasted it when he turned around and spat on the floor. He then rose from the table saying he felt ill, begged everyone to continue with their meal, and retired to his room. He went to bed but rose again to take some salts he carried in his travel case.

At two o'clock the following afternoon Doctor Dentoni was summoned from Parma. He arrived about seven in the evening, by which time the duke's condition had worsened. The last rites were administered, "which [the duke] requested with all the fervor of the ancient Christians." At half past one the following morning, Doctor Levacher, the French surgeon, arrived and found the duke in his bed, uncovered. He felt his feet, and found them cold. The duke asked if he had escaped from peril and then held out his arm for the surgeon to take his pulse. Doctor Levacher exhorted him to have courage, to drink frequently, and to cover himself up. The duke replied that his belly was roiling so tremendously that he could not tolerate any covering on it at all. He protested that dying did not bother him, but he regretted it because of the sadness it would bring to his family. His last words were, "Oh my God, my God, I am dying."

Bodoni went on to speculate about rumors of poisoning. "But who would ever have poisoned him?" he asked. He then reported a conversation he had with Doctor Levacher, in which the surgeon reported that the illness was either cholera or a "twisting," and that the duke's stomach was filled with black bile, which exuded from his eyes, nose, mouth, and ears after his death. (The eyes and ears are exempted from the physicians' official report.) The surgeon also reported that the duke's liver had a large, gangrenous mass.

THAT IS Bodoni's story. His reference to various meals the duke ate and to Doctor Levacher's firsthand testimony has the ring of truth, but it is hard to discount the rumors of poison, rumors that still resound in Parma today.

Luigi Ginetti in *"La Morte di Don Ferdinando di Borbone"* points a finger at a possible culprit, Costantino Anfossi, inspector of the duke's possessions at Colorno, who is said to have died tormented by remorse. Ginetti also cites a report saying that the duke died from poison administered to him in a cup of hot chocolate at the convent.[177] Rumor is a seducer and hard to dispel, so a look at the doctors' report and the autopsy findings may come closer to the truth. In the report attached to Ginetti's article, *"Della Malattie, e successiva repentina Morte del Clementissimo Reale Nostro Sovrano D. Ferdinando I. Infante di Spagna, Duca di Parma, Piacenza, Guastalla,"* [Concerning the Illness, and the subsequent sudden Death of our most Clement Royal Sovereign D. Ferdinano I. Dauphin of Spain, Duke of Parma, Piacenza, Guastalla] the eight attending physicians, who included Levacher and the duke's personal physicians as well as the local doctors, summarized the days leading up to the duke's death and the condition of his body after he expired. They explained how he arrived at Fontevivo with a great pain in his gut, had two evacuations, dosed himself with salts, and had three more evacuations of undigested matter. "His night was rather disturbed." The following morning he drank hot chocolate and said he felt a little better, but two hours later his strength failed him and he was in great pain. He had no appetite, and drank only a little soup, some hot chocolate, and some sips of peppermint water with a sedative. After lunch, the local doctor gave him an enema.

That evening, his pulse was feeble, his fever grew, his belly became grossly distended, he hiccuped whenever he tried to eat or drink and had fierce cramps in his legs. His hiccups worsened. The doctor gave him two more enemas, and he managed to sleep a little although his fever continued to rise and his belly remained distended with gas. At four o'clock the next morning, he was again purged with salts in two liters of water, which resulted in many evacuations of stinking fecal matter and liquid. Even so, his belly remained distended and he continued to hiccup, although his tongue was a good color and he enjoyed a cup of chocolate at six o'clock. At half past nine he took a little soup and drank some burgundy. At eleven o'clock he took two drams of magnesia for heartburn and hiccups. Two hours later he was offered some chocolate, but after a few sips he appeared disgusted by it and by any other food or drink offered to him. His pulse weakened, his fever rose, his belly was taut, and he hiccuped constantly. At five o'clock in the afternoon, he was given a camphor enema and then some laudanum, but he was unable to sleep. Next, the doctors tried quinine and musk, but nothing helped. At eight o'clock he asked for a cup of chocolate, which he found quite good, but at ten o'clock he became very agitated and his pulse weakened even more. At midnight, he vomited black matter flecked with blood, became breathless, and kept asking for spoonfuls of burgundy.

His strength failed, he was administered the last rites, and he died at half past four on the morning of 9 October. The doctors then described their findings after his death:

> Immediately after death, bloody, stinking matter flowed out of his mouth and nose. Nothing extraordinary was found on the exterior of his body, although his stomach was hugely swollen and rubbery. After the body was opened, no other liquid was found except for the usual lymph; the peritoneum was in a body's natural state. The intestines were full of fluid, and the color of the intestinal membrane, particularly in the small intestine, was altered. The belly was full of gas, and its membrane was inflamed. Also in the stomach was a considerable amount of blood concentrated in black bile. The spleen was full of black blood of the same character, the gall bladder vessel contained darkening blood, as was everything else found in the belly. The liver was blackening, and contained a gangrenous adhesion about an inch in diameter. The lungs were flabby and there were adhesions in the upper left pleural cavity, but nothing was wrong with the heart.

Those who claim that the duke was poisoned make much of the fact that Levacher jumped back and cried out when he saw the state of the duke's abdomen. Is it not more likely that he recoiled from the stench of the escaping gas?

Dr. Levacher wrote a report to Moreau de Saint-Méry,[178] the administrator general in Parma (and Bodoni's good friend and admirer). In it, he made it clear that the duke died from *atrabile,* black bile. This condition is usually caused by twisting and blockage of the intestines, which forces matter upwards through the body rather than down. He added that when the duke was presented with the last rites, he felt the need to make a pious speech but his strength did not allow this; instead he asked the priest to make haste.

Moreau de Saint-Méry then wrote a dispatch to the minister of foreign affairs in Paris informing him of the death of the duke, and claiming that the cause of death was gangrene in the liver.[179] He related that the duke died with his faculties intact, and made just two verbal requests. The first was that a regency should be established, composed principally of his wife, Minister Schizzati, and Count Cesare Ventura. The second was that his body should be buried in the parish church at Fontevivo, while his heart would join his ancestors in their tomb in the Capuchin monastery in Parma. He followed this letter with another dispatch to Paris, in which he returned to the question of poisoning: "This rumor has a double source: the opinion of the common people that the death of a prince must be the result of extraordinary causes; and the cry that escaped from the duke in a moment of intense suffering: 'Ah, they have given me something!' Therefore, since he dined with the bishop, the bishop must be accused."

Whether the duke was poisoned or not is a mystery that may never be solved. It is certainly true the French benefitted from his death and were able to put themselves more firmly in charge of Parma as a result. But it is also true that the autopsy report contains a convincing argument for natural causes, the most likely of which is black bile caused by a twisted intestine.

It is puzzling that, in the accounts of the last few days of the duke's life, there is no mention of his family, but there are reasons why they did not show up at his bedside. His oldest daughter, Carolina, was in Dresden with her husband, Prince Maximilian of Saxony. The duke's sickly son and heir, Ludovico, king of Etruria, was in Florence, and may have been bedridden himself because he died the following May. (Ludovico acquired the title "king of Etruria" from Napoleon after the Treaty of Lunéville, when his father relinquished Parma, Piacenza, and Guastalla to the French.) The next two daughters in line had entered holy orders, and all five of the youngest children had died in childhood. This would leave the duchess who was presumably at her preferred residence at Sala Baganza, about 36 kilometers from Fontevivo, not a huge distance for speedy horses and a well-sprung carriage. But she makes no appearance in the reports until the mention of the regency in which she was to play a part.

The duke's body, dressed in a monk's habit, was placed in a covered casket and installed in the parish church at Fontevivo, according to his wishes. It lies there today in an elaborate marble sarcophagus set in a columned niche high on the north wall of the church. On the night of 17 October, his heart was transported to the Capuchin monastery in Parma. Finally, the *Anzianato* (the city fathers) settled on a date and place to celebrate his funeral: 15 December in the church of Santa Maria della Steccata. This elaborately decorated and dearly loved basilica, which became a popular destination for pilgrims, contains a fourteenth-century painting of the Virgin Mary feeding Jesus. Eventually, the pilgrims became so numerous that a fence had to be erected around the church to keep them in order. Hence Santa Maria della Steccata or Saint Mary of the Railing.

Bodoni printed the announcement for the funeral, which was disseminated throughout the city. For the service itself, the poet-lawyer Luigi Uberto Giordani wrote a lengthy, woeful funeral oration, which Bodoni published in folio, quarto, and octavo.

He gave copies to the city fathers, refusing recompense, saying that the gifts were a demonstration of his love for Parma and the late duke. This was a shrewd move. The city fathers finally woke up to the fact that they had a genius in their midst and decided to mint a coin in honor of Bodoni. They chose Luigi Manfredini, a celebrated medal engraver, to design it and ordered four copies in gold: one for Bodoni, one for Napoleon's museum in Paris, the third for Moreau de Saint-Méry, and the fourth to remain in the civic archives. A further 200 medals were to be minted in silver, and 250 in copper. On 24 February 1803, Bodoni was treated to a solemn function in which the president of the Anzianato presented him with a decree announcing the striking of the coin in his honor. Bodoni wept with joy, ". . . and in those delicious moments he forgot all the past adversities, sorrows, odious competition, and stumbling blocks that . . . stood in the way of his progress. No longer did he need to envy Ibarra, Baskerville, and even Didot the idolatry of their countrymen."[180] The date chosen for the announcement, Saint Matthias's day, was the same lucky day on which Bodoni had arrived in Parma 35 years previously. Bodoni finished his letter to Azara about the duke's death claiming that despite all that had transpired, he remained dauntless and tranquil in his little retreat, pursuing his typographic labors in the way he always had. He added, "It is true that [these events] weigh on me, and I find myself not a little upset that, after 33 years of living in this country . . . I must, now that I am old, lose that which I have relied on." However, in his own predictable way,

ORAZIONE FUNEBRE

IN MORTE

DI

FERDINANDO I.

DI BORBONE

INFANTE DI SPAGNA

DUCA

DI PARMA, PIACENZA, GUASTALLA

ECC. ECC. ECC.

COMPOSTA E RECITATA

DA

LUIGI UBERTO GIORDANI

PARMIGIANO

CONSIGLIERE NEL SUPREMO CONSIGLIO DI PIACENZA,
INDIVIDUO ONORARIO DEL CONSIGLIO GENERALE
DELLA COMUNITÀ DI PARMA, E PROFESSORE EMERITO
DELL' UNIVERSITÀ.

PARMA

CO' TIPI BODONIANI

MDCCCIII.

Title page of the funeral oration for the duke of Parma.

Bodoni did not lose all that he relied on. The ducal press remained in operation for a few more years, and it was not long before he was making himself known to those in power and finding new patrons to underwrite some of the greatest publications he ever produced at his private press.

THE REGENCY lasted a mere thirteen days before the French stepped in and took matters into their own hands. They expelled the duchess, and she left Parma forever on 22 October 1802. Rather than returning to Vienna, she settled in Prague, and died there on 18 June 1804. Her body was buried in Saint Vitus cathedral. Her heart, however, was placed in the family's heart crypt in Vienna. A Hapsburg heart to the very end.

Bodoni's good friend Moreau de Saint-Méry was left in charge of governing the duchy, which meant little change in the affairs of the press. On 18 November 1802, Azara wrote from Paris commenting on Moreau's appointment: "Our good Moreau will play the Sovereign, and it seems to me that he will not conduct himself badly." Then he continued: "What has become of the ducal press? the library? the academy, etc.? It is fortunate that the works of Correggio remaining in Parma are not transportable."

Despite the distance between Parma and Paris, the correspondence between Bodoni and Azara continued unabated. On 11 October 1802, Azara wrote: "Right now, I am in good health, and have the pleasure of having acquired a brother, who has arrived from America, and whom I did not know at all. We saw each other once, 37 years ago, but now I hope that we will never be separated again except by death." Prior to arriving in Paris, Féliz de Azara, younger than Nicolás by sixteen years, had spent twenty years in the viceroyalty of the Río de La Plata (which nowadays includes Argentina, Paraguay, Uruguay, and Bolivia). A mathematician and engineer by training, he became an ardent explorer, mapper, and naturalist during his years in South America. He sent his field notes, in which he identified hundreds of birds and quadrupeds, back to his brother in Paris; these notes became the basis for his book, *Voyage dans l'Amerique meridionale depuis 1781 jusqu'en 1801.* It is reassuring to know that, at the end of his life, Nicolás had the companionship of a brother, who not only had interesting stories to recount, but could also provide him with comfort in the last year of his life.

Nicolás's protest to Bodoni that he was in good health was bravado. His friends in Paris had begun to notice that he was not looking well. His legs were swollen, and he was often deathly pale. He himself had written to Bodoni on 8 February

1802: "From the depths of Picardy I write to you dear friend to tell you that I live, if the life I live could be called living. I've been in terrible health for the last few months, and now I have a health crisis. My bladder is inflamed, my urine is bloody, and I have many other symptoms . . . I have been in bed for almost a month, and for me to make the journey to Amiens, they had to set up a bed in the carriage."

By the end of 1803, Azara was sinking fast. Jean-François de Bourgoing, a longtime friend who had been for many years the French ambassador to Spain, describes his last days: "Near his end, his soul was still strong, and he still had hope. He talked ceaselessly about the return of spring. He convinced himself that he would see Italy again, where he had passed such full and happy days . . . he renounced his political life, which had produced so many storms in the evening of his life; he wished to live only for Art, peace, and friendship."

Bourgoing then recounts how, on the day before he died, Azara suddenly went cold. He was moved close to the fireplace, but nothing helped. "It was the coldness of death," states Bourgoing. Azara himself recognized this, and said to his brother, "There is only one step to death from the state I am in. I am going to take it." Even after he lost the power of speech, he retained his reason, and showed no signs of distress or fright. He received the last rites on the morning of 26 January 1804 and died peacefully at five o'clock that evening, his long-lost brother by his side.

Bodoni had written to him on 16 November 1803, just two months before his death, a letter that must have greatly pleased Azara. "In the middle of the strange convulsions in almost all of Italy, and in Parma most particularly, I am better off than many others, and I am very, very busy from morning till night. Next year I will start work on an edition of Homer in Greek, in four volumes, folio imperial."

Nothing could have delighted Azara more than knowing that Bodoni was taking on the classic of all classics in such a magnificent way. How sad it was that he did not live long enough to see the results. They would have thrilled him to the core.

Luigi Lamberti (1759-1813).

15
Napoleon

Citizens! Your emperor and his august wife will soon arrive in your midst. I know that this notice will cause your hearts to explode with joy and love. Let flags on the outside of your houses decorate their Majesties' passage, and in the evening let lights everywhere be another sign of your happiness.

ANNOUNCEMENT OF NAPOLEON'S VISIT TO PARMA ON 26 JUNE 1805

I only want magnificence; my work is not for the common people.

CIAMBATTISTA BODONI

N APOLEON saw Italy as an extension of France. His ancestors were Italian noblemen, and he believed that the country and its art belonged to him. Once he became first consul in France, he set about consolidating his power in Italy. In 1796 his troops occupied Parma, and five years later, according to the terms of the Treaty of Aranjuez, Napoleon forced Don Ferdinando to cede the duchy of Parma, Piacenza, and Guastalla to the French, but left him in place for the moment. In exchange for the duchy, Napoleon ceded Tuscany to the duke's son, Ludovico, giving him the title of king of Etruria. The ceding of

Parma to the French and the duke's subsequent anguish have been suggested as contributing to his mortal illness.

Saluzzo, too, was overrun with French troops. On 27 December 1796, Domenico Bodoni wrote to his brothers complaining that the streets were infested with barbaric soldiers and horses, and that the city was enduring a plague of the most horrible murders, assassinations, fires, pillaging, and stone-throwing.

On 2 December 1804, Napoleon crowned himself emperor of France at the cathedral of Notre Dame in Paris in the presence of Pope Pius VII. On 26 May 1805, in Milan cathedral, he was crowned king of Italy (Italy here referring to just Lombardy and Emilia Romagna), and appointed his stepson Eugène de Beauharnais as viceroy. Once Napoleon had the iron crown of Lombardy firmly on his head, he set off with his wife, the empress Josephine, on a triumphal tour of his new kingdom. On the evening of 26 June 1805, he arrived in Parma. Two days before his arrival, Bodoni had been called upon by Moreau de Saint-Méry to publish the announcement of Napoleon's visit.[181] It was issued from the newly styled *Imprimerie Imperiale* (the Imperial Press).

IT WAS Napoleon's first visit to Parma, but Josephine's second. In August 1796, she had made a point of visiting Bodoni at his studio where she spent a long time in conversation with him. When she expressed interest in buying the sole remaining copy of the Horace in folio, Bodoni demurred, saying that it cost far too much for a book in which the pages had already been cut and whose binding was mediocre.[182] He persuaded her against the purchase, and she settled for other items.

The emperor and empress entered Parma through the San Lazzaro gate, which had been transformed into an elaborate triumphal arch for the occasion. To the cheers of the crowd, they were formally welcomed and presented with the keys to the city. They then made their way to the Palazzo Sanvitale, which Count Sanvitale had made available for their use. Many other noble families relinquished their homes and provided horses for members of Napoleon's retinue. That evening, the citizens of Parma celebrated the royal visit with theatrical presentations, balls, and free ice cream, all the while hoping for a glimpse of the royal couple. They would be disappointed; Napoleon and Josephine were in bed by ten o'clock.

The following morning, Napoleon rose early and sought out Moreau for a lengthy meeting in which they discussed Parma's finances. The discussion became heated when Napoleon demanded a scrupulous rendering of the city's accounts, which Moreau de Saint-Méry was unable to provide in any detail. This would have unfortunate consequences for the administrator general. After their meeting, Napoleon was introduced to some of the city's dignitaries, but disappointed many others who, despite their lengthy wait, were denied the opportunity to "to humble themselves at the august feet of their most gracious sovereign."[183] In the afternoon, Napoleon made a tour of Parma astride his beautiful Arab horse, a tour which included the Citadella, Parma's impressive fortress. There he was forced to seek shelter from a sudden deluge, and rain continued on and off throughout the rest of the day. Continuing his tour of the city, he eventually arrived in the Imperial (no longer Royal) Gardens, where he was treated to the main event of his visit. Moreau de Saint-Méry had organized a giant fair. In a series of pavilions, young men and women displayed Parma's arts and crafts. They offered Napoleon products from Parma and the surrounding countryside and demonstrated how their inventions worked. The first pavilion proved to be of the greatest interest to the emperor. It was that of the papermakers, the founders of letters, the printers, and the bookbinders.

"Where is Bodoni?" asked Napoleon. Chagrined, Bodoni's apprentices were forced to admit that he was suffering from an attack of gout and unable to rise from his bed. They tried to make up for this by immediately printing a madrigal honoring their undefeated emperor, and presenting him with it. It bore the imprint: *Parma, Nel Giardino Imperiale.*

After his tour of the fair and a brief visit to the military hospital, Napoleon galloped back to the Palazzo Sanvitale for dinner with Josephine. By seven o'clock that evening, after a mere 23 hours in Parma, the imperial couple left for Piacenza, the next stop on their whirlwind tour.

LATER THE SAME YEAR, Bodoni was called upon to issue a proclamation from the Imperial Press in celebration of Napoleon's victory at Austerlitz. He then outshone that publication by impeccably printing in folio at his private press *In celeberrimam Victoriam Austerlitii,* an ode in alcaics by Placido Tadini. He followed this in 1806 with *La Descrizione del Foro Bonaparto* [The Description of the Forum of Bonaparte] in folio, which contained double-page etchings of grandiose, utopian, Doric civic architecture. In this way, Bodoni began to ingratiate himself with the emperor.

Bodoni regarded Napoleon and his family as fine opportunities for advancement. Forget Don Ferdinando! Who was he compared to a first consul who became the emperor of France and king of Italy? It was not long before Bodoni started dedicating important volumes to Napoleon; to Napoleon's stepson and viceroy, Eugène de Beauharnais; to Napoleon's sister, Caroline Murat; and to her husband, the dashing cavalry officer and hot dresser, Joachim Murat, who would shortly become the king of Naples. In turn, they all became ardent admirers and supporters of Bodoni's work. Earlier he had also found favor and friendship with Napoleon's oldest brother, Joseph Bonaparte, then the French ambassador to Parma, and had the pleasure of riding around in a carriage with him and being invited to dine with his family. "Before he left Parma," Bodoni added in a letter to Azara on 8 December 1797, "he gave me a present of fifty bottles of the most exquisite Burgundy."

During the first decade of the nineteenth century, and until the end of his life, Bodoni worked on a grand scale. He was consumed by his ambition to outshine every other printer in Europe. He dedicated himself to that end, and he succeeded. In any spare moment when he was not fulfilling a commission, he was hard at work, desperately trying to finish his gigantic *Manuale tipografico,* that specimen book to end all specimen books. He engraved more and more punches for it, replacing those that had lost their sharpness, and adding new ones in both exotic and Roman faces.

By 1803, he had begun work on the *Iliad* for which he cut a large, new Greek font. Such was Bodoni's concern about the new font that he tried it out ahead of time on a lesser work, the *Homeric Hymn to Demeter.* He worked closely with the *Iliad*'s editor, Luigi Lamberti, the classical scholar, to make sure there were as few errors in the text as humanly possible. He was certainly not going to put himself in a position where he could again be the victim of criticism from the Didots. Making sure the text was correct was extremely exacting, in part because of the number and frequency of diacritical marks in Greek. Lamberti turned out to be even more painstaking than Bodoni and, because of his excruciatingly slow pace, weeks, months, and years passed, and still the *Iliad* was not finished. The typographer became impatient; his customers were annoyed by the wait; and the poet, Ugo Foscolo, immortalized the delay in his biting little epigram:

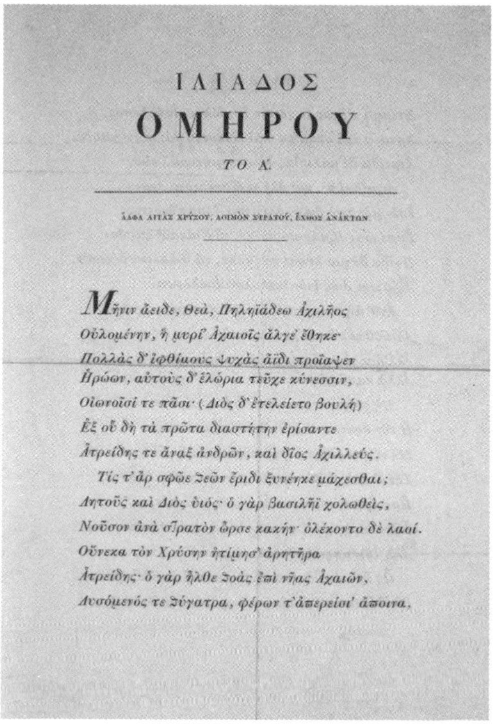

ΙΛΙΑΔΟΣ

ΟΜΗΡΟΥ

ΤΟ Λ.

ΛΔΘΑ ΛΙΤΑΣ ΧΡΥΣΟΥ, ΛΟΙΜΟΝ ΣΤΡΑΤΟΥ, ΕΧΘΟΣ ΑΝΑΚΤΩΝ.

Μῆνιν ἄειδε, Θεὰ, Πηληϊάδεω Ἀχιλῆος
Οὐλομένην, ἣ μυρί᾽ Ἀχαιοῖς ἄλγε᾽ ἔθηκε·
Πολλὰς δ᾽ ἰφθίμους ψυχὰς Ἄϊδι προΐαψεν
Ἡρώων, αὐτοὺς δ᾽ ἑλώρια τεῦχε κύνεσσιν,
Οἰωνοῖσί τε πᾶσι (Διὸς δ᾽ ἐτελείετο βουλή)
Ἐξ οὗ δὴ τὰ πρῶτα διαστήτην ἐρίσαντε
Ἀτρείδης τε ἄναξ ἀνδρῶν, καὶ δῖος Ἀχιλλεύς.

Τίς τ᾽ ἄρ σφωε Θεῶν ἔριδι ξυνέηκε μάχεσθαι;
Λητοῦς καὶ Διὸς υἱός· ὁ γὰρ βασιλῆϊ χολωθεὶς,
Νοῦσον ἀνὰ στρατὸν ὄρσε κακήν· ὀλέκοντο δὲ λαοί.
Οὕνεκα τὸν Χρύσην ἠτίμασ᾽ ἀρητῆρα
Ἀτρείδης· ὁ γὰρ ἦλθε θοὰς ἐπὶ νῆας Ἀχαιῶν,
Λυσόμενός τε θύγατρα, φέρων τ᾽ ἀπερείσι᾽ ἄποινα,

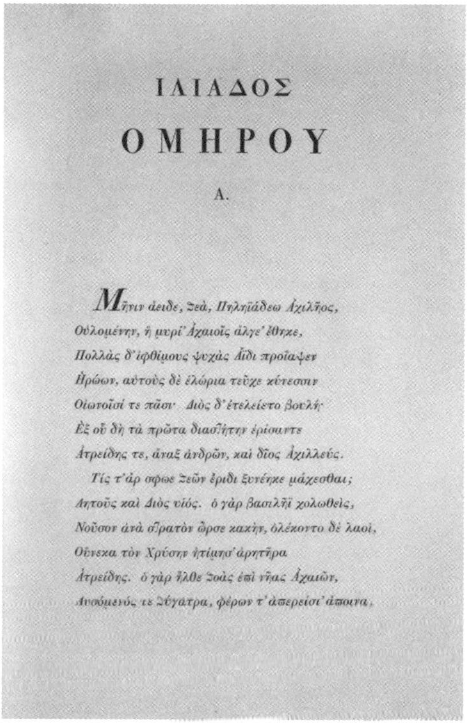

ΙΛΙΑΔΟΣ

ΟΜΗΡΟΥ

Α.

Μῆνιν ἄειδε, Θεὰ, Πηληϊάδεω Ἀχιλῆος,
Οὐλομένην, ἣ μυρί᾽ Ἀχαιοῖς ἄλγε᾽ ἔθηκε,
Πολλὰς δ᾽ ἰφθίμους ψυχὰς Ἄϊδι προΐαψεν
Ἡρώων, αὐτοὺς δὲ ἑλώρια τεῦχε κύνεσσιν
Οἰωνοῖσί τε πᾶσι· Διὸς δ᾽ ἐτελείετο βουλή·
Ἐξ οὗ δὴ τὰ πρῶτα διαστήτην ἐρίσαντε
Ἀτρείδης τε, ἄναξ ἀνδρῶν, καὶ δῖος Ἀχιλλεύς.

Τίς τ᾽ ἄρ σφωε Θεῶν ἔριδι ξυνέηκε μάχεσθαι;
Λητοῦς καὶ Διὸς υἱός. ὁ γὰρ βασιλῆϊ χολωθεὶς,
Νοῦσον ἀνὰ στρατὸν ὄρσε κακήν, ὀλέκοντο δὲ λαοί,
Οὕνεκα τὸν Χρύσην ἠτίμασ᾽ ἀρητῆρα
Ἀτρείδης. ὁ γὰρ ἦλθε θοὰς ἐπὶ νῆας Ἀχαιῶν,
Λυσόμενός τε θύγατρα, φέρων τ᾽ ἀπερείσι᾽ ἄποινα,

Homer, *Iliad*. 1808. Proof of opening page [left] and final printed version.

*C*he fa il Lamberti,
uomo dottissimo?
Stampa un Omero
laboriosissimo.
Commenta? — No.
Traduce. — Oibò.
Dunque che fa?
Le prime prove ripassando va,
Ed ogni mese un foglio dà;
talché in dieci anno la finirà,
se pur Bodoni pria non morrà.
Lavoro eterno!
Paga il Governo.

[What is Lamberti doing,/that most erudite man?/He's publishing a Homer,/very, very slowly./Commentary? No./Translation. No, no./Then what is he doing?/He reviews the first proofs,/and each month he produces one page./In this way, he will finish it in ten years,/if Bodoni doesn't die first./Eternal labor./The Government pays.]

In actual fact, the government did not pay enough. According to Trevisani, most of the costs of the *Iliad* were borne by Bodoni himself and Francesco Melzi d'Eril, at that time vice president of the Italian Republic.[184]

Sensitive as he was to criticism, Bodoni was stung by the poem, and inveighed against Foscolo to Lamberti: "I disregard a certain red-haired *pseudogrecolo* [pseudo Greek geek] and his followers who take a microscope to anatomize our edition; let them stew in their envy, let it gnaw away at them."

Ugo Foscolo (1778-1827).

IT IS NOT SURPRISING that Bodoni undertook the *Iliad* in 1803, for most of his publications that year were of a far less weighty nature, and he needed a challenge. Among other items, his printing included a report to the Society of Medicine in Paris on sinus infections; a letter from Margherita Bodoni to the Accademia Filopatridi, thanking the Academy for admitting her as its first female member; a 46-page booklet about the astronomical events of 1803; a prospectus for geometry and trigonometry exams (one of the few Bodoni publications to contain mathematical symbols); a sixteen-page epigram in praise of Angelica Kauffmann, the famous Swiss-Austrian painter whom Bodoni probably knew during his years in Rome; a catalog of his own work with prices; *Vert-Vert ossia il Pappagallo,* a 65-page poem about a parrot, which he dedicated to Caroline Bonaparte Murat; and a reprint in octavo of Moreau de Saint-Méry's book, *De la Danse,* a history of dance in the West Indies. Azara had complained, with good reason, that the 1801 decimo-sexto edition of this book was impossible to read without glasses as the print was so small.

In 1804, Bodoni published *Annali di C. Cornelio Tacito* [The Annals of Tacitus] in Latin and Italian; it was his first book expressly dedicated to Napoleon. Apart from the *Tacito,* 1804 was a year devoted to grinding out French regulations and proclamations, and of course, sonnets. (In his compendium of Bodoni's works, Brooks lists a staggering 154 sonnets; even this figure is probably too low because of the ephemeral nature of single sheets.) However, behind the façade of all this tedious work, Bodoni was working fanatically on the *Iliad,* the *Manuale tipografico,* and a formidable new endeavor.

Two months before Napoleon's arrival in Parma, Pope Pius VII visited the city and made a point of meeting Bodoni. He had a scheme in mind. He described to Bodoni his meeting with Jean-Joseph Marcel, the young director of the Imperial Press in Paris, who had presented him with his *Oratio Dominica,* a volume containing the Lord's Prayer printed in 150 languages. The Pope then challenged Bodoni to surpass the Frenchman in clarity and quantity. It was the perfect opportunity for Bodoni to show off his skills. It would also be extremely useful to him; he could tie in this effort with his *Manuale tipografico* by using type he had already in hand, as well as creating new type for the new book, which he could in turn use in the *Manuale.* He set to work.

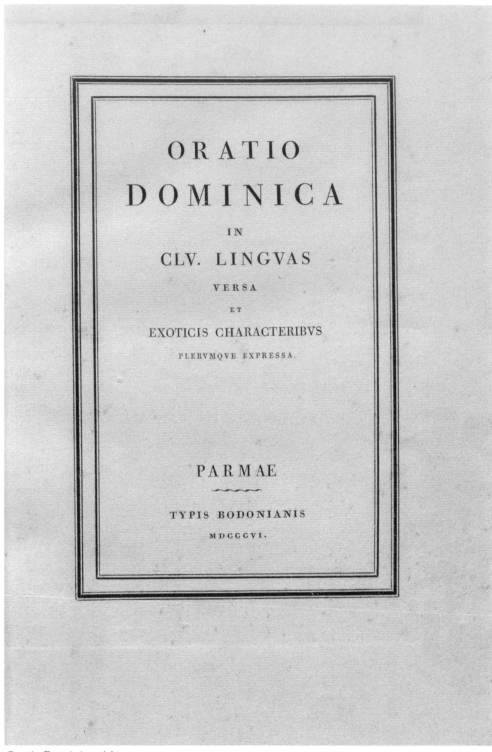

ORATIO
DOMINICA

IN

CLV. LINGVAS

VERSA

ET

EXOTICIS CHARACTERIBVS

PLERVMQVE EXPRESSA.

PARMAE

~~~

TYPIS BODONIANIS

MDCCCVI.

Oratio Dominica, title page.

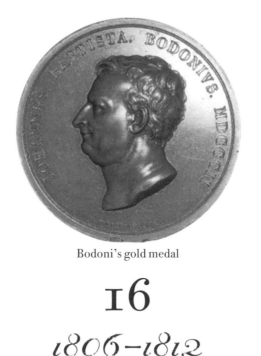

Bodoni's gold medal

16

1806–1812

May this charming old man long live to do honour to his art!

KARL MORGENSTERN

THE POLITICAL situation in Parma remained relatively stable under the stewardship of Moreau de Saint-Méry. He was even able to reintroduce some of Du Tillot's reforms. Among other initiatives, he abolished discrimination against the Jews; abolished torture as a means of proving guilt; promoted the Academy of Medicine; and enforced the Napoleonic Code. He was admired by the people of Parma and greatly liked by Bodoni, but incapable of rendering the city's all-important financial statistics to Napoleon. The beginning of 1806 was a time of colossal upheaval in Parma. Napoleon struck the first hammer blow. Aware of uprisings against him in the Apennines outside Parma because of conscription, he decided to crush the rebellion decisively. He appointed General Jean-Andoche Junot for the purpose. "This general appeared like a comet announcing calamity," wrote De Lama of Junot.[185] With his troops, the general mercilessly slaughtered hundreds of rebels and made a spectacle of their bloody bodies to intimidate the people of Parma lest they, too, dare consider rebelling. Napoleon then named Junot governor general of the Parmesan States. On 28 January, Moreau de Saint-Méry was summarily stripped of his position and pension and recalled to Paris, a grievous loss for Bodoni. Poor Moreau was overcome with sorrow and wrote Bodoni a series of desperate letters about his situation.

General Jean-Andoche Junot (1771-1813).

THEN NATURE struck a blow: on 7 February, Parma was shaken by a tremendous earthquake, which reverberated in Guastalla five days later. Bodoni must have felt as though his entire world were being shaken apart. But did he fall from favor? Certainly not. Fierce Junot took a liking to him and made him one of three deputy mayors of Parma. A great admirer of Bodoni's work, Junot advised him to enter some publications in a contest at the huge national exposition to be held in Paris that May. Not unsurprisingly, Bodoni refused to put his head into that particular French noose. Junot persisted and, not unsurprisingly, prevailed. After much deliberation, Bodoni chose fourteen of his most elegant publications and shipped them to Paris. He won the gold medal. "Signor Bodoni of Parma," wrote the jury, "is one of those men who have contributed most to the progress of typography in the eighteenth century and in our time. He unites numerous talents which are usually found separate, and for each of them he merits the first prize . . . It is worth noting that he has executed all his work in a country where he is alone, left to his own devices. The jury is happy to have the occasion to express its esteem for the talent of this celebrated man, and assign him the gold medal." How this prize and this praise must have delighted Bodoni. This was the first time a competitor from south of the Alps had ever prevailed in the contest. One cannot help wondering what the Didots' reaction was to Bodoni's winning this prestigious French award.

BY 1806, Bodoni had fulfilled the pope's challenge and published his own *Oratio Dominica,* with a dedication to Viceroy Eugène de Beauharnais and his wife, Amalia of Bavaria. It contained the Lord's Prayer in 155 languages. He had bested Marcel. He had created 97 different exotic alphabets, 13 of which did not appear in the Frenchman's book. The remaining pages were printed in Roman type of differing sizes, and 23 were in italics.[186] One of the most interesting pages is that containing the Lord's Prayer in Chinese. For this, Bodoni reverted to his earliest form of printing. He engraved the characters (based on Didot's) in wood. They are exceptionally clean and square and clear.

Not only was the *Oratio Dominica* a book of extraordinary beauty, it was in essence yet another specimen book, with every page containing the Lord's Prayer in a different language, each entry held within a simple rectangular frame. It thus became, in the words of Corrado Mingardi, "... a solemn but not grandiloquent song that from page to page makes an immense polyphony of language and form."[187] (Here again is a musical metaphor in relation to printing.) The viceroy was so pleased with it that he wrote to Napoleon on 12 July 1806: "Bodoni is in Milan right now; he came here to present me with the polyglot *Oratio Dominica*. This is a superb edition, and I must tell Your Majesty that it is much superior to the polyglot edition of the same work put out by Signor Marcel in Paris."[188]

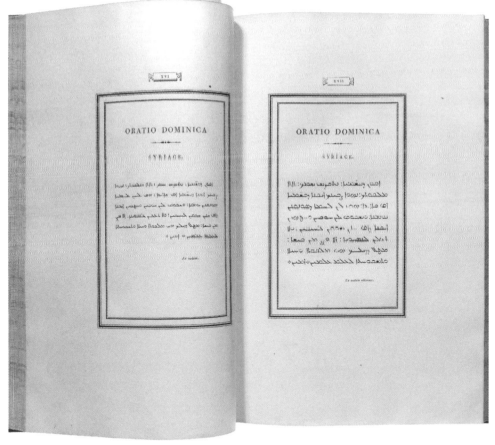

Oratio Dominica, the Lord's Prayer in Syriac.

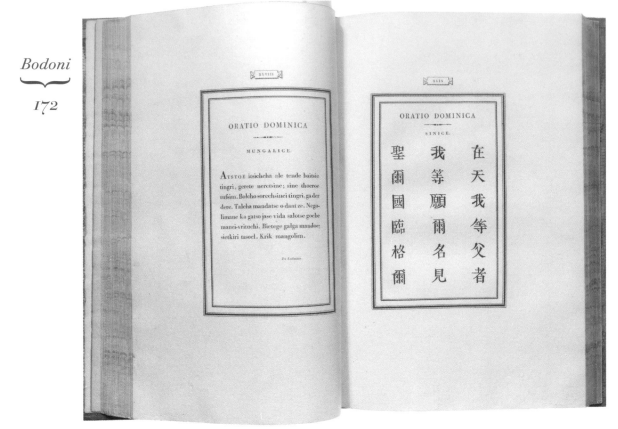

Oratio Dominica, Chinese.

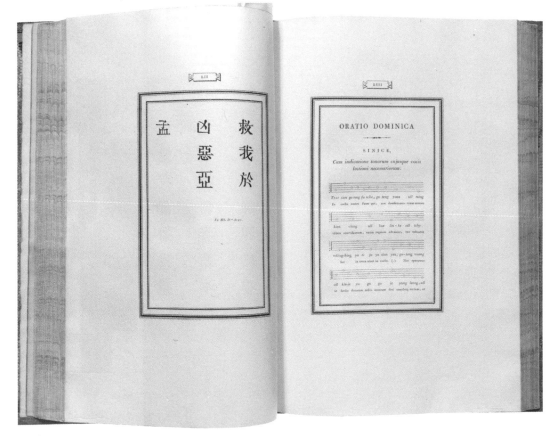

Oratio Dominica, Chinese with chanting tones.

LATER IN THE SAME LETTER the viceroy mentioned another masterwork (Plate 27). This was the epic lyric, *Il Bardo della Selva Nera* [The Bard of the Black Forest] by the Neoclassical poet Vincenzo Monti, an ardent admirer of Napoleon. Bodoni decorated the book with seven headpieces, used previously in the *Epithalamia,* and seven initial capitals, and dedicated it to the emperor. "I informed Signor Bodoni," wrote the viceroy, "that Your Majesty was very satisfied with the beauty of the characters he used for the edition of Monti's poem. He replied that nothing could be more beautiful than publishing a work consecrated to celebrating Your Majesty's achievements." The viceroy was so delighted with his own copy of *Il Bardo* that he gave Bodoni a gold box encrusted with jewels, and invited him and Ghitta for lunch at the palace at Monza. After the meal, the vicereine presented Ghitta with a very valuable pair of diamond and pearl earrings, and the Bodonis were invited for a return visit in the autumn.[189]

Monti, too, wrote to Bodoni, on 11 June saying: "Everyone has hurled themselves avidly on your beautiful edition, and have exclaimed with one voice that they have never seen anything more perfect and magnificent. Méjan himself and other Frenchmen have had to admit that this book alone is enough to position you above any rival."

Bodoni himself was overjoyed with the book. It displayed to advantage his wide range of exotic type, and was a volume he was proud to present to people in power. Napoleon's new prefect in Parma, Henri Dupont-Delporte, was one such lucky recipient. On New Year's Eve in 1810, Bodoni sent him a copy of the *Oratio Dominica,* along with the following letter written in elegant French:

Monsieur le Baron Préfet

If instead of beginning the year on the first of January, that is to say, at the moment when all nature bears the imprint of sadness and grieving, we began it as the astronomers do at the return of spring, or as the Hebrews do when the countryside covers itself with the gifts of Pomona and Bacchus, I could, Monsieur le Baron, again regale you in person with my wishes for your happiness and prosperity, but winter never fails to bring on the gout which forces me to stay in bed in my room . . . [I am] therefore compelled let you know how sorry I am not to be able to present myself in person at your residence along with my colleagues from the town council.

[Instead] . . . I flatter myself, Monsieur le Baron, that you will . . . accept a new year's gift from my vineyard, one of my editions that contains in 155 different languages the prayer that good Christians say every day to the Eternal, a gift which expresses in so many ways the sentiments of esteem and attachment you have inspired in me.

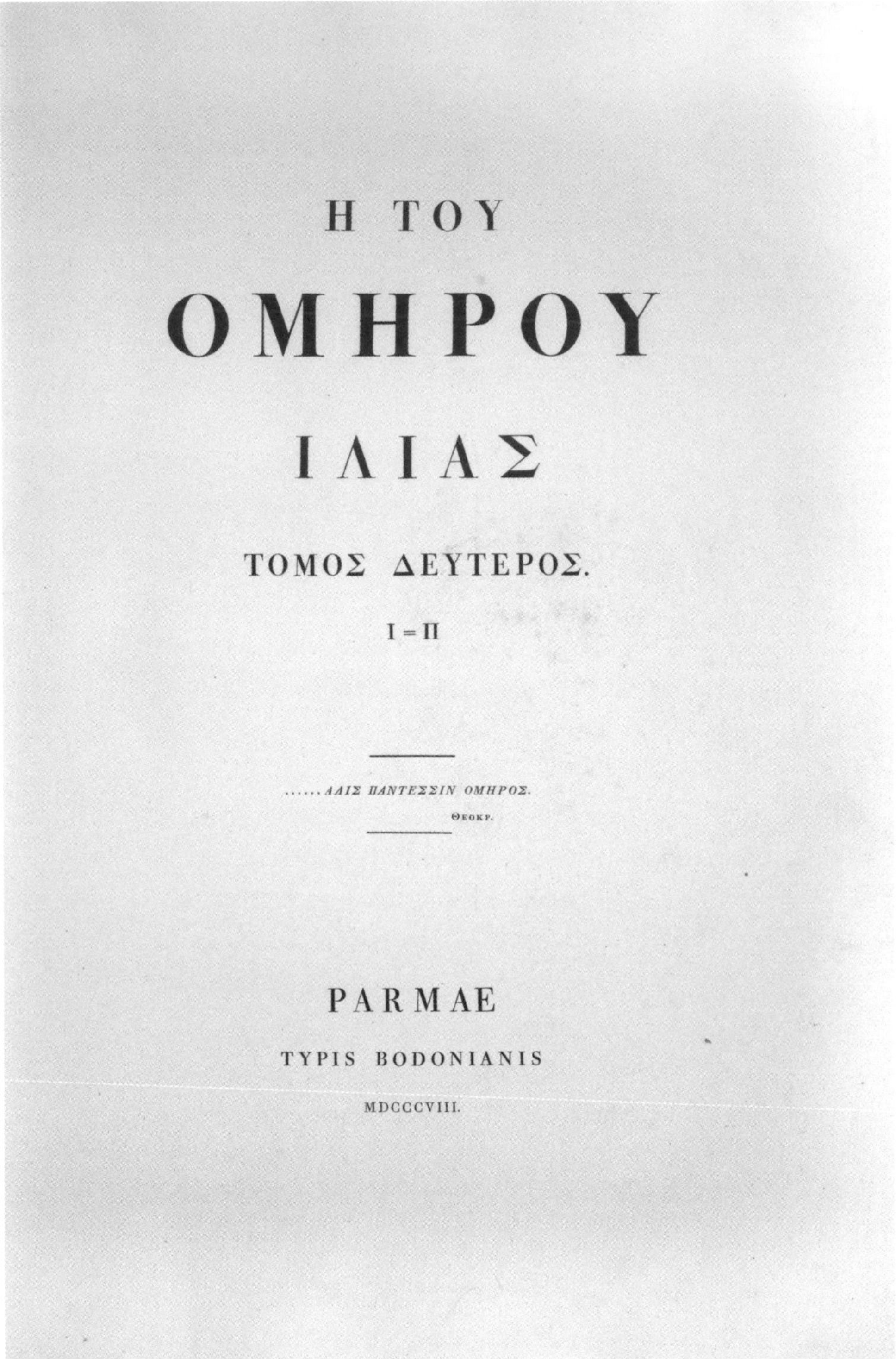

Η ΤΟΥ

ΟΜΗΡΟΥ

ΙΛΙΑΣ

ΤΟΜΟΣ ΔΕΥΤΕΡΟΣ.

Ι = Π

―――――

.... *ΛΛΙΣ ΠΑΝΤΕΣΣΙΝ ΟΜΗΡΟΣ.*
ΘΕΟΚΡ.

―――――

PARMAE

TYPIS BODONIANIS

MDCCCVIII.

Homer, *Iliad.* 1808. Title page.

My little wife, who shares all my feelings, does not wish to be left out and would like to present the Description of the room of Correggio [Pitture di Antonio Allegri detto il Correggio esistenti nel Monistero di San Paolo] *as a new year's gift to Madame la Baronne . . . Can you see, Monsieur le Baron Préfet, in these offerings a new testimony of the respectful sentiments that we both wish you, as well as Madame la Baronne!*

Jean Baptiste Bodoni[190]

Rewards for Bodoni's accomplishments flowed in. Napoleon's family rewarded him materially. In 1808, Viceroy Eugène turned his admiration into gold — a gift of gold coins in a "stupendous tobacco box," which featured the viceroy's portrait inside the lid, surrounded by diamonds. For good measure, he threw in an annual pension, which would revert to Bodoni's wife if he predeceased her. Murat, Napoleon's brother-in-law and now the king of Naples, also awarded Bodoni a pension, and tried once again to woo him to Naples, saying, *"Venez, bon papa, venez; à Naples tout le monde se porte bien; on n'y meurt jamais."* ["Come, dear Papa, come to Naples where everyone is fit and no one ever dies."][191] Pope Pius VII himself, in gratitude to Bodoni for sending Roman and italic matrices for four typefaces to the Propaganda Fide, rewarded him with a mosaic of the "almost living and breathing" *Ecce Homo* by Guido Reni. Bodoni hung the mosaic in the principal room of his apartment so that he could see it each time he passed from his studio to the press.

Even in Parma, Bodoni's accomplishments were being honored in significant ways; Prefect Nardon made sure that Bodoni, elevated to the rank of *Sommo Artista* [Supreme Artist], was exempted from paying taxes and given permission to visit the Camera di San Paolo any time he wished. And finally, the people of Parma acknowledged Bodoni as one of their own by awarding him a long overdue gold medal of honor and lavish paeans of praise.

The *Iliad* was eventually published in three volumes in 1808. It was 779 pages long; 120 copies were printed on paper from Miliani, thirty were printed on French *carta imperiale velina*, eighteen on French *carta velina*, and two copies, one that went to Napoleon and the other to Viceroy Eugène, were on Bavarian vellum. Because of the size of the pages, each page of the two vellum copies required its own sheep skin — for a total of 1,558 sheep! The first volume bore a dedication from Bodoni to Napoleon in Italian, French, and Latin, and Lamberti provided a preface addressed to Homeric scholars. In his *Edizione Bodoniae,* Brooks calls it "a superb edition and one of the most beautiful books ever printed in Italy or anywhere else."[192]

Even after its publication, the delays continued. The official presentation of the copy dedicated to Napoleon was delayed because the emperor was engaged in wars: the brutal Peninsular War and the War of the Fifth Coalition. These wars also impeded the distribution of the paper copies and prevented sales, thus embittering Bodoni, for whom the costs involved in producing such a book were

tremendous. It was in this hiatus between printing and distribution, probably in 1809, that Bodoni received a visit from the eminent philologist Karl Morgenstern (coiner of the word *Bildungsroman*). Morgenstern's account of his visit throws a bright light on the Bodoni establishment.[193]

Karl Morgenstern (1770-1852).

Professor Morgenstern ended a day of sightseeing in Parma by showing up at the Bodonis' door in the early evening, without an introduction. When Dalmastro ushered him in, he asked that he be announced simply as a stranger. Dalmastro led him to an antechamber where Morgenstern had time to admire "a piece of mosaic (a valuable copy of Corregio's [sic] 'Madonna and St Jeremy'), several excellent old portraits, in oil, of Dante, Petrarch, &c." Ghitta then appeared and escorted him to Bodoni's studio. Morgenstern continues: "She is apparently some forty years of age; but he is about seventy, though still a robust and dignified man. He has been deaf for many years past, and his wife, therefore, officiated at first as our interpreter. He was engaged at the time in carving types for his *Manuel Typographique,* and continued at his work; for his house being spacious, open, and lofty, was illuminated for some ten minutes after my entrance by the declining light." Bodoni was never one to waste precious sunlight, but while he worked, he kept Morgenstern entertained by having Ghitta show him the *Oratio Dominica.* Once the sun had set, Bodoni joined them at a large table, produced the copy of the *Iliad* intended for Napoleon and insisted that Morgenstern read the dedication to the emperor. Morgenstern then describes the *Iliad* as being ". . . wrought with great vigour . . . Bodoni's Iliad is far superior in typographical beauty to any other Greek edition that has come under my observation."

As if this were not enough, Bodoni then produced what had been printed so far of the *Manuale tipografico.* Morgenstern was stunned by what he saw: ". . . one hundred and forty specimens of *Latin* characters alone; an astonishing number when compared with what others of the most distinguished founders and printers have produced." He particularly admired the variety of Greek and Russian characters, ". . . but the German department offered me less satisfaction as he might easily have given more copious as well as more beautiful specimens."

While Bodoni continued to bring out volume after volume for appraisal, Morgenstern, the consummate critic, was quick to perceive what Azara had so often complained about, noting, "It cannot be denied, that one consequence of his extreme readiness to oblige, when induced by motives of private intimacy, has been that his extraordinary talent has been sometimes abused in the printing of works of inferior moment." Morgenstern also recognized that while the ". . . accuracy of the text may seldom be such as to satisfy the German philologist, this defect, however, ought to be attributed much less to himself than to his country, which at the present day could not easily produce a philological critic who would rank higher than a supervisor or assistant to Bodoni."

In a description that is firsthand and unbiased, Morgenstern describes the man he met. He calls Bodoni ". . . a vehement old man, still full of vigours, and incessantly intent upon bringing to perfection that art which he has already carried so far. He is fond of fame, in its ancient acceptation, and possesses an abundant share of self-esteem and dignified pride, though at the same time he is plain, ingenuous, and communicative. He contributes in various ways to exalt the celebrity of Parma . . . With all this, he is what good men always are, grateful . . . I spent a full three hours under his roof, and we parted as if we had been old acquaintances. It was only when we bade each other adieu, after he had feasted the stranger's eye with so many delicious treats, and for so long a space of time, during which he abstained in the true Homeric style from interrupting that stranger, by asking him: 'Who are ye?' and 'Whence come you?' that he put any questions to me, and at last requested that I would write down my address for him by way of remembrance. May this charming old man long live to do honour to his art . . . !"

IT WAS NOT until 21 January 1810 that Lamberti was able to travel to Saint Cloud to deliver the *Iliad* to the emperor. Bodoni could not go himself because he had again been stricken with gout and was not fit enough to make the journey. Napoleon was so delighted with the gift that he ordered it displayed in a special place in his private library. (It is now one of the great treasures of the Bibliothèque Nationale in Paris.) Within a few days of its delivery, Lamberti was amply rewarded by Napoleon for his work on the edition, but Bodoni received no acknowledgement for the part he had played. He must have been greatly disappointed, but finally on 6 July, over six months later, he received his reward. It was worth waiting for: a pension for life, a munificent testimony, and a request that he follow the *Iliad* with the publication of the *Odyssey.* This last was an offer that Bodoni found he *could* refuse; by 1810 his life had been almost completely taken over by the *Manuale tipografico.* He did, however, find time that year to publish a less demanding work, which he dedicated to Joseph Bonaparte. This was the poem by Gioachino Ponta, *Il Trionfo della Vaccinia,* a celebration of the success of smallpox vaccination and a paean to Edward Jenner, written in 104 eight-line rhyming verses in six cantos, which takes on the entire history of smallpox and Jenner's discovery of the vaccine.

The same year, Napoleon made a move that would reverberate in Parma. He divorced his wife, Josephine, who had been unable to provide him with an heir, and organized a political marriage for himself, one that would ground his empire more firmly and offer him the potential for descendants. He chose Archduchess Marie Louise of Austria as his second wife. He was 39 and she was 18. Marie Louise had been brought up to hate the French, so an unhappy marriage seemed almost inevitable. But, as it happened, Marie Louise was strangely charmed by the emperor and, for his part, Napoleon was captivated by the young woman for whom the adjective "luscious" seems to have been expressly invented. They were married by proxy in Vienna on 11 March 1810, and Marie Louise suddenly found herself empress of France and queen of Italy. Then she set off in procession for Paris, and Napoleon met her en route at Compiègne on 27 March. They were married in a civil ceremony at Saint Cloud on 1 April, prior to a religious ceremony at the Tuileries later the same day. Their bridal march was composed by Ferdinando Paër, the young composer who appears sitting next to Margherita Bodoni in *Conversazione in Casa Bodoni.* (See front endpaper.)

The king of Rome asleep.

Napoleon had his wish. A year later, Marie Louise gave birth to a son, Napoleon II, who was given the title "king of Rome."

In celebration of the boy's birth, Bodoni published the *Cimelio tipografico-pittorico offerto agli Augustissimi genitori del Re di Roma.* [A typographic-pictorial heirloom offered to the most August parents of the King of Rome.] Napoleon esteemed this work so much that on 28 March 1812 he made Bodoni a knight of the Imperial Order of the Reunion and rewarded him materially. Bodoni could now be addressed as *Cavaliere Bodoni*, an honorific that must have pleased him enormously.

Bodoni published *Le Songe de Poliphile* [The Dream of Polyphilus] in 1811, and dedicated it to another member of the Bonaparte family, this time to his longtime admirer, Napoleon's sister, Caroline Murat. That same year, Bodoni struck a deal with her husband, now styled the king of Two Sicilies, to publish a series of French classics to be used as edifying material for the education of their son, Napoleon Achille. In 1812, Bodoni issued the first of these works, Fénelon's *Les Aventures de Télémaque*, the same work used by Maria Theresa of Austria so many years ago to edify her children, including Maria Amalia, duchess of Parma, and Marie Antoinette, queen of France. Bodoni himself considered the printing of this book to be first among his works.[194]

Cimelio . . . Title page

Parma cathedral by moonlight.

17

Il Bajon

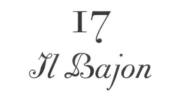

Oh giorno, funestissimo giorno, in cui suonò . . . e diffuse per la città lo squallore quella terribile voce: Bodoni muore: Bodoni è morto!
[Oh dire day! in which rings out . . . and spreads throughout the city the bleakness of that terrible cry: Bodoni dies: Bodoni is dead!]

VINCENZO JACOBACCI

I N 1285, the citizens of Parma raised funds for the creation of a bell that could be heard as far away as Reggio Emilia, 26 kilometers distant. The first bell to be cast was not up to the challenge. A second bell, very beautiful, also failed the test, but in 1287, a third bell, Il Bajon, was struck, and this time the citizens were satisfied. (It is unclear, however, whether it actually made itself heard in Reggio Emilia.) Because of its enormous size, it was subject to rupture, and has been recast seven times since 1287. Strict regulations dictated that Il Bajon, the largest of the six bells in the cathedral tower, would only toll for the deaths of heads of state or members of Parma's most illustrious families. When the populace awoke on 30 November 1813 and heard the great bell tolling, it was clear that someone very important had died.

How Bodoni managed to keep producing work of the highest quality despite his infirmities is nothing short of a miracle. By the beginning of 1812, his gout had progressed so far that it included not only his feet and legs but his arms, and it confined him to bed for two months. Assailed by a nagging cough and frustrated by pain-enforced inactivity, he persisted in examining proofs when he felt well enough to sit up in bed and to point out to an assistant those places where a letter was imperfect or out of line, or where there was a slight smudge — the kinds of flaws that were often invisible to less expert eyes.

In February 1813, Bodoni and Ghitta celebrated their birthdays; Bodoni was 73 and Ghitta was 55. Giuseppe De Lama, who had written a celebratory poem for Ghitta's birthday in 1808, wrote a second in 1813. The first is succinct and charming. It translates as: *"The flower whose name you bear, sweet flower, spring flower of the meadows embellishes the lawn. Her freshness is fleeting; but you, Cloris, are certain to please because of your spirit and your reason, and will always be in season."* In the second poem, De Lama wonders what to give her for her birthday, reflecting that a poor poet cannot afford the baubles that her husband likes to shower upon her. Instead he offers best wishes and verses to celebrate their friendship. Did Bodoni rise from his bed to design the page and print it for her, decorating it with a perfectly wonderful frame? Or did Ghitta see to its printing so that she could give it in turn to Bodoni for his birthday as a demonstration of her developing skills?

In March 1813, De Lama reports that Bodoni came down with a bladder infection so severe that it required medical intervention.[195] The next day, his eyes were full of terror and sadness at the idea that he might be unable to finish the *Manuale tipografico*, but Ghitta and his friends, with their prayers and encouragement, calmed his panic and pulled him back from the brink. Three days later, he rose from bed and started to work, retouching the capital letters for the *Manuale*. He would remain housebound from then on, working ever more feverishly, trying to bring to perfection the huge number of punches and matrices he envisioned using for the *Manuale*. Ghitta tried to persuade him to moderate his efforts, to take a break now and then, but the closer he came to death, the more frantically he worked. One night, exhausted but sleepless, he quietly crept out of bed so as

De Lama's 1808 birthday poem for Ghitta.

De Lama's 1813 birthday poem for Ghitta.

not to disturb Ghitta and went to his desk where he put the final touches on his will. He named his best friends, Giuseppe De Lama, Vincenzo Jacobacci, and Gaetano Ziliani as his executors. (These are the three men appearing on his left in *Conversazione*.)

Ten years previously, Bodoni had importuned Moreau de Saint-Méry to allow him to deviate from the statutes of inheritance in Parma, which then insisted that a widow could only inherit 100 lire from her husband. Bodoni was determined that Ghitta be well-provided for after he died, and Moreau was able to change the statutes, to the benefit of Ghitta and those who followed her. In his final midnight will, Bodoni left everything to her, thus ensuring that she could, at least financially, complete the *Manuale tipografico*, should he die before accomplishing the task himself.

On 17 November 1813, Bodoni seemed to be doing well. In a letter to an unnamed "Dear Friend," he wrote: "My health is good, and I find myself at last liberated from the insults of my untreatable gout; it was relieved at the suggestion of a Piemontese whose gouty father has been perfectly cured for more than eight years. It is a gentle remedy with which I can experiment without fear since it consists of a pad of the finest wool, which is held on the legs and thighs. My Ghitta salutes you cordially . . ."[196] However, on 19 November, he came to the dinner table utterly exhausted, and turned his food away in disgust, saying, "My Ghitta, I am not hungry; I don't feel like chatting. Why should I sit here? Let me go, I beg you. I have something pressing to finish."[197] It was his last meal. The following day, he tried to get up, in vain. His cough worsened, then suddenly ceased. He became thirsty, breathless, and feverish, displaying the symptoms of pneumonia. Ghitta's relative, Dr. Berchet della Trombara (who had been one of Don Ferdinando's physicians) was summoned, but neither his skill nor Ghitta's careful nursing could stay the relentless progress of Bodoni's illness. His fever continued to rise, and his friends gathered around his bedside for the long vigil. While he could still speak, he de-

Bodoni's memorial plaque in the cathedral, with Comolli's bust of him above, and the memorial plaque to Margherita Dall'Aglio Bodoni below.

clared to the grieving crowd that he was dying in the faith of his fathers. On 30 November 1813, eleven days after his final meal, Bodoni received the last rites. At half past seven that morning, he breathed his last.[198]

Il Bajon tolled for twenty minutes early that morning, and repeated this tolling four more times during the day. The bell sounded again two days later, on 2 December, to signify Bodoni's funeral. In his will, he, like Dickens, had stipulated a simple ceremony like those for the poor, but the people's determination to acknowledge the life and work of its most famous citizen overruled his wishes. The municipality ordained that a solemn funeral be celebrated in the cathedral so that the entire city could attend. Unwilling to cede organization of the funeral to others, Ghitta took charge and spared no expense in its execution. She arranged for the cathedral to be dressed in mourning, with the funeral altar set up at one end of the central nave, and a large, stepped catafalque at the other. Bodoni's coffin, decorated with the symbols of typography and the decorations he had received, rested on top of the catafalque. Inside the coffin, De Lama placed a lead tube containing a document extolling the typographer's virtues. On the four sides of the catafalque, inscriptions hung down, lauding Bodoni's achievements.[199]

Ghitta then ordered an extremely large memorial plaque surmounted by a marble bust of her husband, sculpted by Gian Battista Comolli, to be installed in the cathedral, where Bodoni's body was laid to rest. (The bust is said to be an excellent likeness.)

She also ordered a smaller plaque, this one to be placed in Bodoni's parish church of San Bartolomeo, where his heart and viscera were interred. As if this were not enough, she tried to hire Canova to sculpt a bust of Bodoni to be placed in the Pantheon in Rome. Canova was occupied with other commissions but supervised the sculpting done by Antonio d'Este, one of his students, and the bust took its place in the Pantheon in the company of other famous Italians.

The cathedral was thronged for the service. Rich and poor, nobles and peasants, old and young, soldiers, clerics, scholars, artists, poets, and government officials all bowed their heads and prayed for the soul of the man who had brought lasting glory to their city. Vincenzo Jacobacci gave a heart-rending eulogy, which brought the entire congregation to tears. He reminded everyone how Bodoni had been a rare friend, a tender husband, a faithful citizen, a true Christian, the donor of beautiful gifts, and a generous host. He spoke of Bodoni's genius and the kindness of his heart, and he conjured up his spacious brow, his vivacious eyes, his deep voice, and that majestic face so loved by portrait painters. He recalled Bodoni's brilliant, erudite conversation, his prodigious memory, and his ability to lift the spirits and calm the fears of his friends. He concluded by crying out, "Oh Bodoni! You are dead. Ministers, let loose the funeral hymn, and beg the Lord of mercy to grant him peace and rest."[200]

Handwritten layout for typographic treatment in imitation of a Bodoni typeface.

18

La Vedova

La sua determinazione di . . . spingere al di là del sepolcro.
[Her determination to push beyond the grave.]

FRIEDRICH SCHÜRER

IN 1800, when Bodoni was 60 years old and his reputation as the prince of typographers was well established, the precocious young artist Giuseppe Bossi (1777-1815) produced an extraordinary watercolor, *Apoteosi di Bodoni* [The Apostheosis of Bodoni], in which an angel crowns Bodoni with a laurel wreath. Bodoni, in profile, garbed in a toga, rests his left hand rather casually on a plinth. Athena, on top of the plinth, surveys the scene, accompanied by her owl, and wearing her ferocious helmet while holding her spear point down. In the remaining two-thirds of the image, the great classical writers — among them Dante, Petrarch, and Homer — stand, sit, or hover over a large volume. On a hill in the distance, Apollo sits with his lyre, while a small group waits for Bodoni to arrive. Dawn is breaking. In visual terms, Bodoni was already on his way to immortality.

In 1814, remembering the tribute paid to her husband, Ghitta hired the same Giuseppe Bossi to paint her portrait. It shows her wearing the black clothes and dismal expression of the widow *[la vedova]*. Even so, he has managed to portray

Apotheosis of Bodoni.

an attractive woman, whose off-the-shoulder satin dress displays to advantage a creamy neck and shoulders. Her 54-year-old face shows no sign of wrinkles, although she has a small scar just below her lower lip. Her black hair, in ringlets, is parted in the middle; a close look at the parting reveals that her hair may be dyed. On a high bun at the back of her head she wears a coronet; round her neck hang two thick gold chains from which a large diamond cross is suspended. She wears one long gold earring with a ruby at its center. Bossi may not have been able to see the second earring from the angle at which he was painting, or he may have scrubbed it out; there is a pale patch on the canvas where it should have been. It is possible that Ghitta had him do away with the second earring as a symbol representing her solitary status.

As she grieved, she may have turned to writing poetry again. An undated, handwritten poem, reminiscent of Catullus's farewell to his brother, lurks in the Houghton Library at Harvard in a scrapbook of Bodoni miscellany assembled by H.C. Brooks. The frame is typical of Bodoni's decorated frames from his late period, and the poem itself sounds like a farewell from Ghitta to her dear husband.

Tu pur chiudesti que penetranti occhi,
Chiudesti ahi! La melliflua tua bocca
Cimè per sempre: il mio dolor trabocca:
Piu no sarà ch'amico ugual io adocchi.

[You have closed your penetrating eyes,
Closed alas! Your mellifluous mouth.
Alas, forever. My overflowing grief:
I will never set my eyes on such a friend again.][201]

The weight of Bodoni's legacy fell on his wife. Her first duty was to inform his friends and customers all over Europe about his death. She printed death notices in Italian and French, and in a letter of 4 December asked Rosaspina to help her disseminate them.

Oh! how you will grieve to hear that our Bodoni is no longer! His soul went to the Creator, furnished with spiritual comforts, at seven thirty on the morning of Tuesday the 30th of this month. He leaves me drowning in sorrow, the most inconsolable of women. Peace be to his spirit that, without doubt, will soon take place among the elect spirits that in heaven enjoy recompense for their outstanding virtue . . . I beg you, oh warmest friend of my late husband, to distribute this letter to your brother typographers, and to the members of the Institute and the Academy, and others."

One of the most touching letters of condolence came from Moreau de Saint-Méry in Paris, to whom she had written personally about Bodoni's death. His letter of 7 January 1814 expressed his great sorrow at the loss of his dear friend,

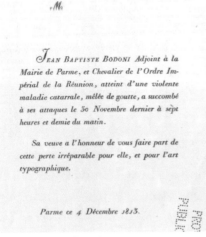

Jean Baptiste Bodoni Adjoint à la Mairie de Parme, et Chevalier de l'Ordre Impérial de la Réunion, atteint d'une violente maladie catarrale, mélée de goutte, a succombé à ses attaques le 30 Novembre dernier à sept heures et demie du matin.

Sa veuve a l'honneur de vous faire part de cette perte irréparable pour elle, et pour l'art typographique.

Parme ce 4 Décembre 1813.

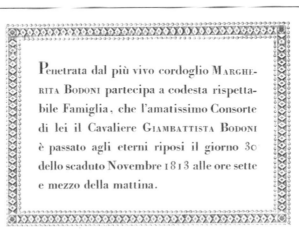

Penetrata dal più vivo cordoglio MARGHE-
RITA BODONI partecipa a codesta rispetta-
bile Famiglia, che l'amatissimo Consorte
di lei il Cavaliere GIAMBATTISTA BODONI
è passato agli eterni riposi il giorno 30
dello scaduto Novembre 1813 alle ore sette
e mezzo della mattina.

Death notice in French.

Death notice in Italian.

and begged Ghitta to send him something that had belonged to her husband, a token that would remind him of Bodoni every day. Although he owned a drawing his daughter had made of Bodoni, Moreau wanted "an affectionate bagatelle," created by Bodoni's own hand, claiming the gift would console his heart. He told her that he also found consolation in the news that Bodoni had assured Ghitta of an "independent fortune."

In the midst of all the letters of condolence, she received a particularly distressing message on another subject, written on 16 December 1813, just two weeks after her husband's death. It came from Nicolò Pedemonte, who informed her that her soldier nephew, Francesco Dall'Aglio, had arrived at the military depot in Metz, in eastern France, having been grievously wounded in battle. Pedemonte begged Ghitta to inform Francesco's relatives about his state, asking them not to forget him in his misery, and to send the fastest possible succor.

THE WIDOW BEGAN overseeing all the major changes at the printing house. Giuseppe Paganino became the director of the imperial press; meanwhile she took over the reins of the private press with Luigi Orsi, Bodoni's foreman, at her side. She thus became the newest arrival in a long line of women printers.

The nuns of the convent of San Jacopo di Ripoli in Florence were the first women on the moveable type printing scene. Active between 1476 and 1484, they were responsible for printing, among other books, the first complete edition of Plato's works. Then, in Venice, Hélizabeth de Rusconibus, a widow like Ghitta, published several works in the early 1500s, including Ovid's *Metamorphoses*. But it was in Paris that widow printers, hanging on to their share of their husbands' estates, really made their mark, usually marrying other printers to strengthen their businesses. Charlotte Guillard (died 1557), the widow of not one but two printers, was perhaps the most famous of all. She was stunningly competent, and her work was valued for its accuracy not just in France but in Italy too; the bishop of Verona chose her above all others as his special publisher.

In America, the first woman printer was Elizabeth Glover, whose husband had died on the long voyage from England. She inherited his press and the tools of his trade, and set up the successful Cambridge Press in Massachusetts in 1638. However, it was Bodoni's fan, Benjamin Franklin, who championed printing as a suitable occupation for women, using his sister-in-law Ann Franklin as a fine example. Widowed in 1735, Ann took over her husband's business, and ran it so competently and profitably that Ben soon recommended printing ". . . for our young Females, as likely to be of more Use to them & their Children in Case of Widowhood than either Music or Dancing, by preserving them from Losses by Imposition of crafty Men."[202]

A direct contemporary of Ghitta's, the duchess of Luynes, did not, however, wait for her husband to die. Instead, she set up a printing office in his castle, where she ran her business for fifteen years. About her, Madame Récamier wrote: "She was highly educated, understood English perfectly, and was enormously well read. What can one say? She printed; she had a press set up in the château at Dampierre, and she was, as indeed she had the pretensions to be, a fine typographic workman."[203]

None of these women, either in Europe or America, was ever faced with a task as great as Ghitta's: the publication of her husband's towering *Manuale tipografico,* the world's most inclusive and ambitious specimen book.

Just four days after Bodoni's death, she wrote to Count Daru, informing him that Baron Pommereul had given her permission to work as a typographer in Parma.[204] She immediately turned her attention to Bodoni's uncompleted commissions and picked up exactly where her husband had left off: with the French classics ordered by Murat. The *Théatre Complet de Jean Racine* (Plate 28) was on the press on the day of Bodoni's death.[205] Even as she grieved the loss of *"il venerato e diletto mio Bodoni"* [206] [my revered and beloved Bodoni], she lost no time in fulfilling his wishes, and the Racine was published before the end of 1813, even though it was not until 11 January 1814 that she received the official imperial printing license.

Early in 1814, Ghitta published at her own expense a memorial volume to her husband, *In Morte del Cavaliere Giambattista Bodoni summo tipografo avvenuta il 30 Novembre 1813.* She presented 500 copies of the slim volume to friends and admirers of Bodoni. She gave the publication information as *Parma presso la Vedova Bodoni* [Parma at the Widow Bodoni's]. The volume contained an image of Bodoni's medal portrait, Vincenzo Jacobacci's oration, a description of the funeral, the various inscriptions, and the text of De Lama's memorial.

Next off the press was *Fables de La Fontaine,* and this time the publication information read: *A Parme de l'Imprimerie de la Veuve Bodoni* [Parma: Press of the Widow Bodoni]. Brooks calls this book one of the most beautiful of all Bodoni's editions. It was shortly followed by the fourth book in the series of French classics for Murat, the *Oeuvres poétiques de Boileau Despréaux.* With infinite care, Bodoni had already cut special punches for the title page so that the

ŒUVRES

POÉTIQUES

DE

BOILEAU DESPRÉAUX

———

TOME PREMIER.

A PARME

DE L'IMPRIMERIE BODONI

MDCCCXI.

words "Boileau Despréaux" could fit comfortably on one line. There is a charming, but probably apocryphal, story about this. It is said that Stendahl visited Bodoni shortly before he died (it is impossible to find any absolute evidence of this) and wrote a much quoted account of the event in which he talked of being completely bowled over by the celebrated typographer, saying: "This man is not conceited, but is truly passionate about his art. After he had shown me all his editions in French, he asked me which I preferred, the *Telemaco,* the Racine or the Boileau. I confessed that they all seemed equally beautiful. 'Ah! sir, but don't you see the title of the Boileau?' I looked at it for a long time, and confessed in the end that I found nothing more perfect in that title than in the others. 'Ah! sir,' exclaimed Bodoni, 'Boileau Despréaux in capitals in just one line!'"[207]

With the French classics behind her, Ghitta turned her hand to other unfinished business. In 1815, she completed the publication of *Memoria ed Orazione del P. Paolo M.a Paciaudi intorno la Biblioteca Parmense,* [Essays and Orations by Paolo Maria Paciaudi from the Parmesan Library], a book that Bodoni had long wanted to print in memory of his great champion.

MEANWHILE, back in Saluzzo, Giuseppe Bodoni was festering. He had left Parma when his health became precarious, some time before Bodoni died. In a disturbing memorandum, written in Saluzzo on 3 September 1815 but apparently never acted upon,[208] he listed a series of complaints about his brother and about the arduous work he had endured at the press. He mentioned physical problems, caused by having to heave cases of type from one place to another, for which his doctor in Parma had provided him with a brace. The brace may have helped his back, but did little to mitigate the effects of the fumes from the molten lead and antimony of the foundry. His asthma became chronic, he was unable to work, and the doctor advised him to return to the good, fresh air of Saluzzo, which he did. Giuseppe reported that he had every intention of returning to Parma, but that his brother wrote and told him to stay at home and attend to domestic affairs. He claimed that he left behind in Parma a large amount of money he and Ciambattista had amassed together, working elbow to elbow, starting from nothing, and that his brother had used these funds to purchase Il Pozzetto. He then complained about the pittance Bodoni left him in his will, a pittance that would not keep a dog alive, much less a man of 67, burdened with troubles, who was the head of a family of ten impoverished people. His intention was to return to Parma to seek out an honest and capable lawyer, and to ask him if Bodoni had the right to leave everything to his widow. If his health prevented his going, he would send his niece's husband, Francesco Lobetti. If the lawyer replied that Bodoni did have this right, he asserted that "I will tell him that Bodoni did not cut a single character. Pancrazio and Giacomo Amoretti prepared all the pieces of steel, and Don Andrea engraved them. Giacomo tempered them and struck and justified the matrices. My brother's will is agonizing to me, but what is worse is that I knew nothing about his illness. It is as though I were illegitimate."

This is a horrifying statement, which turns all preconceived opinions of a generous and loving Bodoni on its head. What is to be made of it?

"This piece of writing appeared like a bolt of lightning out of a serene sky," says Leonardo Farinelli in his essay, "Bodoni senza caratteri." [Bodoni without type.][209] Nothing in the correspondence between the two brothers gives any warning of such a radical change in affection and sentiment. Farinelli continues: "If Bodoni's historians had paid greater attention to this attack, they would surely have transmitted a very different moral picture of the man from Saluzzo than the one commonly accepted, even canonical." It seems that the historians assumed that Giuseppe, bitterly disappointed by his brother's will, was not telling the truth, conveniently enabling them to disregard his manifesto.

What is clear is that Bodoni left practically everything to Ghitta, and that he would stop at nothing to ensure publication of the *Manuale tipografico.* Also clear is that he had lent financial support to his family for decades; he might have wanted to draw the line at continuing this support for his relatives after his death.

Leaning heavily on Ghitta for information, Giuseppe De Lama started work on a biography of Bodoni. (On 15 April 1815, another would-be biographer, Baron Giuseppe Vernazza de Frenay, wrote to Ghitta from Turin, asking for her help too, but nothing seems to have come of that book.) Guided by Ghitta, De Lama made

Count Adam von Niepperg, Maria Luigia's second husband.

sure that Bodoni was a man without flaws, and his efforts resulted in a stunningly hagiographic work. An earlier biography, Father V. Passerini's *Memorie aneddote per servire un giorno alla vita del Signor Giovanbattista Bodoni tipografo di sua Maestà Cattolica e Direttore del Parmense Tipografeo* was not quite so worshipful, and Bodoni was unhappy about it. Published in Parma in 1804 by the Carmignani press, Father Passerini, an old friend, chose to point out on the third page that Bodoni had a deep longing for glory, saying that ". . . day and night he made the virtuous and moderate desire for glory his pasture and his most tasty delight."[210]

De Lama's biography was published by the ducal press in 1816, and is still considered the preferred source for those researching Bodoni's life,

Yes, the press was no longer imperial, it was once again ducal because Parma had a new duchess. Under the terms of the Treaty of Fontainebleu in 1814, the duchy of Parma, Piacenza, and Guastalla was ceded to Napoleon's young wife, Marie Louise, when the emperor abdicated to Elba. First, however, she retreated with her little boy to her family in Vienna, leaving the child there when she moved to Parma two years later. From the moment of her arrival, she became Parma's beloved Maria Luigia. She remains to this day one of the four leading lights of the city, along with Correggio, Bodoni, and Verdi (born the month before Bodoni died). Her colorful life was, and remains, the subject of considerable gossip and speculations.

She arrived in Parma on 18 April 1816 with an escort, the 39-year-old Count Adam Adalbert Niepperg, her majordomo, the man who, on orders from her father, accompanied and kept his eye on her.

The count was a dashing mili-

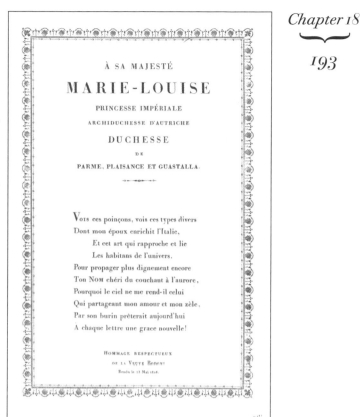

Ghitta's madrigal.

tary man with a history of heroic acts behind him; he wore a black band over his missing eye, which seemed more to attract women than to repel them. With directives from Metternich, he became the power behind the duchess. He also became the father of Maria Luigia's two illegitimate children, secret children, whom they hid away outside Parma with a country doctor, giving them the name Montenuovo (a name translated from Niepperg [new mountain]). Three weeks after hearing about the death of Napoleon, Maria Luigia married Niepperg, and the children were acknowledged. Maria Luigia's arrival came at just the right time for Ghitta. She was enchanted by the duchess, who visited her at the Pilotta just a month after her arrival in Parma. The duchess spent more than an hour with her, conversing about Bodoni while Ghitta showed her his masterworks and his jewel-like punches and matrices. Ghitta immediately celebrated the visit by writing and publishing a poem in which she gave equal glory to the duchess and to Bodoni. Six days later, Countess Scarampi, the duchess's lady-in-waiting, appeared at Ghitta's door, bearing a gift from the duchess, a diamond ring with the duchess's monogram. The ring was accompanied by a note that said: "Her Majesty finds you truly worthy to have been the companion of such a celebrated man, and hopes that this monogram will remind you from time to time of the good opinion that your qualities inspire in her."[211] The following month, on 4 June 1816, Ghitta received a message from Countess Scarampi, inviting her to dine with the duchess at eight o'clock that evening.

Ghitta had made a strong impression on the duchess and Count Niepperg, whom she inundated with gifts of Bodoni's finest editions. So many, and so important, were the gifts that Niepperg was cornered into reciprocating. On 16 October 1816, he wrote to Ghitta: "You have been kind enough to send me such interesting souvenirs of the inimitable art of your immortal husband that I have found the courage to send you something from my country in return. It is not costly, but I dare to hope that you will accept it as a mark of the high esteem and respect I have for you." Unfortunately, there is no record of what it was.

The advent of the duchess and her consort brightened Ghitta's life considerably, and helped ease her grief over her loss.

In 1816, the year of Maria Luigia's arrival, Ghitta was finally able to publish *Le più insigni pitture Parmensi indicate agli amatori delle Belle Arti* [The most important Parmesan paintings dedicated to the lovers of Beaux Arts], to which she added a dedication to the duchess. Seven years earlier, Bodoni had prepared this volume of engravings of Parma's most famous paintings, engravings which Rosaspina had executed before Napoleon snatched the paintings from Parma. When the paintings were finally returned and displayed at the Academy of Beaux Arts, the people of Parma went wild with joy at seeing their treasures again. The publication of *Le più insigni pitture . . .* could not have come at a better time.

Ever since her husband's death, Ghitta had been working on the *Manuale tipografico*. Bodoni had trained her carefully how to go about this, but it was not until five years after his death that Ghitta felt prepared to publish it. Several years before he died, Bodoni had written what became the 72-page introduction to the *Manuale*. He gave it the title, "Giambattista Bodoni to the Reader," and began by saying: "Here are the specimens of my industry and my labours of many years, devoted with great care to an Art which is the accomplishment of the most beautiful, ingenious, and useful invention of man, that is writing. Printing is its best form . . ."[212] The most salient moment of this rambling discourse, which flaunts his erudition and includes classical allusions, printing history, and a long discussion about the challenges of working with exotic type, comes when he insists that the more classical a book, the more the beauty of its type should stand alone, without decoration. Then he lays out what he considered the four basic principles of typography: regularity, neatness and refinement, good taste, and grace, the very principles for which he is remembered with such respect today. He finished his manifesto with the words, "I shall therefore conclude by beseeching the reader to turn his mind with love and attention towards these specimens of mine; and towards the many other things of every kind that I have printed; may he seek to know at least the most beautiful."

Manuale tipografico, frontispiece.

Chitta wrote a shorter, clearer introduction that preceded Bodoni's, entitled, "The Widow Bodoni to the Reader," in which she explained how it fell to her to print her husband's masterwork:

> *Having readied almost everything for the edition of his voluminous Manual, he was preparing to print it; already he had begun to work on this, when acute illness prevented the fulfillment of his desires. Nor did he wish, in the final moments of his sad departure, to burden me with the responsibility of printing and publishing a work on which his reputation would be staked, and of such importance for the art of typography. He believed such an undertaking to be far beyond my ability; and indeed at first I was intimidated by the huge difficulties presented by the task of — at least — gathering and organizing according to the principles of his singular genius the final parts of such an extensive body of work, which he was still amending during the early stages of his illness, and which he only abandoned when his weakness became extreme.*[213]

After defending Bodoni against charges that he "boasted talents not his own" (a clear reference to the Amoretti débâcle) she went on to describe how her husband made decisions about which typefaces to put in the book, and she took care to point out the surprising inclusion of musical type at the end of Volume II, for which "... owing to the extreme precision that is necessary, the process of engraving the punches proved to be very complicated and difficult." Bodoni

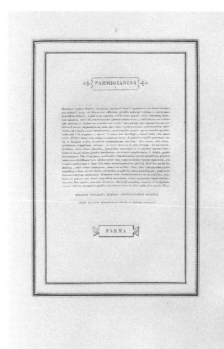

Manuale tipografico, dedication.

Quousqu; tandem . . . Printed in Papale, Bodoni's largest type which he reserved for Saluzzo.

Quousque tandem . . . Printed in Parmigianina, Bodoni's smallest type, which he reserved for Parma.

Quousque tandem . . . Printed in Imperiale italic.

MANUALE

TIPOGRAFICO

DEL CAVALIERE

GIAMBATTISTA BODONI

———

VOLUME PRIMO.

PARMA

PRESSO LA VEDOVA
MDCCCXVIII.

Manuale tipografico, title page.

correctly observed that the difficulty in cutting music type derives from the need, when the notes are strung together to be printed on the ruled staves, for the perpendicular, horizontal, and oblique strokes of the music to meet each other perfectly and produce a seamless whole. She concluded her introduction by saying:

> *. . . after gathering and organizing the various alphabets and all the other elements that should form the whole work, I ordered its casting and then its printing. I was well aware of the weight of such an endeavour: but I gathered all my strength; my love for him and for his glory sustained me. Accordingly I bravely began this enterprise, so that Italy and Europe would not be bereft of such a distinguished monument to the art of typography. Thus I will have attempted to fulfill, to the best of my ability, the expectations of all.*

Ghitta dedicated the *Manuale tipografico* to the duchess of Parma, and the dedication (printed in italics) has all the ring of a Shakespeare sonnet. It includes the lines:

> *Statues, paintings, temples by the most celebrated artists, either perished in ruins, or were devoured by flames: but it was not so for the Press. This art, the most useful of human discoveries, as it speedily diffuses all other discoveries; this art, that spread all over the world from Germany where it originated, endured fires, vicissitudes, time itself. It alone was able to broadcast the virtues of monarchs, the great deeds of our ancestors, and the ideas of the most sublime minds.*
>
> *Encouraged, then, by Your Majesty's generosity of spirit and by the support You lend to the Sciences and the Fine Arts, I presume to dedicate to You a book that will perhaps make history in the annals of the World . . .*

The *Manuale tipografico* was printed in two volumes, with Luigi Orsi doing the actual printing.[214] It was over 600 pages long. The title page indicated that the work was published *"Presso la Vedova"* [at the Widow's] and the first volume included an engraving of Bodoni by Rosaspina from the portrait by Andrea Appiani, followed by the dedication and the two introductions. "The list of contents alone is enough to amaze us," states Corrado Mingardi, "265 pages of Roman characters, imperceptibly declining in size, romans, italics, and script types, and the series of 125 capital letters; 181 pages of Greek and Oriental characters; 1036 decorations and 31 borders; followed in the last 20 pages by symbols, ciphers, numerals, and musical examples; the fruit of forty years of study and, as Bodoni says, 'indefatigable watchfulness.'"

As for the print run and cost of the *Manuale*, Ghitta herself announces them in her letter of 14 November 1817 to a Monsieur Durand of Metz (probably François Durand de Tichemont, an ardent book collector and mayor of Metz):

The Manuale tipografico in 2 vol-
umes in folio on papier velin (the
only paper used) is not yet fin-
ished, but will be without doubt
by the beginning of next year. I
dare to think that bibliophiles will
be grateful to me for having pub-
lished such an interesting book for
typography. The welcome it re-
ceives will recompense me for the
effort it has cost me, even though
Bodoni did leave me outlines and
models, and for the considerable
fore its completion. Above all, be-
cause only 250 copies have been
printed, I cannot give it away

for less than 120 francs, no discounts. Monsieur Rosaspina has engraved the
portrait, after the one that the celebrated Appiani (who has just died in Milan)
painted in oil and which bears an astonishing resemblance.[215]

After five years of painstaking work, Ghitta had prevailed. She had produced
the specimen book that Bodoni had spent forty years preparing, a book that
would indeed make typographic history. On 25 March 1818, she presented a
copy of the *Manuale tipgrafico* to the duchess. Later the same day, she received
a beautifully decorated clock from Maria Luigia in gratitude for the magnificent
work and its dedication.[216] Then Ghitta was free to send copies wherever she
would, to the most influential people she could think of, including Pope Pius VII.
As a measure of his gratitude, he sent her two medals and a message addressed
to Dilectae Filiae Vedovae Bodoni [lovely daughter widow Bodoni]. It included
the words *"un monumento di gloria per nostra Italia"* [a monument of glory for
our Italy]. Ghitta was so delighted with the pope's letter that she had it printed
up in Papale, Bodoni's largest font.

She did not stop working. Much of the labor took the form of inscriptions in
celebration of the duchess, announcements and invitations directly commissioned by the court, and illustrated books about constructions erected during

Chapter 18

199

the duchess's reign. One of these buildings was the Teatro Reggio [the Royal Theatre], the opera house where, upon its completion, Ghitta purchased a box for herself and her friends. She also published a few classics translated into Italian, and many sonnets. Although the commissions slowly petered out, she managed to keep the press running until 1834, twenty-one years after Bodoni's death. According to Brooks, the last work she published was *Catalogo de'libri che trovansi vendibili ne'magazzini della Ducale Tipografia di Parma.* [Catalog of books available for sale in the stores of the Ducal Printworks of Parma.] Brooks points out that this catalog contains some editions not printed in Parma, which is the reason Bodoni's name is not mentioned in the title.

Ghitta had a large stock of Bodoni's books in the storerooms at the Pilotta, and after the press was closed, she maintained a business as his bookseller. She was never asked to leave her premises in the building, and life in her later years must have been relatively pleasant. She had inherited a pension from Bodoni, she had an apartment with a view in the heart of Parma, she owned property in the country, and she had income from the sale of her husband's books. She also had the love of her family and the admiration of the duchess. And she had a box at the opera.

At four o'clock in the afternoon on 25 August 1841, in her bedroom at number 17 della Pilotta, with its two windows looking out towards the bridge and the royal gardens, Margherita Dall'Aglio Bodoni signed her will with a shaky hand in the presence of five typographers. Then she handed the document over to the notary, Giovanni Rondani.[217] It was just in time. Eleven days later, at half past eleven on the morning of 5 September 1841, she died of a stroke (the burial register states *"apoplexia correpta"* [stolen by apoplexy]). Her funeral was celebrated at the parish church of San Bartolomeo; she was buried at seven o'clock in the morning of 8 September, not in a church or a cathedral but at La Villetta, the public cemetery. La Villetta dates from 1817, and was created by decree of Maria Luigia as the direct result of the 1804 Napoleonic edict stating that, for sanitary reasons, bodies were no longer to be buried at churches within a city's perimeter. Ghitta, the guitar player, was in good company at La Villetta; she was preceded there one year earlier by Niccolò Paganini, the celebrated violinist and composer.

She has no large monument at La Villetta. She was buried in a vault, along with others, in the floor of the arcade of the cemetery. A small memorial plaque, which no longer exists there, was placed on the wall above. More to her liking than this small tribute would be the large plaque extolling her virtues that was installed at the base of Bodoni's on the wall of the great cathedral in Parma.

After leaving the major part of her fortune (including Il Pozzetto) to her nephews, Antonio and Francesco Dall'Aglio, Ghitta did not forget those who had helped her during her long life: her domestic servants, her cook, and the workers at the press (except for Luigi Orsi who had predeceased her). She singled out the cook, Carlo Frascati, and two of the workers, Giuseppe Vajarani and Giuseppe Cafferati, and assigned them each a monthly pension, but it was to the faithful Giambattista Zambiagi, who became the director of the ducal press after the death of Bodoni, that she paid the most attention. She left him a large sum of money, a generous monthly pension, all the food and fuel left in her home at the time of her death, and she added more money for his wife and children. She thanked the executors of her will, Angelo Pezzana, the librarian of the Biblioteca Palatina, and Giuseppe Bosi, her lawyer, with the gift of her silver coffee service and two candlesticks.[218]

FOR MANY YEARS after Bodoni died, Ghitta tried to sell Bodoni's immense collection of punches and matrices. Knowing well how valuable the collection was and the importance of keeping it together, she put a price on it of 500,000 francs. She received expressions of interest from royal courts and the Vatican, but no firm commitment. The collection was still unsold at the time of her death, and her heirs were left with the question of what to do with it. Eventually, with the support of Maria Luigia, duchess of Parma, and the persistence of Angelo Pezzana, the collection was purchased for the Palatina library for 50,000 francs.

Much later, during World War II, the Bodoni material was removed to the abbey of Torrechiara for safekeeping, a wise move because on 13 May 1944 much of the Pilotta was destroyed by Allied bombers, including part of the library, the Farnese theatre, and Bodoni's studio, printworks, and living quarters. When the material was restored to the library, it was in a state of disarray, and remained that way until the opening of the Bodoni museum in 1963. Since then, it has been the gleaming heart of the collection.[219]

If you ever have a chance to visit the museum, spend time with Bodoni's 22,618 punches and 42,148 matrices, all neatly arranged in specially made wooden cases. Ask the attendant to remove a punch from its case so that you can hold it. While you marvel at the coldness and perfection of this jewel-like piece of steel, press on its carved face so that the letter makes an ephemeral print on your finger — a print from Bodoni's hand to yours.

EPILOGUE

Parma 30 November 2013

I T IS A BLEAK MORNING; the air is so cold that it hurts to breathe. Parma's wealthy pull on cashmere sweaters and fur coats, and garb their dogs in fashionable canine attire. Students hunch into their down jackets (always black) and drag on leggings and modish boots. African immigrants, all men, huddle together in the Piazza della Pace in front of the Pilotta, swathed in scarves and woolly hats. Housewives bustle to market, their breath whitening the air. At the produce stall, just behind Bodoni's parish church of San Bartolomeo, the vendors wear fingerless gloves as they hand over potatoes, onions, apples, pears, and clementines to their customers. Cafés, bright spaces in a dull world, do a brisk business in hot chocolate. A skim of ice borders the *torrente.* Between the great arches of the Pilotta hangs a three-and-a-half-meter-tall banner announcing a major exhibition in celebration of the two-hundredth anniversary of Bodoni's death.

Just before quarter past ten, a small group gathers in the cathedral at the foot of Bodoni's plaque. The group includes Sabina Magrini, director of the Biblioteca Palatina and the Bodoni museum; Andrea Amoretti, scion of the Amoretti family from San Pancrazio; Andrea De Pasquale, scientific director of the Bodoni museum (and previous director of the Biblioteca Palatina and Bodoni museum); Monsignor Alfredo Chierici, parish priest of the cathedral and of San Bartolomeo; deputations from San Pancrazio and the Bodoni museum; and interested onlookers. Tall, charming, and handsome, Andrea Amoretti welcomes everyone to the celebration; Sabina Magrini reads a succinct and thoughtful speech about the importance of Bodoni in the world at large, and about the Bodoni museum in particular; and Monsignor Chierici gives the benediction and recites Psalm 121, *"Alzo gli occhi verso i monti"* [I will lift mine eyes unto the hills], the great psalm of ascension.

Members of the core group climb into cars, turn the heaters on, and drive seven kilometers from the center of Parma to San Pancrazio on its outskirts. On their arrival in the parking lot of the parish church, Andrea De Pasquale, who has been working with Andrea Amoretti to organize this event, explains the intention of the gathering: to celebrate the work of Bodoni and the Amoretti brothers, combined with a desire to pay tribute to their joint achievements and to bury the hatchet in this anniversary year.

Residents of San Pancrazio, who have known the Amorettis' descendants all their lives, and a small class from the primary school join the group as Andrea Amoretti guides them all out onto the Via Emilia. Traffic is halted so they can stand back and admire two plaques, one new and one restored, on the wall of the original printworks.[220] The restored plaque was originally placed there in 1913 by Ugo Benassi in celebration of the hundredth anniversary of the death of Bodoni. Amoretti points out that no one, not even the oldest people in San Pancrazio, can remember ever being able to read the inscription, so eroded had it been by weather and traffic fumes. Now they can read it perfectly, thanks to the restoration undertaken by the commune of San Pancrazio.

AMORETTI proudly thanks those who have contributed to the event and promises that the plaques will soon be moved to a spot where viewers will be less threatened by busy traffic on the Via Emilia. He then shepherds the crowd into the old printworks, long since converted into apartments. Along a low brick-lined corridor some of the Amorettis' punches and printing are on display in glass-topped cases. For many of the group, this is their first glimpse of the Amorettis' work. Their descendant carefully explains to the children how much preparation and effort were required for printing some two centuries ago.

Then everyone troops out into the courtyard to brave the cold again, gladdened by the promise of refreshments. The wine flows; the savories are appetizing; people admire the quality of the pieces of parmesan; and they fall with delight on two delicious, home-made almond cakes. They converse. Everyone has red noses, but everyone is smiling.

Restored Amoretti plaque.

BACK AT THE PILOTTA, in the newly restored (but unheated) Petitot gallery, Costanza Marchesini, wearing her heavy down coat, boots, and gloves, welcomes visitors to the elegant anniversary exhibition. It includes works printed by Bodoni's predecessors; Bodoni's masterpieces; a reproduction of one of his presses; his tools; and an interactive video display. Across the way, in the wings of the Teatro Farnese and in the Galleria Nazionale, bold posters explaining the significance of the people and places that were important in Bodoni's life stand next to appropriate portraits and maps.

Meanwhile, a two-day conference is in full swing in the Teatro Reggio, Parma's stupendously beautiful opera house. The conference, *"Il segno italiano. Moderno per tradizione"* [Italian design. Modernity by way of tradition], uses Bodoni as the prime exemplar of Italian design as it is perceived abroad, that is, design that is classically elegant but has a modern edge. The audience, composed of journalists, designers, graphic designers, and more than 400 students from all over the country, is reminded again and again of Bodoni's importance in the aesthetics of communication and the printed word.

You may not realize it, but Bodoni is everywhere. His is a favorite font; a headliner; a mark of elegance on the covers of *Vanity Fair* and *Vogue;* he shows up in the texts of books and on their covers; he is featured on albums and posters for Nirvana, Mamma Mia, and Lady Gaga. He has never really disappeared, but even now is a thoroughly modern man. One hundred years from now, at the next centenary celebration when you and I are long gone, he will still be making printing history, delighting the eye, delivering the punch.

Giambattista Bodoni (1740-1813).

ACKNOWLEDGEMENTS

I HAD HOPED to meet Mimi Meyer, whose theft of the *Manuale tipografico* had so intrigued me, to ask her how she chose the books she stole, as well as a host of other questions. Was she interested in how a book was printed? Did she select books because they were on inconspicuous shelves? How did she really conceal the large and often fat volumes? and so on, in what I hoped would be a lengthy and lively conversation. I turned to the Internet and searched for her online, and learned she was a rower and had moved to Chicago. I found her phone number but was nervous about cold calling, so I put it off. A year passed, and then I did another search, only to learn that she had died suddenly at home on 29 December 2009 at the age of 63. I owe her thanks for kindling my interest in Bodoni.

When I admitted to Fred and Barbara Voltmer, my hosts at the dinner party in California where I first heard the word "Bodoni," that I wanted to write about him, they kept nudging me to get going, insisting that the printing community desperately needed a biography in English. They advised me to contact the type designer, Sumner Stone, who not only had a deep knowledge of the historic Bodoni, but also modern, practical experience in designing type for the computer. In March of 2008, I wrote him a letter. Thus began a seven-year correspondence in which Sumner treated me to seminars on, among other things, the history of printing, the hows and satisfactions of type design, the city of Rome and Roman inscriptions, the food in Parma, and the mushrooms that flourish near Alphabet Farm, his studio in California. In turn, I described for him every detail of my journey towards the completion of this book. I have always hated writing a journal (I'm an only child; I need an audience), but writing letters has been part of my life. Since Sumner was already so deeply immersed in my topic, he became the perfect audience, always ready with wise counsel, apt knowledge, and encouragement. To say that I profited from his response to my letters would be an understatement. I owe Sumner, the creator of the Bodoni for our electronic age, an enormous debt of gratitude.

James Mosley kept me honest. His knowledge of printing history is immense, and he has been unflinchingly patient with my questions and rigorous in his answers. I am forever in his debt. He has another great attribute; he is married to the food historian, Gillian Riley. Not only has Gillian helped me enormously with the issue of what Bodoni ate, she has provided some truly memorable meals when I have visited James and her in London.

Gillian in turn introduced me to Oretta Zanini De Vita in Rome, another pre-eminent food historian. Oretta took me into her study one evening and told me exactly what Bodoni would have eaten in Rome during the years 1758-1766. Then she served me one of the most delicious dinners I've ever eaten; it included baked ricotta with orange peel and rosemary.

Bodoni lived in three beautiful places in Italy, and I felt I should spend time in all of them. In Saluzzo, Dr. Giancarla Bertero, librarian of Saluzzo's civic library, befriended me and led me to various Bodoni sites throughout the town. She welcomed me to the library, bringing out treasure after treasure for me to examine. When she staggered out with Bodoni's three-volume *Iliad* on a trolley, heaved the first volume onto my desk, and opened it at random, I thought I would swoon. The sight of those snowy pages, black ink, and perfect Greek characters took my breath away. Such was the grandeur and beauty of the volume that I wanted to lie down in it and die right there. Warmest thanks to Dr. Bertero, for showing me the way in Saluzzo.

In Rome, in 2011, I was lucky enough to be a visiting scholar for five weeks at the American Academy, where I benefitted from its library, its ambiance, and its delicious cuisine. I spent my time wandering around the city, soaking up the atmosphere, visiting Bodoni's sites, and spending time in the archives of the Propaganda Fide. Believe me, it was a challenge to stay focused on the years 1758-1766 when the rest of Roman history was spread out before me. My thanks go to the sculptor, Simon Verity, for leading me down the Janiculum hill, through Trastevere, across the river, and into the thick of things. I am also deeply grateful to my Italian tutor, Dr. Milena Locatelli, whose friendship and fascinating conversation made every session a pleasure.

I went to Parma four times and began to feel I lived there. I stayed in a little apartment in the Palazzo dalla Rosa Prati, the beautiful red building next to the baptistry on the Piazza del Duomo. Half the building is occupied by the Rosa Prati family, and the other half has been converted into a hotel and apartments. I was comfortable and happy there; everything I needed was within walking distance. I thank Vittorio dalla Rosa Prati, Mattia Pizzelli, and Carla Maramotti for all their help, and the Marchesa Zaira dalla Rosa Prati for her friendship and hospitality. Through her I experienced a side of Parma and its people that I would never have seen as a tourist.

Wallis Wilde-Menozzi arrived on her bicycle at my doorstep the day after I arrived in Parma and immediately took me out for lunch (*tortelli d'erbette*).

She was a gift from my friend Gillian Riley, the food historian and author of *The Oxford Companion to Italian Food.* Wallis has written extensively about Parma and Rome, and the conversation we started that day has continued to this. I have learned so much from her about Parma, about what it means to be a writer, and about friendship.

The Biblioteca Palatina then became the center of my universe, and I would like to thank the librarians who helped me in my struggle to decipher the Bodoni correspondence. My thanks in particular go to Dr. Caterina Silva, the vice-curator of the Bodoni Museum Foundation, for providing me with so much useful information and answering so many questions.

On my most recent trip to Parma, I was thrilled to meet Dr. Sabina Magrini, the new director of the Biblioteca Palatina and Bodoni Museum. With her energy, her keen intelligence, her remarkable public relations skills, and her vision for the future of the museum, she will prove a wonderful steward for Bodoni in the 21st century.

My Bodoni education was furthered by regular conversations with Professor Leonardo Farinelli, director emeritus of the Biblioteca Palatina and the Bodoni Museum He patiently dealt with my questions and consistently offered enthusiastic encouragement and insights. It was wonderful to converse with someone who had spent so much time reflecting on Bodoni and his life, and we talked about the maestro as though he were still alive.

It was my great fortune to meet Costanza Marchesini on my first day at the museum. She was working there and at the Biblioteca Palatina as a cultural collaborator. Although almost forty years my junior, she took me under her wing and helped me find my way, not just at the museum but in Parma itself and in the surrounding countryside. She and Andrea Conti, a fine historian, swooped me up on weekends and showed me the palace at Colorno, the duke's hunting lodge and chapel, Torrechiara, Felino, Sabionetta, and the inside of various restaurants, where my food education flourished.

Other friends who helped me on my quest were Lois Clegg and Ermanno Bondi with whom I had many happy adventures, including finding our way to Bodoni's country house in San Prospero — in the teeming rain. Lois and I also made the trek, again in the rain, to the charming library in Busseto to meet Professor Corrado Mingardi, the great Bodoni scholar. One of his treasures among the many he showed us was the album of Vieira's drawings from the Camera di San Paolo, an album which Bodoni himself had owned.

Dr. Rosa Necchi offered me the hand of friendship when we were both working in the scholars' reading room in the Biblioteca Palatina. Since then she has been ever willing to fulfill my requests for material from the library, scanning items when necessary, and always encouraging me.

My visits to Franco Maria Ricci and Laura Casalis in Fontanellato were eye-opening. I am awed by their publishing accomplishments, their knowledge of Bodoni, their extraordinary bamboo labyrinth, and their kindness.

The life of a researcher in a foreign country can be miserably lonely; thanks to my Parma friends, I never suffered that misery.

Everything I read about Bodoni was in Italian or French. Fortunately my French is fluent, but I needed to beef up my vestigial Italian. Initially, I started taking classes at Anne Arundel Community College in Maryland, where I ground down the patience of my instructor, Maria Pitocco, by persistently asking for help in translating snippets of eighteenth-century Italian. In revenge, she brought my grammar up to speed. In Parma, I took an intensive course at the Dante Alighieri Institute, where my instructor Lucia Trocchi energetically shoved my Italian to a higher level. *Grazie mille, professoresse.*

Because I spent so much time in Parma hunched over a desk, and because I was there during the winter when the streets were often icy and the cobblestones treacherous, I joined a gym called Fisilabor. I took various aerobic classes, and there was something magical about exercising in a mirrored *palazzo* with a group of tattooed young women a third my age. Thanks to all at Fisilabor for keeping me sane.

Back in Boston, I enjoyed Italian food with Allan Haley of Monotype, and learned about type and its emergence on the electronic scene. I am grateful for his solid encouragement and lively conversation.

In West Virginia, I spent a couple of nights with Stan and Lucille Nelson, and Stan demonstrated the process of cutting a punch, an act that brought home vividly the immense labor, skill, and time involved in the way Bodoni spent the greater part of his life. For allowing me to witness a skill that has practically disappeared, I thank him deeply.

The libraries and museums I consulted were, first and foremost, the Bodoni museum, the Palatine Library, the Glauco Lombardi Museum, and the National Gallery, all in Parma. They provided me with most of the primary material from which I worked, but I have profited also from the Turin Public Library; the Bibliothèque Nationale; the British Library; the Library of Congress; the

Houghton Library at Harvard; the Providence Public Library; the Butler Library at Columbia; the New York Public Library; the Boston Public Library; the Harry Ransom Research Center; and the Book Arts and Special Collections Center at the San Francisco Public Library. Special thanks go to the Hingham Public Library in Massachusetts for providing me with the perfect environment in which to write. I love libraries.

For bringing me up to scratch electronically and for being so enthusiastic about Bodoni in the twenty-first century, I thank my trainers at the Apple store in Hingham.

As well as Sumner Stone and James Mosley, my readers have been: Diana Phillips; Toby, Alison, and Jane Lester; Miriam Dow; and Marcia and Geoff Thompson. Thank you all so very much. Mary Anne Frye and Michael McPherson have witnessed the evolution of this book and added their wise counsel, good taste, and companionship. Other people whose help means more than I can say are: Andrea Amoretti; Margie and Bill Blackwell; Sarah deLima; Cara Di Edwardo; Sergio Andres Gaiti; Jordan Goffin; Sarah Gregory; Jane Joyce; Pat and Paul Kaplan; Diane Montenegro; Daniela Morena; Dr. Francesca Sandrini; Jane Siegel; and, of course, Fred and Barbara Voltmer, whose legendary hospitality and encouragement continue to this day. At a recent gathering in their studio, they assembled some stars of the San Francisco printing world. Barbara served an elegant brunch (cheese soufflé, asparagus, and briochcs), and we all sat around the same table, where Bodoni was again the center of attention.

My friend Nick Humez, himself published by David Godine, brought my manuscript and his publisher together in what feels like a perfect marriage. I thank David for his conviction that this book should be published, for his scrupulous editing, and for the delight of coming to grips with Bodoni in tandem with him, his team, the brilliant and circumspect Heather Tamarkin, and with the very talented book designer Jerry Kelly.

Two weeks before he died in April 2010, my husband Jim made me promise to finish this book. He has kept my shoulder to the wheel, and I thank him most of all.

APPENDICES

To explain the intricacies of cutting punches, striking matrices, and hand printing, I have relied on modern experts to describe the processes. Stan Nelson, among the few people in the world still practicing the art of cutting punches, striking matrices, and casting type, has volunteered to explain how this is done. Fred and Barbara Voltmer, printers themselves, explain how to set type and print on a hand press. James Mosley takes on the mystery of the Trieste leaf.

APPENDIX I

Cutting a Punch

BY STAN NELSON

To CUT A PUNCH, that is a letter engraved on the end of a steel rod, is to give expression in three dimensions to what will become a two-dimensional character or letter, printed on paper. The medium is steel and the process requires discipline and patience. In most cases an expert engraver can cut a punch in four to six hours, although extremely large or complex punches may take several days. The engraver must sit erect, with the punch held in the left hand against a "bench pin" — a wooden peg — looking through a magnifying lens. At his or her elbow is a range of files from very small to quite large, various clamps and gauges, and a variety of gravers. The gravers are carving tools made of very hard steel and come in a variety of shapes and sizes. The three shapes most used are round, flat, and onglette (a small, pointed graver with curving sides). The punchcutter begins with the round gravers (often called scorpers), turns to the flat gravers to level surfaces and to clean up angles, and employs the onglette graver to make fine adjustments.

Punches are cut in high carbon, water-hardening tool steel, which is square in cross section, comes in a wide range of sizes from 1/8" to 1", and is sold in 3' rods which are cut up into workable lengths. Except for very large punches, most work is done in billets 2 ¼" or 2 ½" inches long.

Traditionally punches were driven into copper with a hammer to form a matrix, that is a mold from which a piece of type is made. Later, in the nineteenth century, special striking presses were employed to push the punch into copper blanks. To avoid hitting a corner during striking, the "hammer end" of the punch is tapered or rounded off.

In order to know which side of the punch is the "bottom" of the letter, a signature mark is made on that side — usually a horizontal line, much like the nick on a piece of type. This same mark is helpful during the polishing of the face, since it allows one to put the punch in various fixtures, always oriented in the same way.

The face of the punch is first polished using a coarse stone that levels the surface fairly quickly. Oil is used to keep the stone from clogging up. If the letter is small, a portion of this face may be gently beveled to reduce the area that has to be polished. Successively smoother stones give a finer and finer finish to the face of the punch.

A final polish is given to the punch using a very smooth Arkansas stone, or a piece of fine, black slate (such as used for blackboards).

After preparing the steel billet, guidelines for the letter are drawn on the polished face of the punch using a sharp steel scribe. Gauges with notches showing all needed dimensions make this easier.

If one is copying an existing design, a soot impression can be transferred from the model to the face of the punch, then meticulously drawn with the scribe. Straight lines are made with tiny "squares" and "angles," while curves are drawn using a series of tiny dots.

Original designs are drawn directly on the face of the punch, again using the face gauges while studying careful drawings reflected in a mirror.

Everything—the entire success of the letter—depends upon making a very careful drawing from the beginning. One does not leave details to be determined later.

A great many successful punchcutters made use of counterpunches to form the inside (counter) of their punches. A small piece of steel is filed to the exact shape of the counter, hardened, and then struck into the face of the punch to a depth of about 1/32" or a bit deeper. Then the sides and face of the punch must be trued up and the face rubbed flat once again and the letter drawn once again.

Although the making of the counterpunch is time consuming, there are some advantages. The counterpunch forms a finished counter that is very clean and even. In some cases one can be used to make several letters such as n and u or b, d, p and q. While commonly used, counterpunches were not suited to ornate designs. Such punches were usually engraved.

If the punchcutter is going to engrave the insides or counters of the letter, then work begins by filing up the outside of the letter. Large files are used to quickly rough away metal from the top third of the punch — metal that would get in the way of the finer work to come.

Then, with finer files, a second, slightly more obtuse angle is created that approaches the desired outline of the letter. The onglette graver is used to shave away the edge of the letter where metal must be removed, and the resulting, tiny bevel (called the indication) reflects light that is easily seen by the punchcutter. When this small reflection disappears one stops filing. Stage by stage the outside contours are perfected.

After checking the letter with the gauge, one begins digging out the counter, or inside of the letter. The round gravers (scorpers) are used to dig a hole that is then enlarged and flattened, following the general contour of the counter. Because one is digging toward the center it is less likely that a damaging slip will occur. This hollow must be kept fairly shallow at first.

The edges of the counter are cleaned up using a series of nearly vertical stabbing motions with the round graver. The angle will match that filed on the outside. (This angle is called the talus.) The gravers must be held at a fairly high angle as the belly or bottom edge of the graver is very likely going to "bruise" the edges of the lines. The first pass of this round graver will leave a scalloped edge, so one must go back and cut away the little ridges — leaving a smoother surface that can then be perfected with the onglette graver.

Successive stages of engraving expand and deepen the counter until the drawing is reached. It is then time to test the letter to see what else must be done. This is accomplished by making soot impressions, called smoke proofs.

Now one must blacken the face of the punch and then press it evenly and crisply against smooth paper. The resulting print has no ink spread as it is pure pigment with no oil.

One continues to refine the letter, making very minute adjustments with successive smoke proofs to test the work deliberately and cautiously. If too much metal is shaved away the repair can add hours to the work, and in some cases ruin the punch.

When the punch is perfect, it is placed with its fellows and the set is heated, letter by letter, and then quenched in cool water. The shock of suddenly going from extreme hot to cold hardens the punch and it becomes hard and brittle. Subsequent tempering of the punch draws the hardness to a specific level where it is not too hard, nor too soft. The punch is ready for striking.

Copper is the best metal for matrices, since it is ductile and easily filed. The punch makes a perfect impression in the copper, usually by being hit by a hammer or striking press. Because metal is being displaced and not removed, the swelling copper must be filed square and flat before measuring the depth and levelness of the impression. While "a matrix well struck is half justified," most punches have sunk into the copper unevenly, so adjustments must be made.

Matrices have traditionally belonged to a specific mold and are fitted to that mold. At first direct measurements are made of the matrix and areas filed. As one approaches the final stage a series of proof castings is made and measured. In this way perfect accuracy is achieved.

These proof castings are made in the same manner as any casting in a hand mold. This mold consists of two nearly identical halves that slide against each other, creating a variable cavity that can be at once wide for a letter like M or W, and narrow for I and l. The size or body of this cavity remains constant, as does its height.

The matrix is fitted in the bottom, where it is gripped between two registers and pressed against a stop called the stool. These guides position the matrix consistently beneath the mold. A long curving spring (the bow) presses up against the matrix to keep it tight against the mold.

Molten metal is poured into the mold through the jet (a funnel) and the mold is given a quick shake to help form a sharp, crisp letter. The metal cools very quickly so there can be no delay. After each letter hardens it is tipped out onto the caster's bench and the process is repeated. Five or six types can be cast in the span of a minute by the hand caster

Type metal is an alloy made up of lead, tin, and antimony. While the percentages vary, a common mixture is 64% lead, 12% tin, and 24% antimony. This forms a durable alloy that is inert and quite safe to handle.

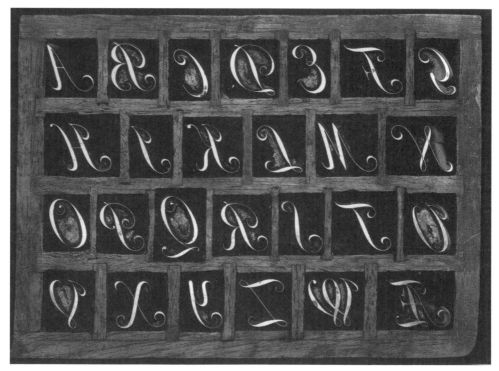

Bodoni's punches for swash italic capitals.

APPENDIX II
Striking and Fitting a Matrix

BY STAN NELSON

A FINISHED PUNCH, no matter how perfect, is of no value whatsoever until it is driven into malleable copper and justified to form a fitted matrix. The dimensions of this matrix are determined by the mold with which it will be used to cast printing types. The most important of these dimensions is its "depth-of-drive." The depth of the impression in the matrix, combined with the "height-to-shoulder" of the mold (I hope these terms are self-explanatory) will produce a type that is of the desired overall height. In the U.S. and England this height is now standardized at .918". In the past it was slightly shorter at .917" — but in Europe several greater heights are used. Of course whatever the standard, it is essential that all the types in the printing office be of the same height so that they will print evenly. So, let's begin with the making of a matrix, which must start with driving the punch. Such may be accomplished with just a hammer and a solid anvil. The eighteenth-century French typefounder Pierre Simon Fournier recommended three fingers, as enough for the job; but other founders then and later employed various gauges and machines to push the punch into a polished copper blank to form a "strike."

Some have said that "with one blow" the punch is driven into copper to form a matrix, but this is an oversimplification. With even a small punch, several repeated hits are made with the hammer in order to sink the punch to a sufficient depth to allow for fitting. When the letter is large much greater amounts of force are needed to push the punch deeply into the copper. First a light tap is made that leaves a faint mark on the face of the matrix blank. The position is adjusted if it is not straight and then heavier blows are made. Each hit is made very deliberately, making sure the punch hasn't moved out of place between blows.

As copper is compressed it becomes much harder and it resists the punch. To counteract this, the metal must be annealed. Strangely, copper reacts to heat in exactly the opposite manner of steel, so by heating the matrix and then quenching it in water the metal is softened (not hardened). This softening of the copper must be repeated multiple times when large matrices are driven. I've done it as many as twelve and thirteen times for one 48-point matrix.

This striking isn't done without risk. It is always with some trepidation that each blow is struck. If misdirected, the unequal force delivered by the hammer can snap off a corner of the letter, ruining both punch and strike. With large punches the vibration can sting the fingers. It is not a task for sissies! One can easily understand why founders invented "striking fixtures" to hold copper matrix blank and punch firmly while being driven, Fournier's prejudices notwithstanding.

Regardless of the manner used to drive the punch, the goal is to push it as level as possible and deeper than the final desired depth. This is necessary because striking merely displaces copper. This ductile metal is pushed about under the enormous pressures generated under the face of the punch. It also often causes the surface around the drive to collapse, leaving a sunken area about the "eye" of the mat.

All the resulting bulges have to be filed or cut away with a special milling machine. Only after the surfaces are flattened and square can one begin to measure the face of the drive in the matrix in relation to the surface of the mat.

There are various special gauges made for taking these measurements, but one can also make trial castings and then get measurements from these sample letters.

At first the fitter makes the face of the strike level with the surface and then reduces the depth until it is exactly correct. The tolerances are to less than one half of a thousandth of an inch (.0005″!) That's really remarkable, especially when one realizes that this was (and still can be) achieved without modern micrometers or other fancy tooling. Just a file, a try-square, and a "straight edge." And lots of patience.

I've skipped describing a multitude of adjustments that make up this process of justifying a matrix. They include determining the width of the cast letter, as well as its "alignment" – putting the letters upon an even baseline so that they don't look like a roller coaster. And more subtly each letter must sit upright, but this is achieved optically since some letters must be tipped a trifle in order not to appear to be leaning.

Suffice to say that all of this work is essential to the success of a typeface. Properly fitted matrices will allow the efficient casting of good type. Good work cannot be done with badly fitted matrices.

Type was routinely cast in hand molds for over four centuries and while type casting machinery was introduced in 1838, in America, it did not immediately replace the hand caster. For a variety of reasons these skilled workmen continued to ply their trade for several more decades.

Their work consisted of using a small spoon to pour a measured amount of liquid type metal into the funnel-shaped "jet" of the type mold. This opening tapers down to the actual casting cavity of the mold, with the matrix firmly clamped at the bottom, so that the liquid metal flows directly to the face of the matrix, then fills the rest of the type's body. Since there is no "pressure" other than gravity, the caster must give the mold a jerk or shake just at the moment of pouring the metal. This helps to accelerate the metal, driving it through the narrow "throat" of the mold, where the jet joins the casting cavity. Varying the shake helps to achieve quality castings although very large types do not need this movement. They just need a very hot mold.

Laboriously sculpting a letter in steel, then hammering it into copper and spending hours filing the impression into a fitted matrix, pouring shining, silvery metal into a mold, only to tip out a beautiful glittering letter is a very gratifying experience — one which becomes even more pleasing as the pile of finished letters grows. For any printer who has run short of letters — has been "out of sorts" — having the ability to cast a requisite supply of letters is like owning a candy store. This must always have been true for printers.

Bodoni's punches for cyrillic capitals.

APPENDIX III
Printing on a Hand Press
BY FRED AND BARBARA VOLTMER

THE GOLD EAGLE on our 1869 Columbian iron handpress looks down on us from the counterpoise lever as we prepare to print a broadside. We have spent the last week going over the text and considering the design. The platen of this press is 19 ¼" x 24 ½" so we can use a sheet of paper roughly the same size. In our mind's eye, we see generous margins. Should we have an illustration? An initial letter? Color? We will be using 14-point Caslon Old Style as the text font. We consider the line length and decide on the size of the margins. The text will be more readable set in two parallel columns. We adjust the type stick and begin setting letters one at a time, justifying left and right. The lead type is cold to the touch but the letters and spacing fall into place. When we have one to two inches of type set, we move the lines to the imposing stone. It takes a day to set the page and another day to proof and correct errors that consist mostly of inverted letters or broken characters. The look of the page becomes clearer now. We will have a title set in 60-point type and print it in blue. At the bottom of the sheet there will be a Bodoni dash followed by a colophon in the shape of an inverted triangle. The handmade paper we have selected is a warm white with deckle edges on two sides. We decide to dampen the paper and tear the other two sides to achieve the appearance of a deckle on all four sides. With this complete we can dampen the paper for the whole edition, a run of 50 copies. We cut blotter paper to the appropriate size and put water into a metal spray can that produces a fine mist. The work surface is ready—stacks of blotters, stacks of paper cut to size, two plastic-laminate-covered boards to start and finish the stack, and a plastic bag which will act as a humidor. The mist from the sprayer rises in the air as we carefully spray both sides of the first blotter. Six sheets of paper make up the first lift, then another wet blotter, more paper, and more blotters until all the sheets are near the dampness of the blotters. The second board goes on top and the stack goes into the plastic bag. We place a light weight on top of the bag.

At the press, we are preparing to lock up the form. We have placed the type in the chase, a metal frame around the type and wooden furniture. We use quoins [blocks] to secure the type and transfer the form to the bed of the press. Inking the corners of the form lightly with a stamp pad, we print an impression on the frisket [a masking device]. Then the paper on the frisket is cut out to expose the portion of the paper to be printed. Mylar, which acts as packing, is secured with cellophane tape. The tympan [a sheet of paper or cloth between the impression surface and the paper to be printed] is in the up position and the frisket is flying above it. The roller and platen bearers are in the bed and we are ready to put the ink on the piece of glass that acts as our inking stone.

We are careful removing the ink from the can as it is becoming harder to purchase ink appropriate for the handpress. We use a knife to put a small amount of ink near the top of the glass. This will serve as our ink fountain. Then we spread some of the ink across the width of the surface. We roll the brayer [a hand roller] back and forth across the glass, each time adding a little ink to the roller. The rolling against the ink on the glass makes a hissing sound as the ink begins to cover the surface. An experienced pressman can sense that he has the right amount of ink by the sound of the roller against the glass.

The first proof will be all black. From this image we will decide if any make-ready [a method of equalizing the impression using overlays or underlays] is necessary. We print a light proof on thin paper and attach it to the tympan. We adjust the platen bearers so the pressure from the platen [the roller of the printer] is even. The roller height is raised with tape on the roller bearers so the ink just touches the top of the form. We put the gauge pins in place.

The first pass looks acceptable. The lower left-hand corner is lighter than the rest of the page but some tissue behind the proof sheet will even out the pressure and correct the problem. We pull several more proofs and turn our attention back to the paper. It is time to reverse the order of the sheets so that all the paper will be uniformly damp. By the next day, all the sheets will have absorbed moisture from the blotters.

Before starting the print run, we remove any type that will be printed in blue and replace it with furniture that is the same dimension. What remains is the text that will be printed in black. We take one sheet of dampened paper from the bag and place it carefully against the gauge pins. We lower the frisket and the tympan and roll the bed of the press under the platen using the rounce, the handle which operates the drum that moves the bed under the platen. We pull the bar and the eagle rises to provide the counterweight. We can feel the pressure of the platen against the type and paper. We allow the platen to dwell in that position for a few seconds and then let the bar move back into place. We roll the bed out, and quickly raise the tympan and frisket—the sound is an audible snap. The sheet is exposed.

We raise the frisket and take a critical look at the first page. The result is satisfactory and we begin the print. If all goes well, we can expect to print 50 to 75 pages in an hour with one person inking and the other placing the paper and pulling the bar. Each sheet is checked against a standard to ensure uniformity. We stack the sheets lightly and store them back in the humidor. It is time to clean the type, glass, and brayer.

Now we are ready to print the second color. We remove all the black text type from the form and lock the letters to be printed in blue into the chase. We have saved enough proof sheets to make sure that the letters to be printed in blue are positioned correctly on the page. After we are satisfied with the registration, we are ready to print the second color. We take the sheets one by one from the plastic bag, place them at the gauge pins, and the printing process continues. We separate the finished pages by slip sheets, and lightly weight them until they are completely dry.

Would Bodoni have used a similar process when he printed on a wooden press? Probably. He would also have designed and cast his own type and made his own ink. He would not have had the benefit of Mylar, cellophane tape, stamp pads, plastic bags and metal quoins which are commonly used in print shops today.

The successful handpress printer, both in Bodoni's time and now, develops a sense of the parameters which ensure fine printing. The aesthetic of typesetting a beautiful page, the quality and dampness of the paper, the position of the text in the form, the amount of ink on the type, the pressure applied by the platen, the dwell of the bar, and the exactness of the registration all contribute to the final result.

impression bar
platen
frisket
ink balls
forme
tympan

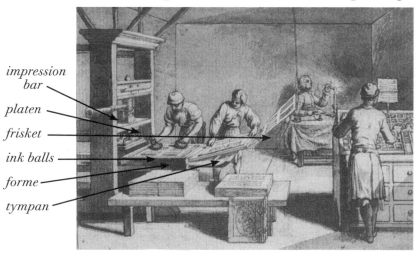

A 1773 wooden hand press similar to the ones Bodoni used.

APPENDIX IV

The Trieste Leaf

BY JAMES MOSLEY

This is an unsolved mystery. It has long been known that copies of Bodoni's *Manuale tipografico* of 1788 lack a leaf numbered 71. This much was noted by Angelo Pezzana (1772-1862), for many years the director of the Palatina Library, Parma, who wrote a note in one of the library's volumes containing the Manuale (Coll. bod. 9) that leaf 71 was never found in it, and that "it was said that it was not printed."

It was not until after the Second World War that a claim was made that the leaf had been deliberately suppressed for political reasons, because it contained a description of Trieste, a city in Austria. In 1948 a dealer and art-critic in Milan called Giampiero Giani published a list of publications by Bodoni, entitled *Catalogo delle autentiche edizioni Bodoniane,* under his own imprint, *Edizioni della Conchiglia.* Although the work appears to be the compilation of an amateur collector, who made additions and corrections to the classic Bodoni bibliography that had been compiled by H. C. Brooks (*Compendiosa bibliografia di edizioni Bodoniane.* Firenze, 1927), there is reason to think that at least some of the items described were available for sale, and that its publication may have been aimed at contemporary collectors and institutions.

One item described in Giani's Catalogo was a single leaf, which is reproduced among his illustrations with a caption saying that it was "the proof of leaf 71 of the *Manuale* of 1788, which concerns the city of Trieste." It should be noted that the text of each leaf of the Manuale of 1788 carries an account of a different city in Italy, and that its leaves are arranged in the order of the size of the type, starting with the smallest, though the name of the size of each type is not given. The source of these accounts of cities has not been discovered. On the leaves numbered from 1 to 50 each text is set in roman with some words in italic. For the larger sizes, from leaf 51 onwards, roman type is used for the text in Italian, which is followed by another leaf with a Roman numeral (starting with LI) showing the same text in French.

In his account of the *Manuale tipografico* of 1788 in his text of 1948, Giani says (*Catalogo,* p. 20), "I have found a proof of the missing leaf in a copy [of the Manuale of 1788] in quarto format, annotated by Bodoni himself, which describes the city of Trieste (!) with the text: 'Trieste, in the age of Augustus was a part, with Venice and Istria, of the tenth region of the Empire. In 1719 Karl VI declared our beautiful and ancient Italian city a free port.' A phrase like this must have been quite audacious at the time of Maria Theresa, and it was certainly the reason for the prohibition placed on the printing of this leaf, a prohibition that Bodoni made conspicuous by numbering [the sequence of the leaves] as 70 and 72, and by not putting another leaf in its place." Did Giani find the text relating to Trieste, or did he write it himself? The specimen is set in a twentieth-century version of Bodoni type. Did he make the proof that he reproduced in his book of 1948, and then sell it to the library in Lugano? I not sure that Giani is innocent of such malficence. In the end these questions which go to the root of the "mystery" that concerns the "Trieste leaf" are still unresolved.[221]

Giani, who was born in 1912 and died in 1964, had been the art correspondent of the Milan journal, *Avanti!* He wrote a number of articles and books about contemporary painting. This is from an unsigned obituary notice in the *Corriere della Sera*: "He had ability, even cunning; but it was allied to a certain frankness, even innocence, enthusiasm, childishness and generosity." [*Era abile, era magari furbo; ma con qualcosa di candido e persino d'ingenuo, con qualcosa d'infantile, e d'entusiastico e di generoso . . .*] The tone of the piece is personal and friendly, but the term cunning (*furbo*) is not explained and it seems worth noting.

Giani's reference in 1948 to a leaf with a description of Trieste is the earliest that I have found. Previous accounts of the *Manuale* of 1788, like those of Pezzana and Brooks (in his bibliography of 1927), do indeed say that leaf 71 is missing, but they do not suggest that it had mentioned Trieste, nor that political censorship had suppressed it.

In 1964 the authoritative Bodoni scholar Sergio Samek Ludovici revealed the location of this leaf as the Biblioteca Cantonale, Lugano, and in the same article ("I 'Manuali tipografici' di G. B. Bodoni." *L'Italia grafica,* volume strenna, 1964) he reproached Giani for failing to reveal the location of the letter by Mazza that he had cited. In his facsimile edition of the *Manuale tipografico* of 1788, Giovanni Mardersteig included the Trieste Leaf in its numerical place as leaf 71, with the number within a typographical tablet (*tabula ansata*). This number, which had not been present on Giani's leaf, was added by Mardersteig himself, as he explains in his introduction, to match those of the other leaves of the *Manuale*.

I first saw the Trieste leaf in Mardersteig's facsimile edition of the *Manuale* of 1788, published in 1968. Mardersteig's reproduction was also cited in an account of the preparation of the image of the leaf for the facsimile in an article by Vanni Scheiwiller in the volume that was published to accompany an exhibition in Verona, *Giovanni Mardersteig: stampatore, editore, umanista* (Verona: Edizioni Valdonega, 1989). When I saw it, it immediately struck me that the type with which the leaf was set was not Bodoni's, but a type of the 20th century, the "Bodoni" of the American Typefounders' Company, New Jersey, which was made in about 1911, and was also cast under license in Italy. Later I found that Luigi Cesare Maletto had also noticed the anomalous identity of this type. He assumed that Mardersteig must have set the page from type in his own possession, but Mardersteig never owned a fount of the ATF Bodoni.

The Biblioteca Cantonale, Lugano, a city which is in Canton Ticino, the

Photograph of the so-called proof of #71, the Trieste leaf.

Mardersteig reproduction of the Trieste leaf.

Italian-speaking region of Switzerland, had a major Bodoni collection that it had acquired some years previously, that of Richard Hadl, of which a catalogue had been published in 1926. It was clearly not unwilling to make additions to it. Writing about its collections in 1976, the director of the library, Adriana Ramelli, wrote this passage in an article about the library's collections, calling *La Carta di Trieste* (the Trieste Leaf—a term that she appears to have been the first to use) "a highly rare printed item, one printed by Bodoni, and probably an unicum [i.e. the only copy in existence]. It is a leaf acquired a few years ago, the so-called 'Trieste Leaf' that Bodoni set for his *Manuale tipografico* of 1788. We read: 'Trieste . . . this beautiful and ancient Italian city of ours'. This is why the leaf, which should have been numbered 71, could not be included in the Manuale. We are proud to possess this leaf, which is a courageous declaration by Bodoni of the Italian identity of one who, serving a prince, was obliged to be loyal and obedient. Our collection is rich in important folios, but we regard the Trieste Leaf as the most precious of our possessions, not only for its absolute rarity, but because his voice—silenced for political reasons—remains alive in this unique document, which is preserved in the library of Italian Switzerland." (*Storia di biblioteconomia e storia del libro in onore di Francesco Barberi*, Roma, 1976, p. 454. An illustration of the library's copy of the Trieste Leaf accompanies her article as plate 41.)

When I made contact with the library at Lugano in 2009, it was planning a Bodoni exhibition made up of items in their own collection, and I was invited to come and give a talk there about the *Carta di Trieste*, which I did in 2010. I thought that this was generous and broad-minded of them, considering my suspicions concerning their treasured possession. I was told that it had been bought in 1948. There remained just one problem: the original leaf could not then be found, and my information is that it seems to be still missing. This is a pity, since an examination of the paper would help to confirm its status.

Giani's reference to the sensibilities of Maria Theresa is explained by the fact that Maria Amalia, who was married to the new duke, Ferdinando, in 1769, and who on her arrival in Parma deliberately destroyed the career of Bodoni's first patron Du Tillot, was—like Marie Antoinette in France—a daughter of the Austrian Empress Maria Theresa. Giani also cited a letter of 1790, in "a private collection in Milan," by one Mazza, which suggested that the political implications of the use in the Manuale of texts relating to "Italian" cities had disturbed the authorities in Parma, thus lending colour to his suggestion that the leaf with the passage relating to Trieste, which would have been numbered 71, was suppressed for political reasons. In his book of 1948 Giani prints a long passage in which Bodoni asserts his "love of Italy and his pride in the name of Italian," but he does does not give its source. It is in fact from Bodoni's preface to his edition of the multilingual *Oratio Dominica* of 1806, a work that was made to rival one produced in 1805 by the Imprimerie impériale, Paris.

Trieste, a port which had an Italian-speaking population though the rural population of the region was largely Slovene, had in the fourteenth century preferred an alliance with Austria in order to escape the overwhelming dominance of the rival city of Venice, which took possession of several cities on the mainland (terra ferma) to the West, including Padua, Vicenza and Verona. My own belief is that the text of the Trieste Leaf, with its overtones of the Italian *irredentismo* that had also laid claim to another former Austrian possession, the Alto Adige (or Südtirol), seems most credibly to derive from the years after the Second World War, when the ultimate status of Trieste (which had been ceded in 1920 by Austria to Italy, but at that date was claimed by Yugoslavia) was under international discussion and was often in the news. Perhaps a word should be added here about irredentismo or "irredentism," since this is an Italian term that has no real English equivalent. The Oxford English Dictionary's definition of 'irredentism', a word which came into English use in the 1880s, is "any policy of seeking the recovery and reunion to one country of a region or regions for the time being subject to another country." A classic example in the twentieth century was the German annexation of the whole of Czechoslovakia for the sake of the German-speaking population of the region known as 'the Sudetenland' that had found itself absorbed into the newly created state. Perhaps this is why neither Samek Ludovici nor Mardersteig suspected the credibility of Giani's suggestion of eighteenth-century censorship. After long negotiation, Trieste was formally made a part of the Italian province of Friuli–Venezia Giulia in 1975. Other cities that are described in the texts in the Manuale are often called "*città d'Italia*" (a city of Italy), but this is the only instance in which the term *italiana* (Italian) with its nineteenth-century irredentist overtones is used. This inevitably makes the wording of leaf 71 somewhat suspect in itself.[221]

SELECTED BIBLIOGRAPHY

Agazzi, Nicoletta, "Testamento della vedova Bodoni." *Aurea Parma*, Maggio-Agosto 1994.

Ajani, Stefano, and Luigi Cesare Maletto, eds. *Conoscere Bodoni.* Collegno: Gianfranco Altieri, 1990.

Andrieux, André. *Daily Life in Papal Rome in the Eighteenth Century.* London: Allen and Unwin, 1968.

Anon., *Il Cuoco Piemontese Perfezionato a Parigi.* Turin: Ricca, 1766.

Antonazzi, Giovanni. *Il Palazzo di Propaganda.* Rome: De Luca, 2005.

Barocelli, Francesco, ed. *Il Correggio nella Camera di San Paolo.* Milan: Electa, 2010.

Beales, Derek. *Joseph II: In the Shadow of Maria Theresa.* Cambridge: Cambridge University Press, 2008.

Bédarida, Henri. *Parme et la France.* Paris: Champion, 1927.

Begheldo, Alfonso. "Giambattista Bodoni, Il Tipografo della Cattolicità." *Missioni Illustrati*, August 1940. XVIII, #8.

Benassi, Umberto. "Il tipografo Giambattista Bodoni e i suoi allievi punzonisti." *Archivio Storico per le province Parmensi. Nuova Serie.* Volume XIII. Parma: Presso La R. Deputazione di Storia Patria, 1913.

Bernardi, Jacopo. *Vita di Giambattista Bodoni.* Saluzzo: Tipografia Fratelli-Bodoni, 1872.

Bernini, F. *Storia di Parma.* Parma: Battei, 1979.

Bertieri, Raffaello. *L'arte di Giambattista Bodoni.* Milan: Bertieri e Vanzetti, 1913.

Biblioteca Angelica, *La Collezione Bodoniana.* Catalogo a cura di Annamaria Palaia e Loana Moscatelli. Rome: Istituto Poligrafico e Zecca dello Stato, 1987.

Bottasso, Enzo. *Dizionario dei bibliotecari e bibliografi italiani dal XVI al XX secolo.* Montevarchi: Accademia Valdarnese del Poggio, 2009.

Brooks, H.C. *Compendiosa bibliografia di edizioni Bodoniane.* Florence: Tipografia Barbèra, 1927.

Burgio, Anna Ceruti. *Donne di Parma.* Parma: Proposte, 1994.

Campanini, Zefirino. "Memorie diverse. Intervista di 28 domande e risposte su bodoni e la sua stamperia." Mss. Parm. 613/615. (Published in the catalog of the Bodoni Museum.)

Casanova, Giacomo. *The Story of My Life.* New York: Penguin, 2001.

Ciavarella, Angelo. "Bodoni e la sua villa del Pozzetto." In *Bollettino del Museo Bodoniano di Parma*, 5, 1983.

——. *Bodoni: L'invenzione della semplicità.* Parma: Guanda, 1990.

——. *Catalogo del Museo Bodoniano di Parma.* Parma: Artegrafica Silva, 1968.

——. *De Azara—Bodoni.* Vols. 1 & 2. Parma: Artegrafica Silva, 1979.

Cleland, T.M. *Giambattista Bodoni of Parma.* Boston: Society of Printers, 1916.

Coke, Lady Mary. *Letters and Journals, 1756-1774.* London: Kingsmead Bookshops, 1889.

Dall'Acqua, Marzio. "Tra antico regime ed età moderna il ducato provvisorio di Parma, Piacenza e Guastalla." *Bodoni (1740-1813) Principe dei tipografi nell'Europa dei Lumi e di Napoleone.* Padua: Studio Esseci, 2013.

De Brosses, Charles. *Lettres familières d'Italie.* Brussels: André Versaille, 2009.

De Lama, Giuseppe. *Vita del Cavaliere Giambattista Bodoni Tipografo Italiano.* Parma, dalla Stamperia Ducale, 1816.

De Pasquale, Andrea. *Allievi e antagonisti di Giambattista Bodoni: gli Amoretti di San Pancrazio.* Parma: Museo Bodoniano, 2009.

——. *Bodoni 1813-2013. Principe dei tipografi nell'Europa dei Lumi e di Napoleone.* Parma: Grafiche Step, 2013.

——. and Andrea Amoretti. *Bodoni e gli Amoretti concorrenti anche a Milano.* San Pancrazio Parmense, 2013.

——. *La fucina dei caratteri di Giambattista Bodoni.* Parma: Monte Università, 2010.

——. *Una donna tra libri e caratteri. Margherita Dall'Aglio Bodoni.* Parma: Museo Bodoniano, 2012.

——. *I capolavori della tipografia di Giambattista Bodoni.* Parma: Monte Università, 2012.

Ellenbog, Ulrich. "On the poisonous evil vapours and fumes of metals such as silver, quicksilver, lead and others . . ." *The Lancet,* 1932, p. 270.

Farinelli, Leonardo. "Bodoni: l'esperienza Romana." In *Bodoni: l'invenzione della semplicità.* Parma: Ugo Guanda, 1990.

——. "Bodoni senza caratteri." In *Bodoni, i Lumi, l'Arcadia. Atti del Convegno.* Parma: Museo Bodoniano, 2008.

Fraser, Antonia. *Marie Antoinette: The Journey.* New York: Anchor, 2002.

Füssel, Stephan. "Bodoni's Typography in Historical Perspective." Introduction to facsimile of Bodoni's 1818 *Manuale tipografico.* Cologne: Taschen, 2010.

Gambara, Ludovic. *Le Ville Parmensi.* Parma: La Nazionale, 1966.

Gasparinetti, Federico, ed. *Bodoni—Miliani.* Parma: Artegrafica Silva, 1970.

Ginetti, Lugini. "La Morte di Don Ferdinando di Borbone." *Aurea Parma*, Anno II. Fasc. 1-2. Parma: Unione Tipografice Parmense, 1913.

Giambattista Bodoni. A special number from the monthly bulletin *La Scuola Fiorentina del Libro.* Anno II. – N. 12. Florence, 1913.

Giorgi, Agostino Antonio. *Alphabetum Tibetanum Missionum Apostolicarum Commodo Editum.* Rome: Propaganda Fide, 1762.

In Morte del Cavaliere Giambattista Bodoni Sommo Tipografo. Parma: Presso La Vedova Bodoni, 1814.

Inventario Generale del 1768. Rome: SC Stamperia.

Lobetti-Bodoni, Giovanni, ed. *Nei parentali di G.B. Bodoni.* Saluzzo: Lobetti-Bodoni, 1913.

Lopresti, Lucia. *Granducato di Parma e Piacenza,* Colognola ai Colli: Demetra, 1999.

Marini, Marino. *Memorie istorico-critiche della città di Santo Arcangelo.* Rome: Propaganda Fide, 1844.

Martini, Carlo. "La Gloria di Giambattista Bodoni cominciò a Roma." In *G.B. Bodoni e la Propaganda Fide.* Parma: Museo Bodoniano, 1959.

Metzler, J., ed. *Sacrae Congregationis de Propaganda Fide Memoria Rerum . . . 1622-1972.* Vol. 2. 1700-1815. Ch. XI. Freiburg im Breisgau: Herder, 1971.

Mingardi, Corrado. *Bodoni.* Parma: Gazzetta di Parma, 2008.

——. *Napoleone & Bodoni, Nel secondo centenario della visita dell'Imperatore a Parma 1805-2005.* Parma: Artegrafica Silva, 2005.

Mörtinger-Grohmann, Pia. "Les débuts de Marie Amélie à Parme à travers les sources autrichiennes de Haus-, Hof- un Staatsarchiv." In *Un Borbone tra Parma e l'Europa, Don Ferdinando e il suo tempo (1751-1802).* Reggio Emilia: Diabasis, 2005.

Natale, Pasquale. *Saluzzo in cattedra: Scuole, maestri e studenti del Piemonte dal Medioevo a oggi.* Saluzzo: Fusta Editore, 2008.

Necchi, Rosa. *I celebrati caratteri.* Parma: Università degli Studi di Parma, 2011.

Nello Vetro, Gaspare. *Il teatro ducale e la vita musicale a Parma dai Farnesi a Maria Luigia (1697-1829).* Rome: Aracne, 2010.

Nisard, Charles. *Guillaume du Tillot, un valet ministre et secrétaire d'etat, épisode de l'histoire de France en Italie de 1749 à 1771.* Paris: Ollendorf, 1887.

Orsenigo, Camilla. "Bodoni e gli inchiostri." In *Bodoni celebrato a Parma.* Parma: Biblioteca Palatina, 1963.

Passerini, V. *Memorie aneddote per servire un giorno alla vita del Signor Giovanbattista Bodoni tipografo di sua Maestà Cattolica e Direttore del Parmense Tipografeo.* Parma: Stamperia Carmignani, 1804.

Pasta, Giuseppe. *Coraggio nelle malattie*, Section XIX. Parma: [G.Bodoni], 1792.

Ricci, Franco Maria. ed. *Bodoni 1740-1813.* Parma: Cariparma/Ricci Editore/Grafiche Step, 2013.

——. Leonardo Farinelli and Corrado Mingardi, eds. *Bodoni nel duecentocinquantesimo anniversario della nascita.* Parma: Casa di Risparmio di Parma/Franco Maria Ricci, 1989.

Riley, Gillian. *The Oxford Companion to Italian Food.* Oxford: Oxford University Press, 2007.

Samek Ludovici, Sergio. "Giovan Battista Bodoni e la Propaganda Fide." *Accademie e biblioteche d'Italia*. Anno XXXIII, N. 3. Roma: Fratelli Palombi, 1965.

Smith, Sir James Edward. *A Sketch of a Tour on the Continent.* Vol. III. London: Longman, 1807.

Stone, Sumner. "Notes from Parma," *U&lc*, Vol. 21, No. 2 (Fall 1994).

Trevisani, Piero. *Bodoni Epoca Vita Arte.* Second edition. Milan: Hoepli, 1951.

Tuki, R., ed. *The services of the Holy Mysteries, except those of the Eucharist and Holy Order, together with the Burial Service, psalms for certain days, and the monthly Katameros.* Rome: Press of the Propaganda Fide, 1763.

Updike, D.B. *Printing Types: Their History, Forms and Use. A Study in Survivals.* Vols. I & II. Third edition. Cambridge, Mass.: Harvard University Press, 1962.

Wilde-Menozzi, Wallis. *Mother Tongue. An American Life in Italy.* New York: Farrar, Straus and Giroux, 1997.

Zanini de Vita, Oretta. *Encyclopedia of Pasta.* Trans. Maureen B. Fant. Berkeley: University of California Press, 2009.

——.*The Food of Rome and Lazio* Trans. Maureen B. Fant. Rome: Alpha*byte*, 1994.

NOTES

THE IMMENSE COLLECTION of correspondence to and from Bodoni is kept in large, heavy cardboard boxes covered with marbled paper in the Biblioteca Palatina in Parma. Each box is closed with an iron rod that runs from one end to the other. The letters themselves are gathered alphabetically and chronologically and held together in groups with a neatly-notched, stiff, sometimes foxed paper band on which is handwritten the name of the writer. We have Margherita Bodoni to thank for the careful cataloging of what she called her husband's immense correspondence. The letter writers are listed in *Catalogo del Museo Bodoniano di Parma,* ed. A. Ciavarella. Parma, Museo Bodoniano, 1968. Rather than citing each piece of correspondence in my already unwieldy notes, I have instead written the date of each quoted letter in the body of the manuscript.

I have followed the same procedure with the voluminous correspondence between Bodoni and Nicolás de Azara, which is collected in (editor) Angelo Ciavarella's *Azara/ Bodoni.* Parma: Artegrafica Silva, 1979.

All translation from Italian and French into English is mine, unless otherwise noted, and I take responsibility for any errors.

PROLOGUE

1 Information about Mimi Meyer comes from news releases from the Harry Ransom Center and from Mark Lisheron's article, "Book Bandit Rocked Ransom," in the *Austin American-Statesman,* Feb.1, 2004, as well as from conversations with people knowledgeable about the case.

2 T.M. Cleland, *Giambattista Bodoni of Parma.* Boston: Society of Printers, 1913.

CHAPTER 1

3 Giuseppe De Lama, *Vita del Cavaliere Giambattista Bodoni Tipografo Italiano.* Parma: Stamperia Ducale, 1816, p. 2.

4 Giambattista Bodoni, "Notizie intorno a vari incisori di caratteri e sopra lacune getterie d'Italia." MS.ital.222, Bibliothèque Nationale, Paris. Translated by James Mosley in 1994.

5 Stephan Füssel, "Bodoni's Typography in Historical Perspective." Introduction to facsimile of Bodoni's 1818 *Manuale tipografico.* Cologne: Taschen, 2010.

6 *Estrazione della Famiglia del celebre Tipografo Parmense: il Signor Cavaliere Giovanni Battista Bodoni di Saluzzo.* Single-page family tree in Bodoni letter collection at the Turin Public Library.

7 E. Nicoli, *Monviso re di pietra,* Cavallermaggiore: Gribaudo, 1993, pp. 307-318.

8 Natale Pasquale, *Saluzzo in cattedra: scuole, maestri e studenti del Piemonte, dal Medioevo a oggi.* Saluzzo: Fusta, 2008, pp. 84-88.

9 Unless otherwise noted, this letter and any other subsequent letters from which I quote come from the Carteggio Bodoni (Bodoni correspondence) in the Biblioteca Palatina in

Parma. The letters are all filed under the writer's name, and arranged chronologically. I have made sure to include the date of each one I mention.

10 Hans Klemer (c. 1480-1512) was a French painter who became a naturalized Italian and made his career in Saluzzo.

11 Anon., *Il Cuoco Piemontese Perfezionato a Parigi.* Turin: Ricca, 1766.

12 Leonardo Farinelli and Corrado Mingardi, eds. *Bodoni 1740-1813.* Parma: Cassa di Risparmio di Parma/Franco Maria Ricci, 1990, Note 2, p. 27.

13 Zefirino Campanini, "Memorie diverse. Intervista di 28 domande e risposte su bodoni e la sua stamperia." *Catalogo del Museo Bodoniano di Parma.* Parma: Artegrafica Silva, 1968, p. 123.

14 V. Passerini, *Memorie aneddote per servire un giorno alla vita del Signor Giovanbattista Bodoni tipografo di sua Maestà Cattolica e Direttore del Parmense Tipografeo.* Parma: Stamperia Carmignani, 1804, p. 9. Passerini's date of 8 February is more reliable than De Lama's 15 February because Passerini, writing while Bodoni was still alive, had access to his subject.

15 Carlo Martini, "La Gloria di Giambattista Bodoni cominciò a Roma." In *G.B. Bodoni e la Propaganda Fide.* Parma: Museo Bodoniano, 1959, p. XIII.

16 Ibid.

17 Tobias Smollett, *Travels through France and Italy.* Evanston, Illinois: Marlboro/Northwestern, 1997, Letter XXIX, 1765, p. 217.

18 I am grateful to the food historian Oretta Zanini de Vita for this information.

CHAPTER 2

19 Smollett, p. 217.

20 Charles de Brosses, *Lettres familières d'Italie.* Brussels: André Versaille, 2009, p. 76.

21 Peter Cunningham, ed. *The Letters of Horace Walpole, Fourth Earl of Oxford,* Vol. 3. London: Bentley, 1891, p. 85.

22 "Benedict XIV," *Encyclopedia of World Biography,* 2004.

23 Maurice Andrieux, *Daily Life in Papal Rome in the Eighteenth Century.* London: Allen and Unwin, 1968, pp. 74-75.

24 Ibid.

25 Jacopo Bernardi, *Vita di Giambattista Bodoni.* Saluzzo: Tipografia Fratelli Lobetti-Bodoni, 1872, p. 12.

26 Campanini, p. 123.

27 De Lama, p. 4.

28 Alfonso M. Begheldo, SX, "Giambattista Bodoni, Il Tipografo della Cattolicità." *Missioni Illustrati,* August 1940. XVIII, #8.

29 Farinelli and Mingardi, fn. 6, p. 6.

30 Bernardi, p. 12.

31 Campanini, p. 124.

32 Ibid.

33 Excavations beneath the Palazzo Valentini have revealed a domus, the home of a patrician

family. It is now possible to visit the domus and its impressive baths. One walks on glass floors (a somewhat unnerving experience) to view the rooms and the mosaics, while lights play on them and reinvent the missing bits.

34 Martini, p. xiv.

35 *Encyclopedia of Library and Information Science,* Vol. 23. New York, N.Y.: Marcel Decker, 1978, p. 441.

36 The building has been turned into a museum, and one is forced to go through it in haste during its limited visiting hours with a guide who is ignorant about the press.

37 J. Metzler, ed. *Sacrae Congregationis de Propaganda Fide Memoria Rerum . . . 1622-1972.* Vol. 2. 1700-1815. Ch. XI. Herder: Freiburg im Breisgau, 1971, pp. 299-315.

38 Marino Marini, *Memorie istorico-critiche della città di Santo Arcangelo.* Rome: Propaganda Fide, 1844, p. 118.

39 De Lama, p. 131.

40 Passerini, p. 2.

41 *Inventario Generale del 1768,* Rome: SC Stamperia, vol. 2, pp. 699,782 ff.

42 Giovanni Antonazzi, *Il Palazzo di Propaganda.* Rome: De Luca, 2005, p. 56.

43 Passerini, p. 9. "Jealously guarded and saved"? Where are they today?

44 Email from James Mosley, 3 Nov. 2011.

45 Passerini, p. 10.

46 Passserini, p. 11.

47 Sergio Samek Ludovici, "Giovan Battista Bodoni e la Propaganda Fide." *Accademie e Biblioteche d'Italia.* Anno xxxiii, N. 3. Roma: Fratelli Palombi, 1965, p. 145.

48 The university moved out of those premises in 1935, and the palazzo now houses the archives of state; its library, also designed by Borromini, is the site of exhibitions.

49 Begheldo, #8.

50 I am grateful to Hope Mayo, Philip Hofer Curator of Printing and Graphic Arts at Havard's Houghton Library, for the following information: Coptic type first appears at the Propaganda Fide in a specimen datable to 1626-1634. (Houghton Library, TypTS 625.70.262.) See letter of 21 March 1629 from Pietro della Valle in Rome to Jean Morin in Paris, which states that the Coptic type "has now been cast." This is the same type that Bodoni set in the *Pontificiale.*

51 Samek Ludovici, p. 150.

52 Information from email correspondence with Robert T. Pomplun, translator of the *Alphabetum Tibetanum.*

53 I have used the words "disconcerting" and "ill-suited" in describing Bodoni's decorations for the *Pontificale* and the *Alphabetum,* but of course my opinion is subjective. I should bow to the prevailing mood in Rome in the Baroque era. Indeed, I have been gently reminded by Robert Pomplun that "the baroque world saw itself as expansive and indeed global . . . and the juxtaposition would not have seemed odd for educated readers of the eighteenth century."

54 Samek Ludovici, pp. 144 ff.

55 While I was in Rome, trudging in Bodoni's footsteps, I hoped to unearth treasure troves of books he had printed, as well as references to him in the Propaganda Fide records (now housed in the Collegio Urbano on the Janiculum hill). Nothing. I had been warned that this

was the case by others who had trodden the same path. Of course I didn't believe them, so confident was I in my own ability to ferret out information. I believe them now. So much of value to researchers is in private hands.

56 Here's what James Boswell (diarist, author of *Life of Johnson*, the same age as Bodoni, and in Rome at the same time) has to say about the city: "Nine months in this delicious country have done more for me than all the sage lessons which books, or men formed by books, could have taught me . . . I remembered the rakish deeds of Horace and other amorous Roman poets, and I thought that one might well allow one's self a little indulgence in a city where there are prostitutes licensed by the Cardinal Vicar."

57 De Brosses, p. 81.

58 De Brosses, p. 75.

59 See Casanova's seduction of Mariuccia in his *The Story of My Life*. New York: Penguin, p. 321.

60 Passerini, p. 13.

61 Passerini, p. 12.

62 See Leonardo Farinelli, "Bodoni: L'Esperienza Romana." In *Bodoni: L'invenzione della semplicità*. Parma: Ugo Guanda, 1990, p. 73.

63 Smollett, XXIX, p. 223.

64 Casanova, p. 316.

65 Cheap wine.

66 Liqueur.

67 Gillian Riley, *The Oxford Companion to Italian Food*. Oxford: Oxford University Press, 2007, p. 452.

68 Boswell, p. 50.

69 De Lama, p. 7. There he goes again, implying that Bodoni did absolutely nothing but work.

70 Ruggieri's date of death is a moving target and has been variously attributed to 1762, 1769, and 1766. I am convinced that 1766 is the correct date, and take as my sources Enzo Bottasso's *Dizionario dei bibliotecari e bibliografi italiani dal XVI al XX secolo*. Montevarchi: Accademia Valdarnese del Poggio, 2009, p. 395; A. Montanari, "Amaduzzi, illuminista cristiano," Romagna arte e storia, 67/2003, p. 67; and the email confirming 1766 as the correct date that I received on 20 Sept. 2013 from Mons. Luis M. Cuña Ramos, the archivist at the Archivio Storico di Propaganda Fide in Rome, which states *"Dalla informazione in nostro possesso, Costantino Ruggieri muore a Roma il 16 novembre 1766."*

71 Farinelli and Mingardi, Note 7, p. 29.

72 Passerini, p. 13.

73 The suicide is the subject of constant debate in Bodoni circles. One famous historian lowers his voice when he talks about it, saying "There's a whiff of something strange going on here."

CHAPTER 3

74 Bernardi, p. 19.

75 In Bernardi, p. 20. (Letter from Paciaudi to Berta, 19 January 1766. In Vicenzo Promis, *Miscellanea*. Vol. XI. Turin: Fratelli Bocca, 1871, p. 452.)

76 Ibid.

77 De Lama, p. 11.

78 *"Bodoni mi ha scritto di proprio pugno di essere giunto in Parma il giorno di san Mattia dell'anno 1768 alle ore dodici mattutine."* (Bodoni wrote to me in his own hand that he arrived in Parma on St Mattias's day 1768 at 12 noon.) Margin note by Passerini on p. 19 of *Memorie . . .*, alluded to by Trevisani (see below), p. 21.

79 Henri Bédarida, *Parme et la France.* Paris: Champion, 1927, p. 96.

80 Bédarida, p. 164-166.

81 Umberto Benassi, "Il tipografo Giambattista Bodoni e i suoi allievi punzonisti." *Archivio Storico per le province Parmensi.* Nuova Serie. Volume XIII–Anno 1913. Parma: Presso La R. Deputazione di Storia Patria, 1913, p. 52.

82 Bédarida, p. 113.

83 Gossip that Don Filippo was poisoned or that he died after falling off his horse and being torn apart by his hounds immediately began its whispered round at the court. However, according to the experts Ubaldo Delsante and Manlio Mora, there is absolutely no basis for the gossip. All the evidence points to smallpox. Email from Ubaldo Delsante, 14 June 2012.

84 Piero Trevisani, *Bodoni, Epoca Vita Arte.* Milan: Hoepli, p. 76.

85 Benassi, p. 53.

86 Sensualism is a philosophical theory which holds that perceptions and sensations are necessary components of true knowledge.

87 Bédarida, p. 148.

88 Lady Mary Coke, *Letters and Journals*, 1756-1774. London: Kingsmead Bookshops, 1889.

89 In Derek Beales, *Joseph II: In the Shadow of Maria Theresa.* Cambridge: Cambridge University Press, 2008, p. 262.

90 Marzio Dall'Acqua, "Tra antico regime ed età moderna il ducato provvisorio di Parma, Piacenza e Guastalla." In *Bodoni (1740-1813) Principe dei tipografi nell'Europa dei Lumi e di Napoleone.* Padua: Studio Esseci, 2013, p. 208.

91 Gossip heard by me in Parma in 2011.

92 Trevisani, p. 22.

93 Trevisani, p. 24.

94 Benassi, p. 97.

95 Benassi, p. 70.

96 De Lama, p. 11.

97 A tympan is a large pad that is used to soften and equalize pressure between the page to be printed and the platen.

98 Probably 20" x 15", a standard English size.

99 The coffin was a moveable cart for transporting type.

100 A "forme" is a metal frame to contain already composed type.

101 This apparently was the very best kind of skin for the purpose, but it begs the question of how fond the Parmigiani actually were of their dogs.

102 Many thanks to James Mosley for his help with translating this document.

103 Draft of a letter from Bodoni, perhaps to a prelate at the Propaganda Fide. In *G.B. Bodoni e la Propaganda Fide,* p. 13. Undated but presumably before the death of Baskerville in 1775.

104 Trevisani, p. 27.

105 Trevisani, p. 29.

106 Bédarida, p. 181.

107 Bédarida, pp. 500-501.

108 Bédarida, p. 556.

109 Dall'Acqua, p. 200.

110 Oretta Zanini de Vita, *Encyclopedia of Pasta.* Berkeley: University of California Press, 2009, p. 36.

CHAPTER 5

111 F. Bernini, *Storia di Parma.* Parma: Battei, 1979, p. 139.

112 Pia Mörtinger-Grohmann, "Les débuts de Marie Amélie à Parme à travers les sources autrichiennes de Haus-, Hof- un Staatsarchiv." In *Un Borbone tra Parma e l'Europa, Don Ferdinando e il suo tempo (1751-1802).* Reggio Emilia: Diabasis, 2005, p. 41.

113 Mörtinger-Grohmann, p. 42.

114 Letter from Marie Antoinette at Versailles to Maria Amalia, 5 Oct. 1770. In P. Vogt de Honolstein, *Correspondance inedite de Marie-Antoinette.* Paris, 1864.

115 Pierre Jean Mariette to Paciaudi, Paris, 8 April 1771. In Farinelli and Mingardi, p. 226.

116 Benigno Bossi, *Mascarade à la Grecque.* Parma, (1771?). This mysterious little album is without publication information or date. It is likely that Bodoni ran it off at the press as a favor to his friends.

117 *Dizionario Biografico degli Italiani.* Maria Amalia d'Asburgo Lorena, duchessa di Parma, Piacenza e Guastalla. Vol. 70, 2007.

118 Charles Nisard, *Guillaume du Tillot, un valet ministre et secrétaire d'etat, épisode de l'histoire de France en Italie de 1749 à 1771.* Paris: Ollendorf, 1887, p. 124.

119 Füssel, pp. 6 7.

120 *Fregi e majuscule.* Parma: Stamperia Reale, 1771, p vii.

121 De Lama, p. 15.

122 Louis XV to Ferdinando, Fontainebleau, 1 Nov. 1769. In Nisard, p. 126-127.

123 "Quand on est prince, on ne peut sans ridicule être moine." In Roberto Lasagni, *Dizionario Biografico dei Parmigiani,* p. 632.

124 Nisard, p. 97.

125 Lucia Lopresti, *Granducato di Parma e Piacenza,* Colognola ai Colli: Demetra, 1999, p. 108.

126 Nisard, p. 231.

127 Letter from De Dufort to the duke of Aiguillon, 23 Aug. 1771. In Nisard, p. 232.

128 Nisard, p. 213.

129 Du Tillot to Count Algarotti, 14 February 1762. In Bédarida, p. 36.

CHAPTER 6

130 Camilla Orsenigo, "Bodoni e gli inchiostri." *Bodoni celebrato a Parma.* Parma: Biblioteca Palatina, 1963, p. 243.

131 Allen Hutt, *Fournier, the compleat typographer.* Totowa, NJ: Rowman and Littlefield, 1972.

132 Letter from Paciaudi to Rufino Rossi, the duke's private librarian. In Bernardi, p. 47.

133 Trevisani, p. 36.

134 Dall'Acqua, p. 208.

135 Leonardo Farinelli, "Bodoni senza caratteri." In *Bodoni, i Lumi, l'Arcadia.* Eds. Andrea Gatti and Caterina Silva. Parma: Museo Bodoniano, 2008, p. 27.

CHAPTER 7

136 Angelo, Ciavarella, ed. *Azara-Bodoni.* Vol. 1. Parma: Artegrafica Silva, 1979, p. XVIII.

137 Ciavarella, p. XVII.

138 Ibid.

139 Paula Zanardi, "Giambattista Bodoni: Le Scelte Editoriali, La Circolazione Libraria e i Vincoli della Censura." In *Bodoni, i Lumi, l'Arcadia.* Parma: Museo Bodoniano, 2008, p. 169.

140 Passerini, p. 32.

141 Sir James Edward Smith, *A Sketch of a Tour on the Continent.* Vol. III. London: Longman, 1807, p. 128.

142 Where is this letter today? Still entombed somewhere? Hoarded in a private collection? Inadvertently discarded? Filed incorrectly? It would be quite the find.

143 Passerini, pp. 78-79.

144 Henry Lewis Bullen, "Giambattista Bodoni, Printer and Typographer." *The Inland Printer.* Sept. 1921, p. 773.

145 De Lama, p. 34.

146 Ibid.

147 As far as I know, nothing came of this idea.

CHAPTER 8

148 Trevisani, p. 92.

149 Anna Ceruti Burgio, *Donne di Parma.* Parma: Proposte, 1994, p. 125.

150 Passerini, p. 4.

CHAPTER 9

151 Zeffirino Campanini in an 1810 interview with Angelo Pezzana. In *Catalogo del Museo Bodoniano di Parma.* Parma: Artegrafica Silva, 1968, pp. 115-116.

152 Andrea De Pasquale. *Allievi e antagonisti di Giambattista Bodoni: gli Amoretti di San Pancrazio.* Parma: Museo Bodoniano, 2009, p. 31.

153 In D.B. Updike, *Printing Types,* Vol. II. Cambridge, Mass.: Harvard University Press, p. 56.

154 Updike, Vol. II, p. 57.

155 James Mosley, email of 18 Sept. 2012, in which he quotes Updike, Vol. 1., p. 219.

156 In Corrado Mingardi, *Bodoni.* Parma: Gazzetta di Parma, 2008, p. 61.

157 Mingardi, p. 62.

158 Antonia Fraser, *Marie Antoinette: The Journey.* New York: Anchor, 2002, p. 440.

159 Thomas Gray, *Poems by Mr. Gray.* Parma, Bodoni, 1793.

160 Francesco Barocelli, ed. *Il Correggio nella Camera di San Paolo.* Milan: Electa, 2010, p. 15.

CHAPTER 10

161 Ulrich Ellenbog, "On the poisonous evil vapours and fumes of metals such as silver, quick-silver, lead and others . . ." *The Lancet,* 1932, p. 270. In Richard P. Wedeen, *Poison in the Pot.* Carbondale, IL: Southern Illinois University Press, 1984, p. 16.

162 Giuseppe Pasta, *Coraggio nelle malattie,* Section XIX. Parma, [G.Bodoni], 1792.

163 Giuseppe Bodoni, 3 Sept. 1815.

164 In Trevisani, p. 131.

165 Published in the *Giornale del Taro,* 1813, p. 422.

166 De Lama, p. 158.

CHAPTER 11

167 Trevisani, p 119.

168 Gaspare Nello Vetro, *Il Teatro Ducale e la Vita Musicale a Parma dai Farnese a Maria Luigia (1697-1829).* Rome: Aracne, 2010, p. 428. This play is actually listed in the carnival season for 1802, rather than in the fall season of 1801. The theatre's carnival season often began at Christmastime.

169 De Lama, p. 94.

CHAPTER 12

170 Trevisani, p. 106.

171 De Lama's letter, in *Passerini,* pp. 54-72.

172 Passerini, p. 62.

173 Ibid.

174 Ludovic Gambara, *Le Ville Parmensi.* Parma: La Nazionale, 1966, p. 35.

175 Gambara, p. 36.

176 Angelo Ciavarella, "Bodoni e la sua villa del Pozzetto." In *Bollettino del Museo Bodoniano di Parma,* 5, 1983, pp. 102-109.

CHAPTER 14

177 Lugini Ginetti, "La Morte di Don Ferdinando di Borbone," *Aurea Parma,* Anno II. Fasc. 1-2. Parma: Unione Tipografice Parmense, 1913, pp. 86-87.

178 In Ginetti, pp. 93-94.

179 Ginetti, p. 100.

180 De Lama, p. 97.

CHAPTER 15

181 Corrado Mingardi, *Napoleone & Bodoni, Nel secondo centenario della visita dell'Imperatore a Parma 1805-2005*. Parma: Artegrafica Silva, 2005, p. 11.

182 *Napoleone & Bodoni,* p. 20.

183 Ibid.

184 Trevisani, p. 128.

CHAPTER 16

185 De Lama, p. 122.

186 Brooks, p. 173.

187 Mingardi, p. 70.

188 *Napoleone & Bodoni,* p. 38.

189 *Napoleone & Bodoni,* p. 41.

190 This letter is bound into the Houghton Library's copy of the *Oratio Dominica*. It is written in Bodoni's most careful hand and is such pristine condition that on reading it, touching the crisp, bright paper, one feels that the ink has only just dried.

191 De Lama, p. 134.

192 Brooks, p. 181.

193 Karl Morgenstern. Letter to the editors, Dec. 1, 1816. *New Monthly Magazine,* Vol. 6, pp. 393-395.

194 *Napoleone & Bodoni,* p. 57.

CHAPTER 17

195 De Lama, p. 160.

196 Biblioteca Angelica, *La Collezione Bodoniana. Catalogo a cura di Annamaria Palaia e Loana Moscatelli.* Rome: Istituto Poligrafico e Zecca dello Stato, 1987, 498/5.

197 In De Lama, p. 162.

198 Bodoni's death that day was a huge loss for Parma, but its citizens soon found a worthy replacement for their hero. Even as Bodoni's breath rattled in death, in nearby Le Roncole di Busseto five-week-old Giuseppe Verdi was emitting those infant wails that signaled the beginning of his extraordinary career as an opera composer.

199 In *Morte del Cavaliere Giambattista Bodoni Sommo Tipografo.* Parma: Presso La Vedova Bodoni, 1814.

200 In *Morte,* p. 20.

CHAPTER 18

201 Houghton Library, Harvard University. TypTS825.18.224F Miscellanea Bodoniano (ca. 1771-1818).

202 Benjamin Franklin, *Autobiography of Benjamin Franklin,* Section 41.

203 Emmanuelle Toulet, "The Private Press in France. Part III: The Revolution." *The Private Library,* Vol 4:4, Winter 2011, p. 202.

204 Andrea De Pasquale, *Una donna tra libri e caratteri. Margherita Dall'Aglio Bodoni*. Parma: Museo Bodoniano, 2012, p. 16.

205 Mingardi, p. 92.

206 Letter from Margherita Bodoni to the Municipality of Saluzzo, 23 May 1818. In Bernardi, p. 223.

207 Mingardi, p. 44-45.

208 Coll: Dir.B.52, Biblioteca Palatina, Parma.

209 Farinelli, "Bodoni senza caratteri," p. 41.

210 Passerini, p. 3.

211 Farinelli and Mingardi, FN. 54, p. 134.

212 In Füssel, p. 49, translated by Joan Clough, who is responsible for the translations of the two introductions and the dedication.

213 Füssel, p. 41.

214 Trevisani, p. 136.

215 This letter is in the D.B. Updike Collection at the Providence Public Library. It was brought to my attention by Philip Weimerskirch, who has written an extremely useful article about it, "A Letter from Bodoni's Widow." *Printing History*, Whole Number 25 (Volume 14, No. 1) 1991. pp. 19-22. Also included in the article is an inflammatory paragraph by Bodoni scholar Robert F. Lane in a letter to Stuart C. Sherman, librarian of the Providence Public Library. Lane states, without supporting evidence, "Bodoni did not write a single word of [the introduction], and nowhere among the thousands of letters written by Bodoni is there any hint of such ridiculous aesthetic and typographic nonsense. In no way is it anything but polite padding to decorate Volume I of the Manuale . . ." I don't know where Lane thinks these thousands of letters are. Yes, there are hundreds of letters TO Bodoni, but relatively few FROM Bodoni remain, even in Parma.

216 Angelo Ciavarella, "I Manuali Tipografici." In *Bodoni*, p. 189.

217 Nicoletta Aguzzi, "Testamento della vedova Bodoni." *Aurea Parma*, Maggio Agosto 1994, p. 138. (The actual will can be found in the acts of the notary Rondani at the Archivio Notarile in Parma.)

218 Ibid.

219 Andrea De Pasquale, *La fucina dei caratteri di Giambattista Bodoni*. Parma: Monte Università, 2010, p. 34.

EPILOGUE

220 The new plaque reads: "On the second Bodoni centenary, the commune of Parma, the Bodoni museum foundation, and the citizens of San Pancrazio unite here to celebrate the skill of their ancestors. 30 November 2013."

    The restored plaque reads: "In this house stood the workshop and the habitation of the AMORETTI FAMILY, expert ironworkers and founders of printing type. — DON ANDREA, worthy disciple, punchcutter and emulator of the great Bodoni, created here from 1795 to 1807 type of rare beauty. Teacher of his brothers Giovanni, Pietro, Vittorino. — GIACOMO their paternal uncle, chief magistrate of this commune. From 23 March 1806 he also crafted punches and constructed clocks of miraculous precision. – The commune and citizens wish to record these principal glories of San Pancrazio. – 1913."

APPENDIX III

221 For more information, go to James Mosley's blog "Typography" http://typefoundry. blogspot.co.uk/2009/03/trieste-leaf-bodoni-forgery.html"

PORTRAIT PLATES

Following page 32

1. Pietro Melchiore Ferrari. Portrait of Don Ferdinando di Borbone. Su concessione del Ministero per i Beni e le Attività Culturali e del Turismo - Galleria Nazionale di Parma.

2. Giuseppe Lucatelli. Portrait of Paolo Maria Paciaudi. Museo Glauco Lombardi, Parma. Inv. 28.

3. Domenico Muzzi. Portrait of Ennemond Petitot. Accademia di Belle Arti, Parma.

4. Pietro Melchiore Ferrari. Portrait of Guillaume Du Tillot. Su concessione del Ministero per i Beni e le Attività Culturali e del Turismo - Galleria Nazionale di Parma.

5. Johann Zoffany. Portrait of Don Ferdinando di Borbone. Su concessione del Ministero per i Beni e le Attività Culturali e del Turismo - Galleria Nazionale di Parma.

6. Johann Zoffany. Portrait of Maria Amalia, duchess of Parma. Su concessione del Ministero per i Beni e le Attività Culturali e del Turismo - Galleria Nazionale di Parma.

7. Anton Raphael Mengs. Portrait of José Nicolás de Azara. Private collection, Madrid. Album, Art Resource, NY.

8. François Gérard. Portrait of Joachim Murat. Châteaux de Versailles et de Trianon, Versailles. ©Rnb-Grand Palais/Art Resource, NY.

9. Unsigned (perhaps Andrea Appiani) Ritratto virile. From a group of drawings in Bodoni's collection. Museo Glauco Lombardi, Parma. Inv. 372.

10. Andrea Appiani. Portrait of Bodoni. Su concessione del Ministero per i Beni e le Attività Culturali e del Turismo - Galleria Nazionale di Parma.

11. Andrea Appiani. Portrait of Napoleon in garb of the king of Italy. Musée de l'Ile d'Aix, Ile d'Aix. Art Resource, NY.

12. Robert Lefèvre. Portrait of Empress Marie Louise. Museo Glauco Lombardi, Parma. Inv. 23.

13. Artist Unknown. Don Ferdinando in maturity. Parma, Deputazione di storia patria per le province parmensi, Sala delle Conferenze.

14. Artist Unknown. Maria Amalia in maturity. Parma, Deputazione di storia patria per le province parmensi, Sala delle Conferenze.

15. Giuseppe Turchi. Portrait of Bodoni, 1797. Parma, Museo Bodoniano.

16. Giuseppe Lucatelli. Portrait of Bodoni. Museo Glauco Lombardi, Parma. Inv. 167.

17. Giuseppe Bossi. Portrait of Margherita Dall'Aglio Bodoni. Museo Glauco Lombardi, Inv. 166.

18. Antonio Allegri da Correggio. Camera di San Paolo. Su concessione del Ministero per i beni e le attività Culturali e del Turismo - Galleria Nazionale di Parma.

PLATES OF PRINTED WORK

Following page 76

ILLUSTRATIONS IN THE TEXT

p. 170. French school. Nineteenth century. Jean Andoche Junot. Wikimedia Commons.

p. 171. *Oratio dominica.* Syriac. Private collection. Photo: 42-line.

p. 172. *Oratio dominica.* Chinese; and Chinese with chanting tones. Private collection. Photo: 42-line.

p. 174. Homer. *Iliad.* Alessandro Bianchi/Archive Franco Maria Ricci.

p. 176. Joseph Kriehuber. Karl Morgenstern. Wikimedia Commons.

p. 178. Anonymous. Copy of drawing by Pierre Paul Prud'hon. The King of Rome Asleep. Parma, Museo Glauco Lombardi, Inv. 660.

p. 179. *Cimelio.* Title page. Alessandro Bianchi/Archive Franco Maria Ricci.

p. 180. Parma cathedral by moonlight. VL.

p. 182. Giuseppe De Lama. À Madame Marguerite Bodoni . . . (1808) and À Madame Marguerite Bodoni . . . (1813). Updike Collection, Providence Public Library, Providence, RI.

p. 183. Bodoni's memorial. Parma Cathedral. VL.

p. 185. Lament. Houghton Library, Harvard University, fTypTs 825.18.225.

p. 186. Giuseppe Bossi. Apotheosis of Bodoni. Alessandro Bianchi/Archive Franco Maria Ricci.

p. 187. Bodoni's death notice in Italian and French. Updike Collection, Providence Public Library, Providence, RI.

p. 190. *Boileau Despréaux.* Title page. Alessandro Bianchi/Archive Franco Maria Ricci.

p. 192. Artist unknown. Count Adam Niepperg. Wikimedia Commons.

p. 193. "A Sa Majesté Marie Louise . . ." Updike Collection, Providence Public Library, Providence, RI.

p. 195. Engraving by Rosaspina from painting by Appiani. *Manuale tipografico.* Frontispiece. Private collection. Photos: 42-line.

p. 196. *Manuale tipografico.* Dedication; Papale; Parmigianina; Imperiale italic. Private collection. Photos: 42-line.

p. 197. *Manuale tipografico.* Title page. Private collection. Photo: 42-line.

p. 199. Letter from the widow Bodoni to Monsieur Durand, 14 November 1817. Updike Collection, Providence Public Library, Providence, RI.

p. 203. Restored Amoretti plaque. Photo: Andrea Amoretti.

p. 204. Biagio Martini. Giambattista Bodoni. Location unknown. In *Conoscere Bodoni.*

p. 214. Bodoni's punches. Alessandro Bianchi/Archive Franco Maria Ricci.

p. 217. Bodoni's matrices. Alessandro Bianchi/Archive Franco Maria Ricci.

p. 217. Bodoni's matrices. Alessandro Bianchi/Archive Franco Maria Ricci.

p. 223. Mardersteig reproduction of the Trieste leaf. Courtesy of Jerry Kelly.

p. 223. The image was published in an article by Vanni Scheiwiller in the volume accompanying the exhibition, *Giovanni Mardersteig: stampatore, editore, umanista.* Verona: Edizioni Valdonega, 1989. Courtesy of James Mosley.

Page numbers in italics refer to illustrations.

Set in
ITC Bodoni and Bauer Bodoni,
both modern digital versions of the type designs
of Giambattista Bodoni.
Book design by
Jerry Kelly.